Network Simulation
Experiments Manual

Network Simulation Experiments Manual

Third Edition

Prepared by Emad Aboelela, Ph.D.

University of Massachusetts, Dartmouth

AMSTERDAM • BOSTON • HEIDELBERG • LONDON
NEW YORK • OXFORD • PARIS • SAN DIEGO
SAN FRANCISCO • SINGAPORE • SYDNEY • TOKYO

Morgan Kaufmann Publishers is an imprint of Elsevier

Acquiring Editor: Rick Adams
Development Editor: David Bevans
Project Manager: Sarah Binns
Designer: Eric DeCicco

Morgan Kaufmann Publishers is an imprint of Elsevier.
30 Corporate Drive, Suite 400, Burlington, MA 01803, USA

Library of Congress Cataloging-in-Publication Data
Aboelela, Emad.
  Network simulation experiments manual / Emad Aboelela.—3rd ed.
    p. cm.
  Experiments associated with: Computer networks : a systems approach / by Larry L. Peterson and Bruce S. Davie.
  ISBN 978-0-12-385210-6 (pbk.)
  1. Computer networks—Computer simulation—Handbooks, manuals, etc. I. Peterson, Larry L. Computer networks.
  II. Title.
  TK5105.5.A24 2011
  004.601′13—dc22
                                    2010051758

British Library Cataloguing-in-Publication Data
A catalogue record for this book is available from the British Library.

Printed and bound by CPI Group (UK) Ltd, Croydon, CR0 4YY

Transferred to digital print 2013

Typeset by: diacriTech, Chennai, India

Working together to grow
libraries in developing countries

www.elsevier.com | www.bookaid.org | www.sabre.org

ELSEVIER   BOOK AID International   Sabre Foundation

For information on all Morgan Kaufmann publications, visit our Web site at *www.mkp.com* or *www.elsevierdirect.com*

CONTENTS

v

Welcome to the *Network Simulation Experiments Manual, Third Edition*. As networking systems have become more complex and enormous, hands-on experiments based on networking simulation have become essential for teaching the key computer networking topics to students and professionals. The simulation approach is highly useful because it provides a virtual environment for a variety of desirable features such as modeling a network based on specified criteria and analyzing its performance under different scenarios.

This, the third edition of this manual, has 15 laboratory experiments in addition to two old experiments that have been moved to the appendices. The experiments discuss a variety of networking designs and protocols. They do not require programming skills as a prerequisite. They are generic and can be easily expanded to utilize new technologies and networking standards. With the free, easy-to-install software, the OPNET IT Guru Academic Edition, networking students and professionals can implement the experiments from the convenience of their homes or workplaces. The manual is suitable for a single-semester course on computer networking at the undergraduate or beginning graduate level. Instructors can pick the experiments that are appropriate to their course contents. The sequence of the experiments matches the order in which the corresponding topics appear in the textbook, *Computer Networks: A Systems Approach, Fifth Edition*. However, instructors can assign the experiments in any sequence that matches their syllabus.

The new materials in the third edition of the manual include two new experiments: the virtual local area networks (VLANs) experiment and the Web caching and data compression experiment. In the VLANs experiment, students will learn how to divide a physical network into a number of separate logical networks using VLANs, with the benefit of decreasing collision domain and adding more security. In the Web caching and data compression experiment, students will study the effect of Web caching and data compression on the response time of accessing Web pages and on the load on the Web server. Two old experiments have been moved to the appendices. The token ring experiment is now in Appendix A and the ATM experiment is in Appendix B. The topics of these two experiments are outdated. They were kept in the manual for instructors who need to cover the principles of the protocols involved those experiments.

The references to animations from the Net-SEAL project (www.net-seal.net)[1] are included in this edition. These animations are intended to reinforce the student's understanding of the concepts related to the topics discussed in the laboratory.

I would like to extend my appreciation to Professor Larry Peterson and Dr. Bruce Davie for giving me the opportunity to associate the laboratory experiments of this manual with their valuable textbook. I want to thank the folks at Morgan Kaufmann who have helped to bring this project to life. Finally, I want to thank you for choosing the manual. I welcome your e-mails to report bugs or to suggest improvements.

Emad Aboelela, Ph.D.
emad@computer.org
Taibah University, Saudi Arabia
January 2011

[1] The materials in the www.net-seal.net Web site are based on work supported by the National Science Foundation under Grant No. DUE-0536388. Any opinions, findings and conclusions, or recommendations expressed on this Web site are those of the Net-SEAL project team and do not necessarily reflect the views of the National Science Foundation (NSF).

Basics of OPNET IT Guru Academic Edition

OBJECTIVES

This lab teaches you the basics of using OPNET IT Guru Academic Edition. OPNET IT Guru Academic Edition enables students to better understand the core concepts of networking and equips them to effectively troubleshoot and manage real-world network infrastructures.

OVERVIEW

OPNET's IT Guru provides a virtual network environment that models the behavior of your entire network, including its routers, switches, protocols, servers, and individual applications. By working in the virtual network environment, IT managers, network and system planners, and operations staffs are empowered to diagnose difficult problems more effectively, validate changes before they are implemented, and plan for future scenarios, including growth and failure.

OPNET's Application Characterization Environment (ACE) module for IT Guru enables enterprises to identify the root cause of end-to-end application performance problems and to solve them cost-effectively by understanding the impact of changes.

In this lab, you will learn the basics of the OPNET IT Guru Academic Edition software. You will learn how to set up and run OPNET IT Guru Academic Edition. You will become familiar with some of its capabilities by running some tutorials.

The labs in this manual are implemented with OPNET IT Guru Academic Edition release 9.1.A (Build 1999). If you want to download the software, you can visit the following site to register with OPNET technology: www.opnet.com/university_program/itguru_academic_edition/

Recommended system configuration, platforms, and software:

- 1.5-GHz processor or higher, 512-MB to 2-GB RAM, and 1-GB disk space
- Display: 1024 × 768 or higher resolution, 256 or more colors
- Adobe Acrobat Reader
- The English-language versions of the following operating systems are supported:
  - ◦ Microsoft Windows NT (Service Pack 3, 5, or 6a)
  - ◦ Windows 2000 (Service Pack 1, 2, and 4 are supported but not required)
  - ◦ Windows XP (Service Pack 1 or 2 is required)
  - ◦ Windows Vista (Service Pack 1 is required)

PRE-LAB ACTIVITIES

📖 Read Chapter 1 from *Computer Networks: A Systems Approach, 5th Edition.*

💻 Go to *www.net-seal.net* and play the following animation:
  ○ No Network

PROCEDURE
Start OPNET IT Guru Academic Edition

To start OPNET IT Guru Academic Edition:

1. Click on **Start → All Programs → OPNET IT Guru Academic Edition x.x → OPNET IT Guru Academic Edition**, where *x.x* is the software version (e.g., 9.1).
2. Read the **Restricted Use Agreement** and if you agree, click **I have read this SOFTWARE AGREEMENT and I understand and accept the terms and conditions described herein.**

Now you should see the starting window of OPNET IT Guru Academic Edition as shown:

CHECK THE OPNET PREFERENCES

The OPNET Preferences let you display and edit environment attributes, which control program operations. In this lab, you will check three of these attributes.

1. After starting OPNET, from the **Edit** menu, choose **Preferences**.
2. The list of environment attributes is sorted alphabetically according to name. You can locate attributes faster by typing any part of the attribute's name in the **Find** field.

3. Check the value of the **license_server** attribute. It has the name of the License Server's host. If IT Guru is getting its license from the local host (i.e., the computer on which the software was installed), the value of **license_server** should be **localhost** as shown in the following figure.
4. Set the **license_server_standalone** attribute to **TRUE**. This attribute specifies whether the program acts as its own license server.
5. A model directory is a directory that contains OPNET model files. If the directory is listed in the **mod_dirs** environment attribute, then OPNET programs will use the models in that directory. Check the value of the **mod_dirs** attribute. The first directory in the list is where your own models will be saved. In the future, you might need to access that directory to back up, copy, or move your models. IT Guru saves numerous files for every single project you create.
6. Click **OK** to close the dialog box.

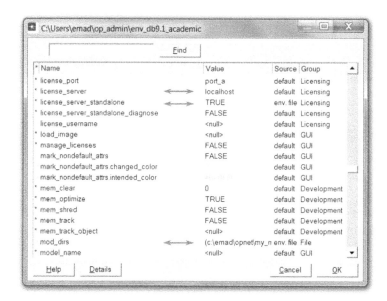

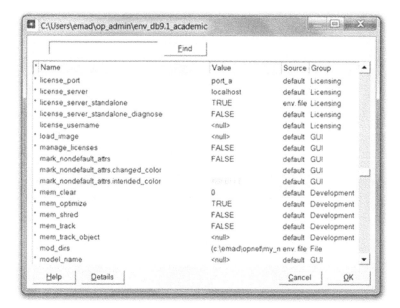

Run the Introduction Tutorial

Now you will run the introductory tutorial that teaches you the basics of using OPNET IT Guru.

1. From the **Help** menu, select **Tutorial**.
2. Go over the **Introduction** lesson from the list of *Basic Lessons*.

Run the Small Internetworks Tutorial

In this tutorial, you will learn how to use OPNET IT Guru features to build and analyze network models.

1. From the **Help** menu, select **Tutorial**.
2. Carry out the **Small Internetworks** tutorial from the list of *Basic Lessons*.

EXERCISE

1. In the project you created for the **Small Internetworks** tutorial, add a new scenario as a duplicate of the **first_floor** scenario. Name the new scenario **expansion2**. In the **expansion2** scenario, expand the network the same way as you did in the **expansion** scenario but with 30 nodes in the second floor instead of 15 nodes. Run the simulation and compare the load and delay graphs of this new scenario with the corresponding graphs of the **first_floor** and **expansion** scenarios.

LAB REPORT

The laboratory report for all labs in this manual, including this one, should incorporate the following items/sections:

- A cover page with your name, course information, lab number and title, and date of submission.
- A summary of the addressed topic and objectives of the lab.
- Implementation: a brief description of the process you followed in conducting the implementation of the lab scenarios.
- Results obtained throughout the lab implementation, the analysis of these results, and a comparison of these results with your expectations.
- Answers to the given exercises at the end of the lab. If an answer incorporates new graphs, analysis of these graphs should be included here.
- A conclusion that includes what you learned, difficulties you faced, and any suggested extensions/improvements to the lab.

CSMA
A Direct Link Network with Media Access Control

OBJECTIVES

This lab is designed to demonstrate the operation of the Ethernet network. The simulation in this lab will help you examine the performance of the Ethernet network under different scenarios.

OVERVIEW

The Ethernet is a working example of the more general carrier sense multiple access with collision detect (CSMA/CD) local area network technology. The Ethernet is a multiple-access network, meaning that a set of nodes sends and receives frames over a shared link. The "carrier sense" in CSMA/CD means that all the nodes can distinguish between an idle and a busy link. The "collision detect" means that a node listens as it transmits and can, therefore, detect when a frame it is transmitting has interfered (collided) with a frame transmitted by another node. The Ethernet is said to be a 1-persistent protocol because an adaptor transmits its ready frame with probability 1 whenever a busy line goes idle.

In this lab, you will set up an Ethernet with 30 nodes connected through a coaxial link in a bus topology. The coaxial link is operating at a data rate of 10 Mbps. You will study how the throughput of the network is affected by the network load as well as the size of the packets.

1

PRE-LAB ACTIVITIES

📖   Read Section 2.6 from *Computer Networks: A Systems Approach, 5th Edition.*

💻   Go to www.net-seal.net and play the following animation:
  ○ Hub

PROCEDURE
Create a New Project

To create a new project for the Ethernet network:

1. Start **OPNET IT Guru Academic Edition** → Choose **New** from the **File** menu.
2. Select **Project** → Click **OK** → Name the project **<your initials>_Ethernet**, and the scenario **Coax** → Click **OK**.

Local area networks (LANs) are designed to span distances of up to a few thousand meters.

3. In the *Startup Wizard: Initial Topology* dialog box, make sure that **Create Empty Scenario** is selected → Click **Next** → Choose **Office** from the *Network Scale* list → Click **Next** → Assign **200** to **X Span** and keep **Y Span** as **100** → Click **Next** twice → Click **OK**.

4. Close the *Object Palette* dialog box.

Create the Network

To create our coaxial Ethernet network:

1. To create the network configuration, select **Topology** → **Rapid Configuration**. From the drop-down menu choose **Bus** and click **OK**.

2. Click the **Select Models** button in the *Rapid Configuration* dialog box. From the *Model List* drop-down menu choose **ethcoax** and click **OK**.

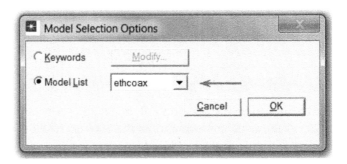

The **eth_tap** is an Ethernet bus tap that connects a node with the bus.

The **eth_coax** is an Ethernet bus that can connect nodes with bus receivers and transmitters through taps.

3. In the *Rapid Configuration* dialog box, set the following eight values, and click **OK**.

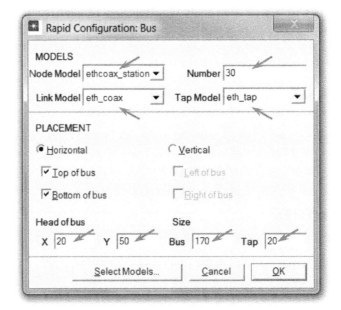

A **higher delay** is used here as an alternative to generating higher traffic, which would require much longer simulation time.

Thickness specifies the thickness of the line used to "draw" the bus link.

4. To configure the coaxial bus, right-click on the horizontal link → Select **Advanced Edit Attributes** from the menu:

   a. Click on the value of the **model** attribute → Select **Edit** from the drop-down menu → Choose the **eth_coax_adv** model.

   b. Assign the value **0.05** to the **delay** attribute (propagation delay in seconds per meter).

   c. Assign **5** to the **thickness** attribute.

   d. Click **OK**.

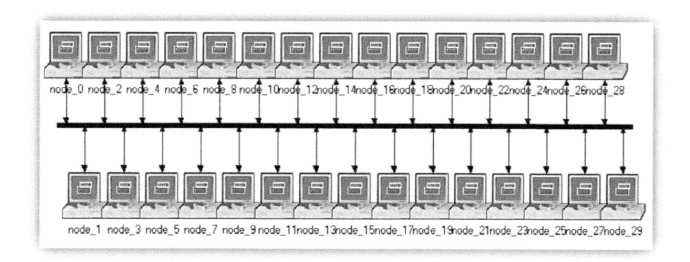

Attribute	Value
name	bus_0
model	eth_coax_adv
ber	0.0
channel count	1
closure model	dbu_closure
coll model	dbu_coll
color	RGB000
condition	enabled
cost	0.0
data rate	10,000,000
delay	0.05
ecc model	dbu_ecc
error model	dbu_error
financial cost	0.00
line style	solid
packet formats	ethernet
propdel model	dbu_propdel
symbol	none
thickness	5

Redefine Path   Extended Attrs.

☐ Apply Changes to Selected Objects   ☑ Advanced

Find Next   Cancel   OK

5. Now you have created the network. It should look like the following illustration.

node_0 node_2 node_4 node_6 node_8 node_10 node_12 node_14 node_16 node_18 node_20 node_22 node_24 node_26 node_28

node_1 node_3 node_5 node_7 node_9 node_11 node_13 node_15 node_17 node_19 node_21 node_23 node_25 node_27 node_29

Configure the Network Nodes

To configure the traffic generated by the nodes:

1. Right-click on any of the 30 nodes → **Select Similar Nodes** to select all 30 nodes in the network.

The argument of the **exponential** distribution is the mean of the interval between successive events. In the exponential distribution, the probability of occurrence of the next event by a given time is not at all dependent on the time of occurrence of the last event or the elapsed time since that event.

The **interarrival time** is the time between successive packet generations in the "ON" state.

2. Right-click on any of the 30 nodes → **Edit Attributes**.
3. Check the **Apply Changes to Selected Objects** check box to avoid reconfiguring each node individually.
4. Expand the **Traffic Generation Parameters** hierarchy:
   a. Change the value of the **ON State Time** to **exponential(100)** → Change the value of the **OFF State Time** to **exponential(0)**. (*Note:* Packets are generated only in the "ON" state.)

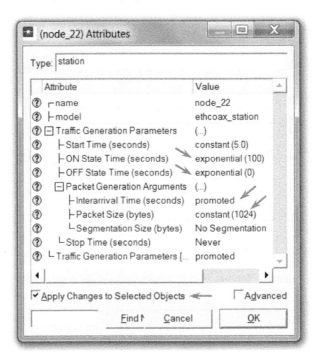

4

5. Expand the **Packet Generation Arguments** hierarchy:
   a. Change the value of the **Packet Size** attribute to **constant(1024)**.
   b. Right-click on the **Interarrival Time** attribute and choose **Promote Attribute to Higher Level**. This allows us to assign multiple values to the **Interarrival Time** attribute and hence to test the network performance under different loads.
6. Click **OK** to return to the *Project Editor*, and **Save** your project.

Configure the Simulation

To examine the network performance under different loads, you need to run the simulation several times by changing the load into the network. There is an easy way to do that. Recall that we promoted the **Interarrival Time** attribute for package generation. Here, we will assign different values to that attribute:

1. Click on the **Configure/Run Simulation** button: 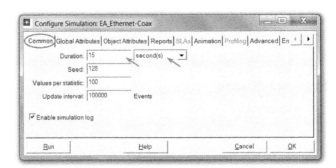 → Make sure that the **Common** tab is chosen → Assign **15** s to the **Duration**.

2. Click on the **Object Attributes** tab.
3. Click the **Add** button. The *Add Attribute* dialog box should appear filled with the promoted attributes of all nodes in the network (if you do not see the attributes in the list,
   close the whole project and reopen it). Add the **Interarrival Time** attribute for all nodes
   as follows:

   a. Click on (**Office Network.node_0.Traffic Generation ….**) → Click the **Wildcard**
   button → Click on **node_0** and choose (*) from the drop-down menu → Click **OK**.

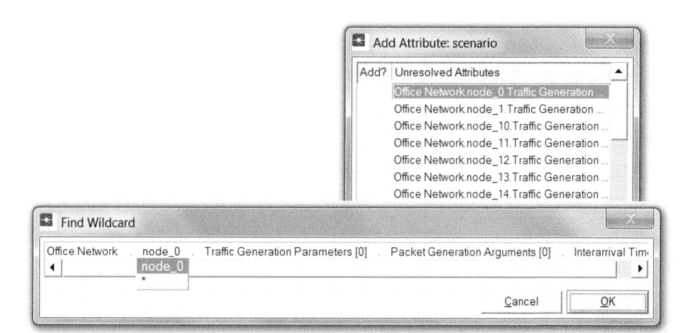

   b. A new attribute is now generated containing the asterisk (the second one in the list).
   Click on the empty cell to the left of this attribute to add it as shown → Click **OK**.

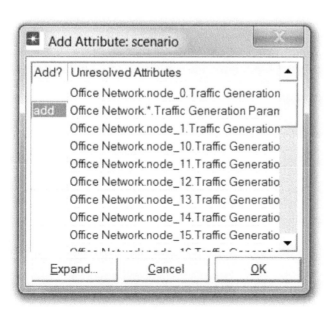

4. Now you should see the **Office Network.*.Traffic Generation Parameter ...** in the list of simulation object attributes. Click on that attribute to select it → Click the **Values** button of the dialog box as shown.

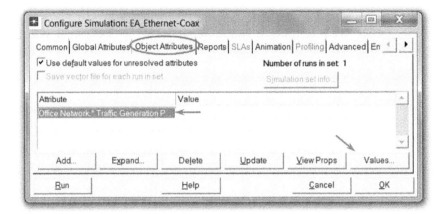

5. Add the nine shown values. (*Note:* To add the first value, double-click on the first cell under the **Value** column → Type "exponential (2)" into the textbox and press **Enter**. Repeat this process for all nine values.)

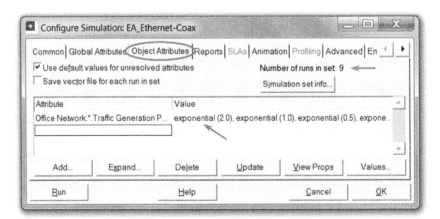

6. Click **OK**. Now look at the upper-right corner of the *Simulation Configuration* dialog box and make sure that the *Number of runs in set* is **9**.

7. For each simulation of the nine runs, we need the simulator to save a "scalar" value that represents the "average" load in the network and to save another scalar value that represents the average throughput of the network. To save these scalars we need to configure the simulator to save them in a file. Click on the **Advanced** tab in the *Configure Simulation* dialog box.
8. Assign **<your initials>_Ethernet_Coax** to the *Scalar file* text field.
9. Click **OK** and then save your project.

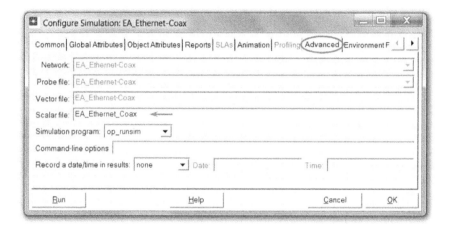

Choose the Statistics

To choose the statistics to be collected during the simulation:

1. Right-click anywhere in the project workspace (but not on one of the nodes or links) and select **Choose Individual Statistics** from the pop-up menu → Expand the **Global Statistics** hierarchy.
   a. Expand the **Traffic Sink** hierarchy → Click the check box next to **Traffic Received (packets/sec)** (make sure you select the statistic with units of packets/sec).
   b. Expand the **Traffic Source** hierarchy → Click the check box next to **Traffic Sent (packets/sec)**.
   c. Click **OK**.
2. Now to collect the average of the above statistics as a scalar value by the end of each simulation run, do the following:
   a. Select **Choose Statistics (Advanced)** from the *Simulation* menu.
   b. The **Traffic Sent** and **Traffic Received** probes should appear under the **Global Statistic Probes**.
   c. Right-click on **Traffic Received** probe → **Edit Attributes**. Set the **scalar data** attribute to **enabled** → Set the **scalar type** attribute to **time average** → Compare to the following figure and click **OK**.
   d. Repeat the previous step with the **Traffic Sent** probe.
   e. Select **Save** from the **File** menu in the *Probe Model* window.
   f. Select **Close** from the **File** menu in the *Probe Model* window.
3. Now you are back to the *Project Editor*. Make sure to save your project.

A **probe** represents a request by the user to collect a particular piece of data about a simulation.

Run the Simulation

To run the simulation:

1. Click on the **Configure/Run Simulation** button: ➜ Make sure that **15 second(s)** (not hours) is assigned to the **Duration** ➜ Click **Run**. Depending on the speed of your processor, this process may take several minutes to complete.
2. Now the simulator is completing nine runs, one for each traffic generation interarrival time (representing the load into the network). Notice that each successive run takes longer to complete because the traffic intensity is increasing.
3. After the completion of nine simulation runs, click **Close**.
4. **Save** your project.

When you rerun the simulation, OPNET IT Guru will "append" the new results to the results already in the scalar file. To avoid that, delete the scalar file *before* you start a new run. (*Note*: Deleting the scalar file *after* a run will result in losing the collected results from that run.)

- Go to the File menu ➜ Select **Model Files** ➜ **Delete Model Files** ➜ other model files ➜ Select (.os): **Output Scalars** ➜ Select the scalar file to be deleted; in this lab it is **<your initials>_Ethernet_Coax** ➜ Confirm the deletion by clicking **OK** ➜ Click **Close**.

View the Results

To view and analyze the results:

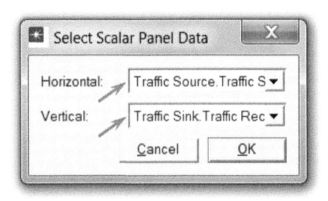

1. Select **View Results (Advanced)** from the **Results** menu. Now the **Analysis Configuration** tool is open.
2. Recall that we saved the average results in a scalar file. To load this file, select **Load Output Scalar File** from the **File** menu ➜ Select **<your initials>_Ethernet-Coax** from the pop-up menu.
3. Select **Create Scalar Panel** from the **Panels** menu ➜ Assign **Traffic Source.Traffic Sent (packets/sec). average** to Horizontal ➜ Assign **Traffic Sink. Traffic Received (packets/sec).average** to Vertical ➜ Click **OK**.
4. The resulting graph should resemble the one below:

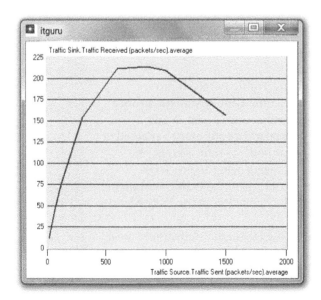

FURTHER READING

IEEE 802.3 Ethernet Working Group: www.ieee802.org/3/

EXERCISES

1. Explain the graph we received in the simulation that shows the relationship between the received (throughput) and sent (load) packets. Why does the throughput drop when the load is either very low or very high?

2. Create three duplicates of the simulation scenario implemented in this lab. Name these scenarios **Coax_Q2a**, **Coax_Q2b**, and **Coax_Q2c**. Set the **Interarrival Time** attribute of the *Packet Generation Arguments* for all nodes in the new scenarios as follows:
   ○ **Coax_Q2a** scenario: exponential(0.1)
   ○ **Coax_Q2b** scenario: exponential(0.05)
   ○ **Coax_Q2c** scenario: exponential(0.025)
   In all these new scenarios, open the *Configure Simulation* dialog box, and from the *Object Attributes*, delete the multiple-value attribute (the only attribute shown in the list). Choose the following statistic for node 0: **Ethcoax → Collision Count**. Make sure that the following global statistic is chosen: **Global Statistics → Traffic Sink → Traffic Received (packet/sec)**. (Refer to the "Choose the Statistics" section in the lab.) Run the simulation for all three new scenarios. Get two graphs: one to compare node 0's collision counts in these three scenarios and the other graph to compare the received traffic from the three scenarios. Explain the graphs and comment on the results. (*Note:* To compare results you need to select **Compare Results** from the **Results** menu after the simulation run is done.)

3. To study the effect of the number of stations on Ethernet segment performance, create a duplicate of the **Coax_Q2c** scenario, which you created in Exercise 2. Name the new scenario **Coax_Q3**. In the new scenario, remove the odd-numbered nodes, a total of 15 nodes (node 1, node 3, …, and node 29). Run the simulation for the new scenario. Create a graph that compares node 0's collision counts in scenarios **Coax_Q2c** and **Coax_Q3**. Explain the graph and comment on the results.

4. In the simulation, a packet size of 1024 bytes is used. (*Note:* Each Ethernet packet can contain up to 1500 bytes of data.) To study the effect of the packet size on the throughput of the created Ethernet network, create a duplicate of the **Coax_Q2c** scenario, which you created in Exercise 2. Name the new scenario **Coax_Q4**. In the new scenario, use a packet size of 512 bytes (for all nodes). For both **Coax_Q2c** and **Coax_Q4** scenarios, choose the following global statistic: **Global Statistics → Traffic Sink → Traffic Received (bits/sec)**. Rerun the simulation of **Coax_Q2c** and **Coax_Q4** scenarios. Create the following graphs and explain them:
   a. A graph that compares the throughput as packets per second in **Coax_Q2c** and **Coax_Q4** scenarios
   b. A graph that compares the throughput as bits per second in **Coax_Q2c** and **Coax_Q4** scenarios

LAB REPORT

Prepare a report that follows the guidelines explained in the Introduction Lab. The report should include the answers to the preceding exercises as well as the graphs you generated from the simulation scenarios. Discuss the results you obtained and compare these results with your expectations. Mention any anomalies or unexplained behaviors.

Wireless Local Area Network
Medium Access Control for Wirelessly Connected Stations

OBJECTIVES

This lab addresses the Medium Access Control (MAC) sublayer of the IEEE 802.11 standard for the wireless local area network (WLAN). Various options of this standard are studied in this lab. The performance of these options is analyzed under multiple scenarios.

OVERVIEW

The IEEE 802.11 standard provides wireless connectivity to computerized stations that require rapid deployment, such as portable computers. The Medium Access Control (MAC) sublayer in the standard includes two fundamental access methods: distributed coordination function (DCF) and point coordination function (PCF). DCF utilizes the carrier sense multiple access with collision avoidance (CSMA/CA) approach. DCF is implemented in all stations in the wireless local area network (WLAN). PCF is based on polling to determine the station that can transmit next. Stations in an infrastructure network optionally implement the PCF access method.

In addition to the physical CSMA/CA, DCF and PCF utilize a virtual carrier-sense mechanism to determine the state of the medium. This virtual mechanism is implemented by means of the network allocation vector (NAV), which provides each station with a prediction of future traffic on the medium. Each station uses NAV as an indicator of time periods during which transmission will not be initiated even if the station senses that the wireless medium is not busy. NAV gets the information about future traffic from management frames and the header of regular frames being exchanged in the network.

With DCF, every station senses the medium before transmitting. The transmitting station defers as long as the medium is busy. After deferral and while the medium is idle, the transmitting station has to wait for a random backoff interval. After the backoff interval and if the medium is still idle, the station initiates data transmission or optionally exchanges request to send (RTS) and clear to send (CTS) frames with the receiving station. The effect of RTS and CTS frames will be studied in the Mobile WLAN lab.

With PCF, the access point (AP) in the network acts as a point coordinator (PC). The PC uses polling to determine which station can initiate data transmission. It is optional for the stations in the network to participate in PCF and hence respond to polls received from the PC. Such stations are called CF-Pollable stations. The PCF requires the PC to gain control of the medium. To gain such control, the PC utilizes the Beacon management frames to set the NAV in the network stations. Because the mechanism used to set NAV is based on the DCF, all stations comply with the PC request to set their NAV, whether or not they are CF-Pollable. This way the PC can control frame transmissions in the network by generating contention-free periods (CFPs). The PC and the CF-Pollable stations do not use RTS/CTS in the CFP.

The standard allows for fragmentation of the MAC data units into smaller frames. Fragmentation is favorable in case the wireless channel is not reliable enough to transmit longer frames. Only frames with a length greater than a fragmentation threshold will be fragmented. Each fragment will be sent independently and will be separately acknowledged. During a contention period, all fragments of a single frame will be sent as bursts with a single invocation of the DCF medium access procedure. In case of PCF and during a contention-free period, fragments are sent individually following the rules of the point coordinator (PC).

PRE-LAB ACTIVITIES

📖 Read Section 2.7 from *Computer Networks: A Systems Approach, 5th Edition*.

💻 Go to *www.net-seal.net* and play the following animation:
   ○ Wireless Network and Multiple Access with Collision Avoidance

PROCEDURE
Create a New Project

To create a new project for the Ethernet network:

1. Start **OPNET IT Guru Academic Edition** → Choose **New** from the **File** menu.
2. Select **Project** → Click **OK** → Name the project **<your initials>_WirelessLAN**, and name the scenario **DCF** → Click **OK**.
3. In the *Startup Wizard: Initial Topology* dialog box, make sure that **Create Empty Scenario** is selected → Click **Next** → Choose **Office** from the *Network Scale* list and check **Use Metric Units** → Click **Next** twice → Click **OK**.

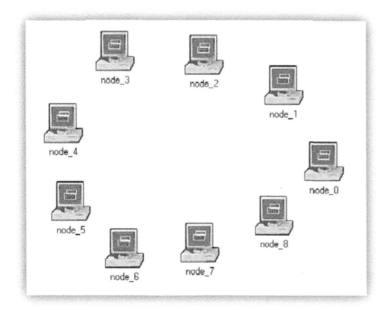

Create and Configure the Network

To create our wireless network:

1. The *Object Palette* dialog box should be now on the top of your project space. If it is not there, open it by clicking 📖. Make sure that the **wireless_lan** is selected from the pull-down menu on the object palette.
2. Add to the project workspace the nine **wlan_station_adv (fix)** from the palette.
   a. To add an object from a palette, click its icon in the object palette → Move your mouse to the workspace → Left-click to place the object. Right-click when finished.
3. Close the *Object Palette* dialog box → Arrange the stations in the workspace as shown in the following figure → **Save** your project.

Configure the Wireless Nodes

1. Repeat the following for each of the nine nodes:
   Right-click on the node → **Edit Attributes** → Assign to the **Wireless LAN MAC Address** attribute a value equals to the node number (e.g., address 1 is assigned to node_1) → Assign to the **Destination Address** attribute the corresponding value shown in the following table → Click **OK**.

Node Name	Destination Address
node_0	Random
node_1	5
node_2	8
node_3	6
node_4	7
node_5	1
node_6	3
node_7	4
node_8	2

13

a. The following figure shows the values assigned to the **Destination Address** and **Wireless LAN MAC Address** attributes for node_1.

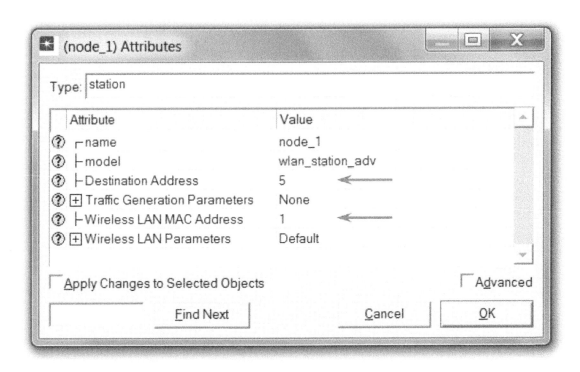

Traffic Generation Parameters

1. Select all nodes in the network simultaneously **except node_0** (click on all of them while holding the **Shift** key) → Right-click on any of the selected nodes → **Edit Attributes** → Check the **Apply Changes to Selected Objects** check box.
2. Expand the **Traffic Generation Parameters** and the **Packet Generation Arguments** hierarchies → Edit the attributes to match the following figure → Click **OK**.

Buffer Size specifies the maximum size of the higher-layer data buffer in bits. Once the buffer limit is reached, the data packets arriving from the higher layer will be discarded until some packets are removed from the buffer so that the buffer has some free space to store these new packets.

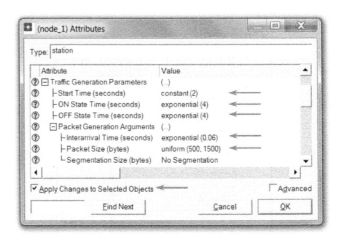

14

3. Select all nodes in the network simultaneously, including **node_0** → Right-click on any of the selected nodes → **Edit Attributes** → Check the **Apply Changes to Selected Objects** check box.
4. Expand the hierarchy of the **Wireless LAN Parameters** attribute → Assign the value 4608000 to the **Buffer Size (bits)** attribute → Click **OK**.
5. Right-click on **node_0** → **Edit Attributes** → Expand the **Wireless LAN Parameters** hierarchy and set the **Access Point Functionality** to **Enabled** → Click **OK**.
6. **Save** the project.

Choose the Statistics

To test the performance of the network in our DCF scenario, we will collect some of the available statistics as follows:

1. Right-click anywhere in the project workspace and select **Choose Individual Statistics** from the pop-up menu.
2. In the *Choose Results* dialog box, expand the **Global Statistics** and **Node Statistics** hierarchies → Choose the five statistics shown.
3. Click **OK**.

Configure the Simulation

Here we will configure the simulation parameters:

1. Click on 🖳 and the *Configure Simulation* window should appear.
2. Set the duration to be **10.0 minutes**.
3. Click **OK** and then **Save** your project.

Duplicate the Scenario

In the network we just created, we did not utilize many of the features explained in the overview section. By default, the distributed coordination function (DCF) method is used for the Medium Access Control (MAC) sublayer. We will create three more scenarios to utilize the features available from the IEEE 802.11 standard. In the DCF_Frag scenario, we will allow fragmentation of the MAC data units into smaller frames and test its effect on the network performance. The DCF_PCF scenario utilizes the point coordination function (PCF) method for the MAC sublayer along with the DCF method. Finally, in the DCF_PCF_Frag scenario we will allow fragmentation of the MAC data and check its effect along with PCF.

THE DCF_FRAG SCENARIO

1. Select **Duplicate Scenario** from the **Scenarios** menu and give it the name **DCF_Frag** → Click **OK**.
2. Select all the nodes in the DCF_ Frag scenario simultaneously → Right-click on any one of them → **Edit Attributes** → Check the **Apply Changes to Selected Objects** check box.
3. Expand the hierarchy of the **Wireless LAN Parameters** attribute → Assign the value 256 to the **Fragmentation Threshold (bytes)** attribute → Click **OK**.

Fragmentation Threshold specifies the fragmentation threshold in bytes. Any data packet received from a higher layer with a size greater than this threshold will be divided into fragments, which will be transmitted separately over the radio interface.

Regardless of the value of this attribute, if the size of a higher-layer packet is larger than the maximum MSDU size allowed by the IEEE 802.11 WLAN standard, which is 2304 bytes, then such a packet will not be transmitted by the MAC, and it will be immediately discarded when received.

15

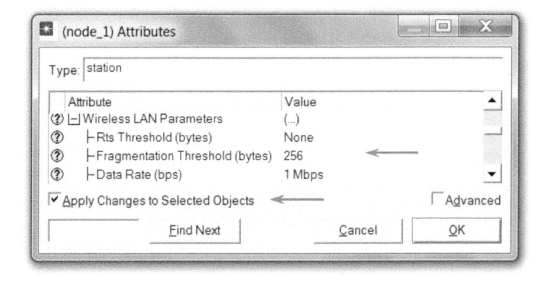

4. Right-click on **node_0** → **Edit Attributes** → Expand the **Wireless LAN Parameters** hierarchy and set the **Access Point Functionality** to **Enabled** → Click **OK**.

THE DCF_PCF SCENARIO

1. Switch to the **DCF scenario,** select **Duplicate Scenario** from the **Scenarios** menu and give it the name **DCF_PCF** → Click **OK** → **Save** your project.
2. Select **node_0**, **node_1**, **node_3**, **node_5**, and **node_7** in the DCF_PCF scenario simultaneously (click on these nodes while holding the **Shift** key) → Right-click on any one of the selected nodes → **Edit Attributes**.
3. Check **Apply Changes to Selected Objects** → Expand the hierarchy of the **Wireless LAN Parameters** attribute → Expand the hierarchy of the **PCF Parameters** attribute → **Enable** the **PCF Functionality** attribute → Click **OK**.

To switch to a scenario, choose **Switch to Scenario** from the **Scenarios** menu or just press **Ctrl+<scenario number>**.

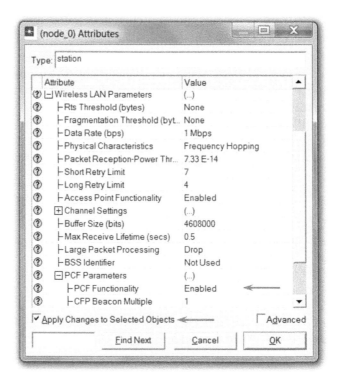

4. Right-click on **node_0** → **Edit Attributes** → Expand the **Wireless LAN Parameters** hierarchy and set the **Access Point Functionality** to **Enabled** → Click **OK**.

THE DCF_PCF_FRAG SCENARIO

1. Switch to the **DCF_Frag scenario**, select **Duplicate Scenario** from the **Scenarios** menu and give it the name **DCF_PCF_Frag** → Click **OK** → **Save** your project.
2. Select **node_0**, **node_1**, **node_3**, **node_5**, and **node_7** in the DCF_PCF_Frag scenario simultaneously → Right-click on any one of the selected nodes → **Edit Attributes**.
3. Check **Apply Changes to Selected Objects** → Expand the hierarchy of the **Wireless LAN Parameters** attribute → Expand the hierarchy of the **PCF Parameters** attribute → **Enable** the **PCF Functionality** attribute → Click **OK**.
4. Right-click on **node_0** → **Edit Attributes** → Expand the **Wireless LAN Parameters** hierarchy and set the **Access Point Functionality** to **Enabled** → Click **OK**.

Run the Simulation

To run the simulation for the four scenarios simultaneously:

1. Go to the **Scenarios** menu → Select **Manage Scenarios**.
2. Click on the row of each scenario and click the **Collect Results** button. This should change the values under the **Results** column to **<collect>** as shown.

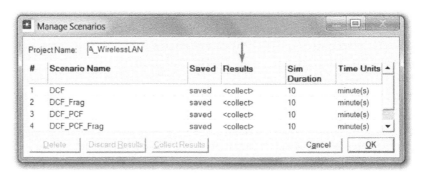

3. Click **OK** to run the four simulations. Depending on the speed of your processor, this process may take several seconds to complete.
4. After the simulation of the four scenarios completes, click **Close** → **Save** your project.

View the Results

To view and analyze the results (*Note:* Actual results will vary slightly based on the actual node positioning in the project):

1. Select **Compare Results** from the **Result** menu.
2. Change the drop-down menu in the lower-right part of the *Compare Results* dialog box from **As Is** to **time_average** → Select the **Delay (sec)** statistic from the **Wireless LAN** hierarchy as shown.

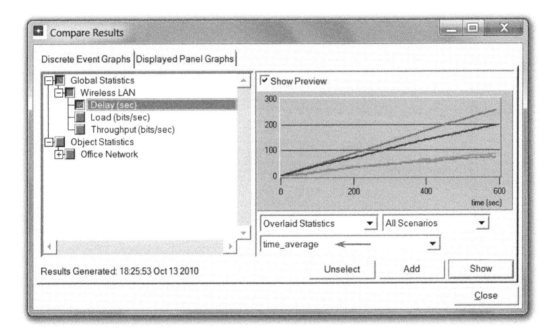

time_average is the average value over time of the values generated during the collection window. This average is performed assuming a "sample-and-hold" behavior of the data set (i.e., each value is weighted by the amount of time separating it from the following update and the sum of all the weighted values is divided by the width of the collection window).

17

3. Click **Show** to show the result in a new panel. The resulting graph should resemble the following one.

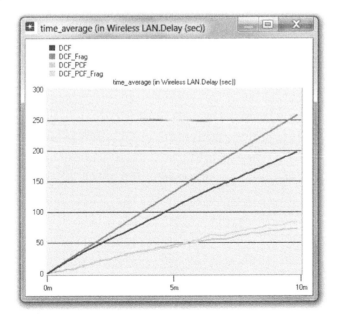

Delay represents the end-to-end delay of all the packets received by the wireless LAN MACs of all WLAN nodes in the network and forwarded to the higher layer.

This delay includes medium access delay at the source MAC, reception of all the fragments individually, and transfer of the frames through AP, if access point functionality is enabled.

4. Go to the *Compare Results* dialog box → Follow the same procedure to show the graphs of the following statistics from the **Wireless LAN** hierarchy: **Load (bits/sec)** and **Throughput (bits/sec)**. The resulting graphs should resemble the following ones.

Load represents the total load (in bits/sec) submitted to wireless LAN layers by all other higher layers in all WLAN nodes of the network.

This statistic does not include the bits of the higher-layer packets that are dropped by WLAN MACs upon arrival and not considered for transmission because of, for example, insufficient space left in the higher-layer packet buffer of the MAC.

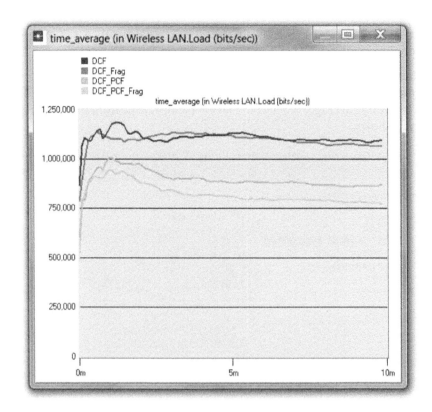

Throughput represents the total number of bits (in bits/sec) forwarded from wireless LAN layers to higher layers in all WLAN nodes of the network.

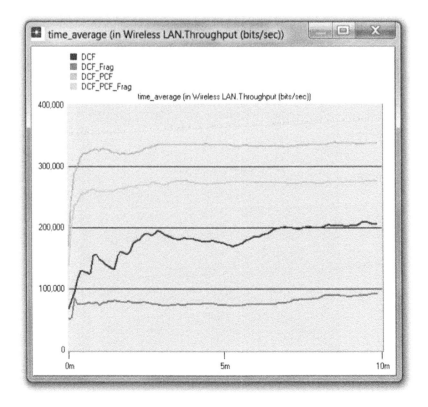

5. Go to the *Compare Results* dialog box → Expand the **Object Statistics** hierarchy → Expand the **Office Network** hierarchy → Expand the hierarchy of two nodes. One node should have PCF enabled in the DCF_PCF scenario (e.g., node_3) and the other node should have PCF disabled (e.g., node_2) → Show the result of the **Delay (sec)** statistic for the chosen nodes. The resulting graphs should resemble the following ones.

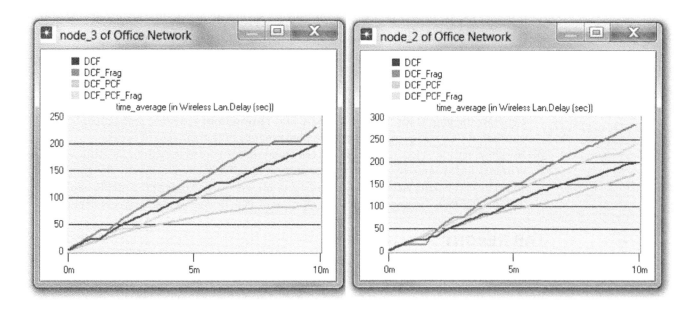

6. Repeat Step 5 above but for the **Retransmission Attempts (packets)** statistic. The resulting graphs should resemble the following ones.

19

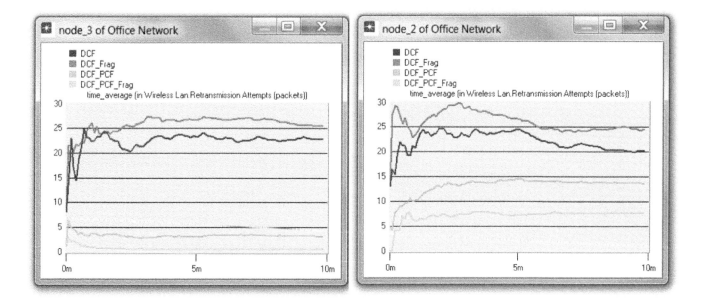

7. Close all graphs and the *Compare Results* dialog box → **Save** your project.

FURTHER READING

ANSI/IEEE Standard 802.11, 1999 Edition: Wireless LAN Medium Access Control (MAC) and Physical Layer (PHY) Specifications.

EXERCISES

1. Based on the definition of the statistic **Load**, explain why with PCF enabled the load is lower than if DCF is used without PCF.

2. Analyze the graphs that compare the **Delay** and **Throughput** of the four scenarios. What are the effects of utilizing PCF and fragmentation on these two statistics?

3. From the last four graphs, explain how the performance of a node without PCF is affected by having PCF enabled in other nodes in the network.

4. Create two new scenarios as duplicates of the DCF_PCF scenario. Name the first new scenario **DCF_allPCF** and the second new scenario **DCF_twoPCF**. In **DCF_allPCF**, enable the PCF attribute in all eight nodes: node_1 through node_8. (*Note:* Do not include node_0 in any of your attribute editing.) In **DCF_twoPCF**, disable the PCF attribute in node_3 and node_5 (this will leave only node_1 and node_7 with PCF enabled). Generate the graphs for the **Delay**, **Load**, and **Throughput** statistics, and explain how the number of PCF nodes might affect the performance of the wireless network.

5. For all scenarios, select the **Media Access Delay** statistic from the Global Statistics → **Wireless LAN hierarchy**. Rerun the simulation for all scenarios. Generate the graph that compares the **Media Access Delay** statistic of all scenarios. Analyze the graph, explaining the effect of PCF, fragmentation, and number of PCF nodes on media access delay.

LAB REPORT

Prepare a report that follows the guidelines explained in the Introduction Lab. The report should include the answers to the preceding exercises as well as the graphs you generated from the simulation scenarios. Discuss the results you obtained and compare these results with your expectations. Mention any anomalies or unexplained behaviors.

Switched LANs
A Set of Local Area Networks Interconnected by Switches

OBJECTIVES

This lab is designed to demonstrate the implementation of switched local area networks. The simulation in this lab will help you examine the performance of different implementations of local area networks connected by switches and hubs.

OVERVIEW

There is a limit as to how many hosts can be attached to a single network and to the size of a geographic area that a single network can serve. Computer networks use switches to enable the communication between one host and another, even when no direct connection exists between the hosts. A switch is a device with several inputs and outputs leading to and from the hosts that the switch interconnects. The core job of a switch is to take packets that arrive on an input and forward (or switch) them to the right output so that they will reach their appropriate destination.

A key problem that a switch must deal with is the finite bandwidth of its outputs. If packets destined for a certain output arrive at a switch and their arrival rate exceeds the capacity of that output, then we have a problem of contention. In this case, the switch will queue, or buffer, the packets until the contention subsides. If the contention lasts too long, however, the switch will run out of buffer space and be forced to discard packets. When packets are discarded too frequently, the switch is said to be congested.

In this lab, you will set up switched LANs using two different switching devices: hubs and switches. A hub forwards the packet that arrives on any of its inputs to all the outputs regardless of the destination of the packet. However, a switch forwards incoming packets to one or more outputs, depending on the destination(s) of the packets. You will study how the throughput and collision of packets in a switched network are affected by the configuration of the network and the types of switching devices that are used.

PRE-LAB ACTIVITIES

📖 Read Section 3.1 from *Computer Networks: A Systems Approach, 5th Edition.*

💻 Go to www.net-seal.net and play the following animations:
   ○ Switch
   ○ Switched Network With No Server
   ○ Switched Network With Server

PROCEDURE

Create a New Project

1. Start the **OPNET IT Guru Academic Edition** → Choose **New** from the **File** menu.
2. Select **Project** and click **OK** → Name the project **<your initials>_SwitchedLAN**, and the scenario **OnlyHub**→ Click **OK**.
3. In the *Startup Wizard: Initial Topology* dialog box, make sure that **Create Empty Scenario** is selected → Click **Next** → Choose **Office** from the *Network Scale* list → Click **Next** three times → Click **OK**.
4. Close the *Object Palette* dialog box.

Create the Network

To create a switched LAN:

1. Select **Topology** → **Rapid Configuration**. From the drop-down menu choose **Star** and click **OK**.
2. Click the **Select Models** button in the *Rapid Configuration* dialog box. From the *Model List* drop-down menu choose **ethernet** and click **OK**.

The prefix **ethernet16_** indicates that the device supports up to 16 Ethernet connections.

3. In the *Rapid Configuration* dialog box, set the following five values: **Center Node Model = ethernet16_hub**, **Periphery Node Model = ethernet_station**, **Link Model = 10BaseT**, **Number = 16**, **Y = 50**, and **Radius = 42** → Click **OK**.

The **10BaseT** link represents an Ethernet connection operating at 10 Mbps.

4. Right-click on **node_16**, which is the hub → **Edit Attributes** → Change the **name** attribute to **Hub1** and click **OK**.
5. Now that you have created the network, it should look like the following one.
6. Make sure to save your project.

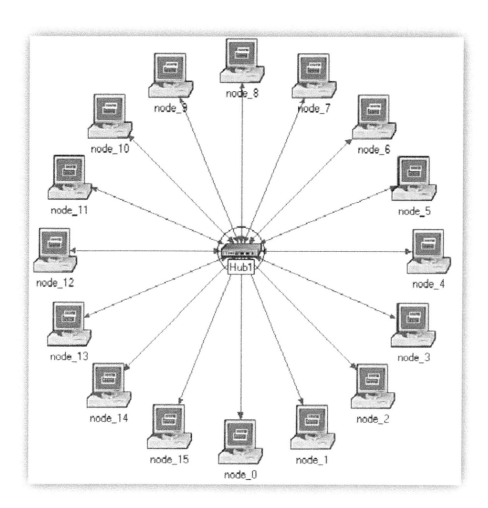

Configure the Network Nodes

Here you will configure the traffic generated by the stations.

1. Right-click on any of the 16 stations (node_0 to node_15) → **Select Similar Nodes**. Now all stations in the network are selected.
2. Right-click on any of the 16 stations → **Edit Attributes**.
   a. Check the **Apply Changes to Selected Objects** check box. This is important to avoid reconfiguring each node individually.
3. Expand the hierarchies of the **Traffic Generation Parameters** attribute and the **Packet Generation Arguments** attribute → Set the four values indicated by the arrows in the figure to the right.
4. Click **OK** to close the attribute editing window(s).
5. **Save** your project.

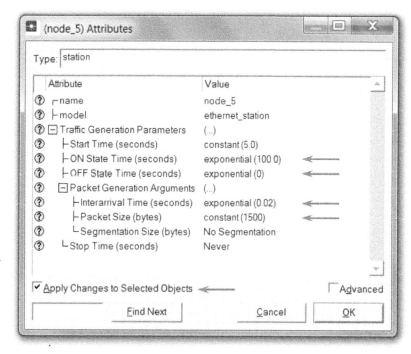

Choose Statistics

The **Ethernet Delay** represents the end-end delay of all packets received by all the stations.

Traffic Received (in packets/sec) by the traffic sinks across all nodes.

Traffic Sent (in packets/sec) by the traffic sources across all nodes.

Collision Count is the total number of collisions encountered by the hub during packet transmissions.

To choose the statistics to be collected during the simulation:

1. Right-click anywhere in the project workspace and select **Choose Individual Statistics** from the pop-up menu.
2. In the *Choose Results* dialog box, choose the shown four statistics.
3. Click **OK**.

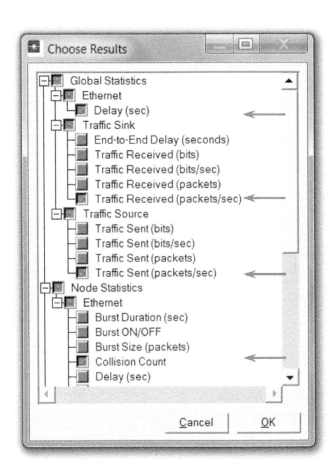

Configure the Simulation

Here we need to configure the duration of the simulation:

1. Click on the **Configure/Run Simulation** button: 🗙
2. Set the duration to **2.0 minutes**.
3. Click **OK**.

Duplicate the Scenario

The network we just created utilizes only one hub to connect the 16 stations. We need to create another network that utilizes a switch and see how this will affect the performance of the network. To do that, we will create a duplicate of the current network:

1. Select **Duplicate Scenario** from the **Scenarios** menu and give it the name **HubAndSwitch** → Click **OK**.
2. Open the **Object Palette** by clicking on 🗙. Make sure that **Ethernet** is selected in the pull-down menu on the object palette.

3. We need to place the hub and switch shown here in the new scenario.

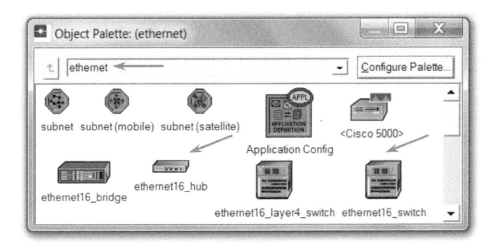

4. To add the **Hub**, click its icon in the object palette → Move your mouse to the workspace → Click to drop the hub at a location you select. Right-click to indicate you are done deploying hub objects.

5. Similarly, add the **Switch**, and then close the **Object Palette**.

6. Right-click on the new hub → **Edit Attributes** → Name it **Hub2** and click **OK**.

7. Right-click on the switch → **Edit Attributes** → Name it **Switch** and click **OK**.

8. Reconfigure the network to look like the following one.

   a. To remove a link, select it and choose **Cut** from the **Edit** menu (or simply press the **Delete** key). You can select multiple links and delete all of them at once.

   b. To add a new link, use the **10BaseT** link available in the **Object Palette**.

25

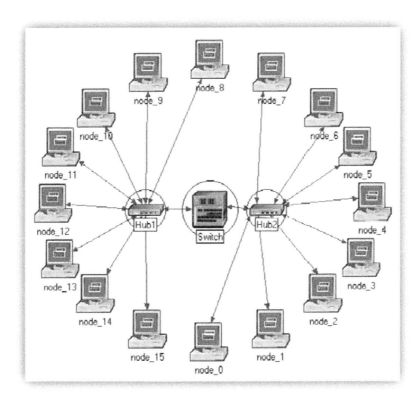

Run the Simulation

To run the simulation for both scenarios simultaneously:

1. Select **Manage Scenarios** from the **Scenarios** menu.
2. Change the values under the **Results** column to **<collect>** (or **<recollect>**) for both scenarios. Compare with the following figure.

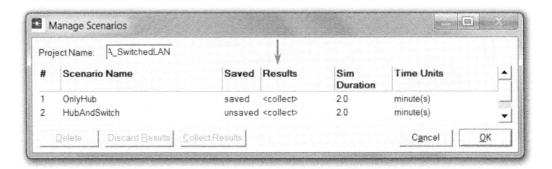

3. Click **OK** to run the two simulations. Depending on the speed of your processor, this may take several minutes to complete.
4. After the two simulation runs complete, one for each scenario, click **Close**.
5. **Save** your project.

View the Results

To view and analyze the results:

1. Select **Compare Results** from the **Results** menu.
2. Change the drop-down menu in the lower-right part of the *Compare Results* dialog box from **As Is** to **time_average**, as shown.

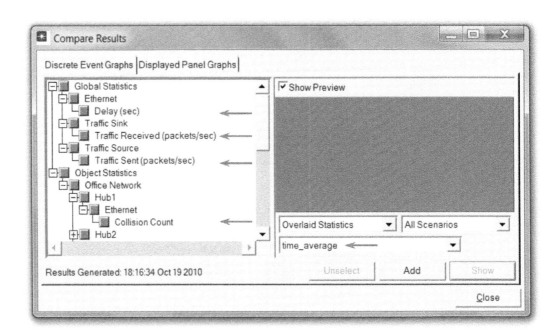

3. Select the **Traffic Sent (packets/sec)** statistic and click **Show**. The resulting graph should resemble the one below. As you can see, the traffic sent in both scenarios is almost identical.

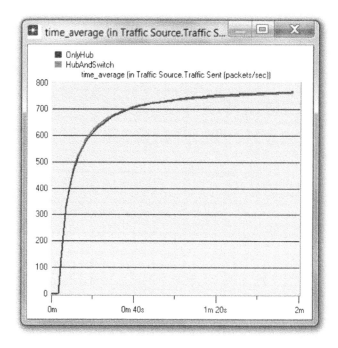

The **time_average** is the average value over time of the values generated during the collection window. This average is performed assuming a "sample-and-hold" behavior of the data set (i.e., each value is weighted by the amount of time separating it from the following update, and the sum of all the weighted values is divided by the width of the collection window). For example, suppose you have a 1-s bucket in which 10 values have been generated. The first seven values were generated between 0 and 0.3 s, the eighth value at 0.4 seconds, the ninth value at 0.6 s, and the tenth at 0.99 s. Because the last three values have higher durations, they are weighted more heavily in calculating the time average.

4. Select the **Traffic Received (packets/sec)** statistic and click **Show**. The resulting graph should resemble the one following. As you see, the traffic received with the second scenario, **HubAndSwitch**, is higher than that of the **OnlyHub** scenario.

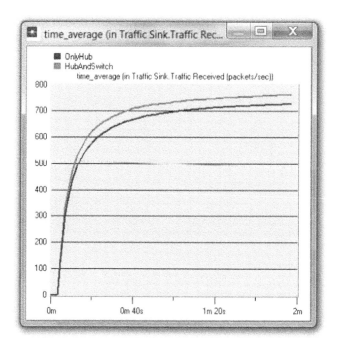

5. Select the **Delay (sec)** statistic and click **Show**. The resulting graph should resemble the one that follows. (*Note:* Results may vary slightly due to different node placement.)

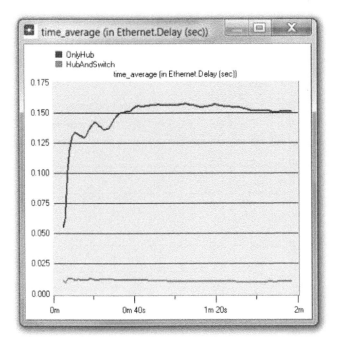

6. Select the **Collision Count** statistic for **Hub1** and click **Show**.
7. On the resulting graph, right-click anywhere on the *graph area* → Choose **Add Statistic** → Expand the hierarchies as shown below → Select the **Collision Count** statistic for **Hub2** → Change **As Is** to **time_average** → Click **Add** → Click **Close**.

The resulting graph should resemble the one that follows.

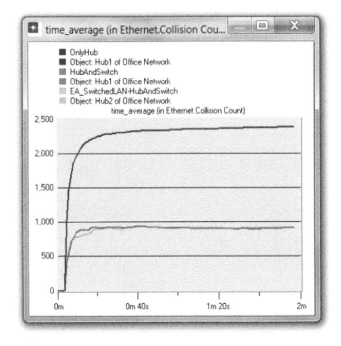

8. Save your project.

FURTHER READING

OPNET Building Networks: From the **Protocols** menu, select **Methodologies** → **Building Network Topologies**.

EXERCISES

1. Explain why adding a switch makes the network perform better in terms of throughput and delay.
2. We analyzed the collision counts of the hubs. Can you analyze the collision count of the "switch"? Explain your answer.
3. Create two new scenarios. The first new scenario is the same as the **OnlyHub** scenario with the hub replaced by a switch. The second new scenario is the same as the **HubAndSwitch** scenario with both hubs replaced by two switches, the old switch removed, and the two switches you just added together connected with a 10BaseT link. Compare the performance of the four scenarios in terms of delay, throughput, and collision count. Analyze the results.

Note: To replace a hub with a switch, right-click on the hub and assign **ethernet16_switch** to its **model** attribute.

LAB REPORT

Prepare a report that follows the guidelines explained in the Introduction Lab. The report should include the answers to the preceding exercises as well as the graphs you generated from the simulation scenarios. Discuss the results you obtained and compare these results with your expectations. Mention any anomalies or unexplained behaviors.

VLANs: Virtual Local Area Networks

Logically Partitioning a Physical Network into Several Separate LANs

OBJECTIVES

The objective of this lab is to study how to divide a physical network into a number of separate logical networks using virtual local area networks (VLANs) with the benefit of decreasing collision domain and adding more security.

OVERVIEW

Virtual LANs (VLANs) allow a single extended LAN to be partitioned into several seemingly separate LANs. Each virtual LAN is assigned an identifier (sometimes called a color), and packets can only travel from one segment to another if both segments have the same identifier. This has the effect of limiting the number of segments in an extended LAN that will receive any given broadcast packet. An attractive feature of VLANs is that it is possible to change the logical topology without moving any wires or changing any addresses.

In this lab, we will build a network for a university with two departments. Each department has three local area networks. One LAN is for the professors, the second is for the staff members, and the third is for the students. The university has three servers: one server is for research, the second is for human resources databases, and the third server is for online courses (e-learning). In the first scenario, the setting of the network allows all members of both departments to have access to all three servers. Even a hacker who plugs his or her computer into any of the network switches can also have access to the network servers.

The second scenario uses VLANs to allow access to the research server only by professors. The staff members are allowed to access only the human resources server. The students can only access the e-learning server. The VLANs settings will not allow a hacker to have access to any of the servers.

In the third scenario, a router is added to allow for communication between different VLANs. Here we will allow both the professors and students to communicate with each other and to have access to both the research and e-learning servers. The simulation results show us that VLANs also decrease the load on some of the links in the networks.

PRE-LAB ACTIVITIES

📖 Read Section 3.1.4 from *Computer Networks: A Systems Approach*, 5th Edition.

PROCEDURE

Create a New Project

1. Start OPNET IT Guru Academic Edition → Choose New from the File menu.
2. Select Project and click OK → Name the project <your initials>_VLAN, and the scenario NoVLAN → Click OK.
3. In the *Startup Wizard: Initial Topology* dialog box, make sure that Create Empty Scenario is selected → Click Next → Choose Campus from the *Network Scale* list → In the *Startup Wizard: Specify Size* dialog box, assign the following: Size = Kilometers, X Span = 1, and Y Span = 1 → Click Next two times → Click OK.

Create and Configure the Network

Network components:

1. Open the *Object Palette* dialog box by clicking ▣. Make sure that the **internet_toolbox** item is selected from the pull-down menu on the object palette. Add the following objects from the palette to the project workspace (see the following figure for placement):
   a. Six **10BaseT_LAN**, four **ethernet16_switch**, three **Ethernet_server**, and one **ethernet_wkstn**.
   b. Connect the objects using **100BaseT** links and *rename* them as shown.
2. **Save** your project.

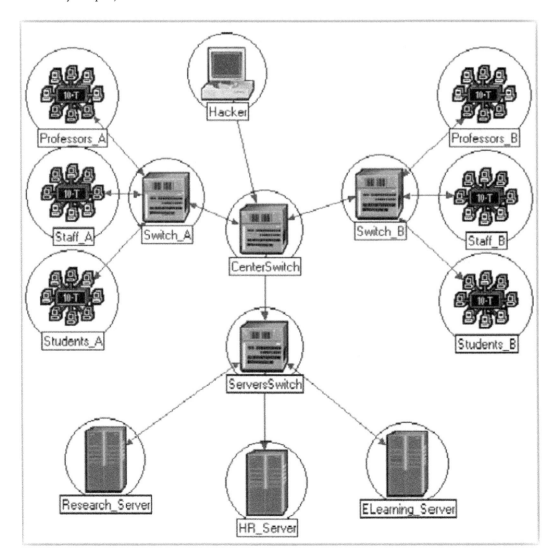

Configure the traffic demands:

1. Simultaneously select the **Research_Server**, the **Hacker**, and all six **LANs** → Select the **Protocols** menu → **IP** → **Demands** → **Create Traffic Demands**.
2. Select **From All** to **Research_Server** as shown → Click **Create**.

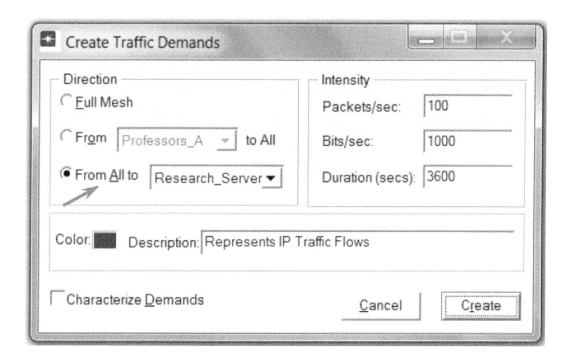

Here we have created traffic demands from all LANs and the Hacker to the Research_Server. Notice the dotted lines representing the demands.

3. Repeat for the HR_Server: Simultaneously select the **HR_Server**, the **Hacker**, and all six **LANs** → Select the **Protocols** menu → **IP** → **Demands** → **Create Traffic Demands** → Select the **From All** to **HR_Server** → Click **Create**.
4. Repeat for the ELearning_Server: Simultaneously select the **ELearning_Server**, the **Hacker**, and all six **LANs** → Select the **Protocols** menu → **IP** → **Demands** → **Create Traffic Demands** → Select the **From All** to **ELearning_Server** → Click **Create**.
5. Press **Ctrl + Shift + M** to hide all traffic demands and **Ctrl + M** to show them again.
6. **Save** your project.

Configure the links ports:

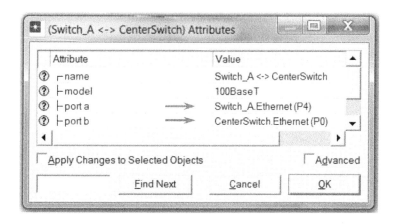

1. Edit the attributes of the network links so that their ports connected to the switches have the numbers indicated in the following figure. The preceding figure shows an example of the ports assigned to the link connecting Switch_A with the CenterSwitch.

Note: If any one of the required ports is not available in the drop-down menu, pick another link to change first because you cannot choose a port that is already in use, and then go back to the previous link.

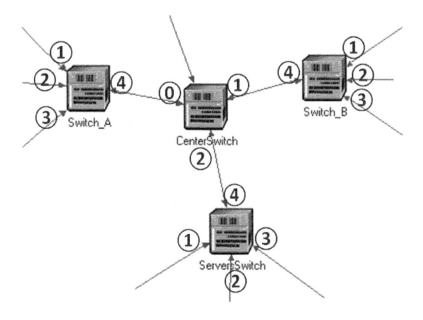

Choose the Statistics

1. Right-click on the link connecting the **Research_Server** and the **ServersSwitch** → Select **Choose Individual Statistics** from the pop-up menu → Check the **throughput (bits/sec)** statistics as shown → Click **OK**.
2. Right-click on the link connecting the **CentralSwitch** and the **ServersSwitch** → Select **Choose Individual Statistics** from the pop-up menu → Check the **throughput (bits/sec)** statistics as shown → Click **OK**.
3. **Save** your project.

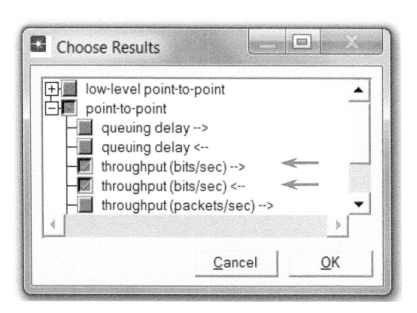

The VLAN Scenario

In the network we just created, the professors, students, staff, and even the hacker have access to the network of three servers. We need to create VLANs so that professors have access only to the Research_Server, staff members have access only to the HR_Server, and students have access only to the ELearning_Server. The hacker will not be granted access to any server. The following table shows the VLANs we plan to create and the members of each VLAN.

VLAN Identifier (VID)	VLAN Members
111	Professors_A LAN, Professors_B LAN, and Research_Server.
222	Staff_A LAN, Staff_B LAN, and HR_Server.
333	Students_A LAN, Students_B LAN, and ELearning_Server.

1. Select **Duplicate Scenario** from the **Scenarios** menu and name it **VLAN** → Click **OK**.
2. In the new scenario, select **Switch_A**, **Switch_B**, and **ServersSwitch** simultaneously → Right-click on any of them → Select **Edit Attributes** → Check the **Apply Changes to Selected Objects** check-box.
3. Expand the **VLAN Parameters** hierarchy → Assign **Port-Based VLAN** to the **Scheme** attribute → Edit the **Supported VLANs** attribute as shown in the following figure → Click **OK**.

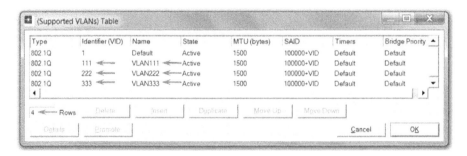

4. Expand the **Switch Port Configuration** hierarchy.
5. Expand **row 1** hierarchy → Expand the **VLAN Parameters** hierarchy → Change the attributes for row 1 as shown in the following figure (recall that, in the selected switches, port 1 is connected to the members of VLAN 111):

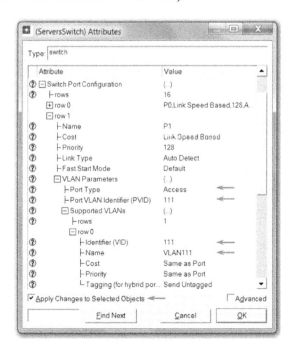

Access ports strip VLAN information from the packets before forwarding, while **trunk** ports always send packets VLAN-tagged, so they always contain VLAN information.

In typical configurations, access ports are used to connect end-nodes and VLAN-unaware nodes to the VLAN-aware bridged network, while trunk ports are used to connect the VLAN-ware bridges/switches of the bridged network to each other.

Regardless of their type, the ports can support as many VLANs as they want as long as these VLANs are supported by the surrounding node. Trunk ports are expected to support multiple VLANs, but they need to be configured under the sibling attribute "Supported VLANs" (i.e., they don't support all the VLANs by default).

6. Expand **row 2** hierarchy → Expand the **VLAN Parameters** hierarchy → Change the attributes for row 2 as we did for row 1 but assign VLAN 222 instead (recall that, in the selected switches, port 2 is connected to the members of VLAN 222).

7. Expand **row 3** hierarchy → Expand the **VLAN Parameters** hierarchy → Change the attributes for row 3 as we did for row 1 but assign VLAN 333 instead (recall that, in the selected switches, port 3 is connected to the members of VLAN 333).

8. Expand **row 4** hierarchy → Expand the **VLAN Parameters** hierarchy → Change the attributes for row 4 as shown in the following figure.

9. Click **OK** → **Save** your project.

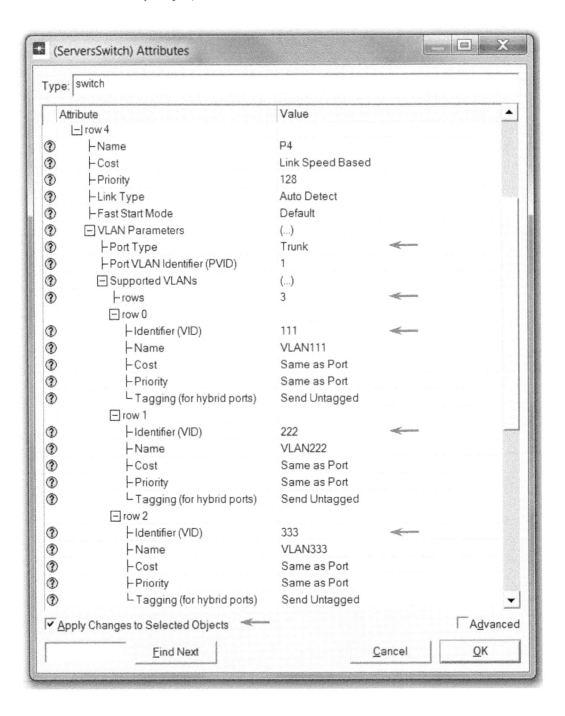

10. Right-click on **CentralSwitch** only → Select **Edit Attributes**.

11. Expand the **VLAN Parameters** hierarchy → Assign **Port-Based VLAN** to the **Scheme** attribute → Edit the **Supported VLANs** attribute as in step 3 above → Click **OK**.
12. Expand the **Switch Port Configuration** hierarchy.
13. Change the attributes of **row 0**, **row 1**, and **row 2** exactly the same way we did in Step 8 with row 4 of the ServersSwitch.
14. Go to the **Protocols** menu → **VLAN** → **Visualize VLANs** → Take a note of the colors listed in the list → Click **OK**. Double check the following:
    a. All members to a VLAN have links with the same color.
    b. All trunk links have their assigned color.
    c. The hacker's link belongs to VID 1.

If you have any problem with the results of the visualization, go back and verify the steps of this configuring scenario.

15. Click **OK** → **Save** your project.

The VLAN_Comm Scenario

The VLAN scenario members of each VLAN are not allowed to communicate with members of any other VLAN. Assume that we need students to have access to the Research_Server and we need the professors to have access to the ELearning_Server. In this case, we need VLAN111 to communicate with VLAN333. This can be done on the IP layer by configuring a router to forward traffic between the two VLANs. Each VLAN will be assigned its own IP subnetwork.

1. While you are in the VLAN scenario, select **Duplicate Scenario** from the **Scenarios** menu and name it **VLAN_Comm** → Click **OK**.
2. Add to the project **ethernet_one_armed_router** from the **VLANs Palette** → Connect it to the **CenterSwitch** using **100BaseT** link → Click on the new link and record the port number in the CenterSwitch connected to it (it is P10 in the following figure).

The **one-armed router** node model represents an IP-based, one-armed router supporting one Ethernet interface. IP packets arriving on the interface are routed to the same interface. This gateway is typically used for inter-VLAN communication.

37

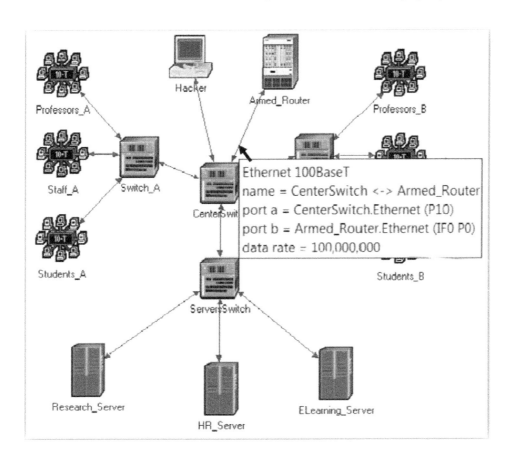

Ethernet 100BaseT
name = CenterSwitch <-> Armed_Router
port a = CenterSwitch.Ethernet (P10)
port b = Armed_Router.Ethernet (IF0 P0)
data rate = 100,000,000

3. Right-click on **CentralSwitch** only → Select **Edit Attributes** → Expand the **Switch Port Configuration** hierarchy → Expand the row of the port you recorded in the previous step (in my project, it is **row 10**) → Change its **VLAN Parameters** and **Supported VLANs** the same way we did with row 0 in the same switch.

4. Click **OK** → **Save** your project.

Now we need to assign the members of each VLAN to the same IP subnetwork, as shown in the following table.

VLAN ID	VLAN Members	IP/Mask
111	Professors_A LAN	192.11.1.1 / 255.255.255.0
	Professors_B LAN	192.11.1.2 / 255.255.255.0
	Research_Server	192.11.1.3 / 255.255.255.0
222	Staff_A LAN	192.22.2.1 / 255.255.255.0
	Staff_B LAN	192.22.2.2 / 255.255.255.0
	HR_Server	192.22.2.3 / 255.255.255.0
333	Students_A LAN	192.33.3.1 / 255.255.255.0
	Students_B LAN	192.33.3.2 / 255.255.255.0
	ELearning_Server	192.33.3.3 / 255.255.255.0

5. Right-click on each of the VLAN members in the previous table → **Edit Attributes** → **IP Host Parameters** → **Interface info** → Assign the **Address** and **Subnet Mask** shown in the previous table. (*Hint:* You can select multiple members and change their attributes at once, then revisit them one by one to edit the IP addresses to match those in the table.)

6. Right-click on the **Armed_Router** → **Edit Attributes** → **IP Routing Parameters** → **Interface Information** → **row 0** → Assign **Address = NO IP Address** → Expand the **Subinterface Information** hierarchy → Assign 2 to the rows.

7. Set the attributes of **row 0** as shown in the following figure:

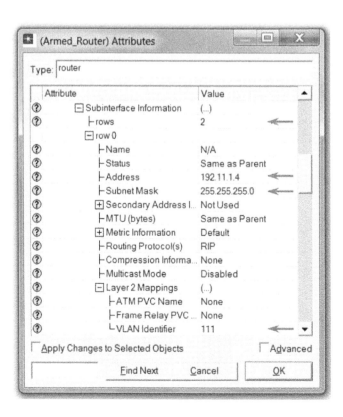

Layer 2 Mappings: **VLAN Identifier** specifies the identifier of the VLAN to which this subinterface belongs. There should not be another subinterface of the same physical interface belonging to the same VLAN. In other words, within the domain of a physical interface, there has to be a 1:1 relation between the subinterfaces and the VLANs.

8. Set the same attributes for **row 1**, but assign 192.33.3.4 to the Address and 333 to the VLAN.
9. Click **OK** and **Save** your project.

Run the Simulation

To run the simulation for the three scenarios simultaneously:

1. Go to the **Scenarios** menu → Select **Manage Scenarios**.
2. Change the values under the **Results** column to **<collect>** (or **<recollect>**) for the three scenarios. Set the **Sim Duration** to 0.5 hour, as shown in the following figure.

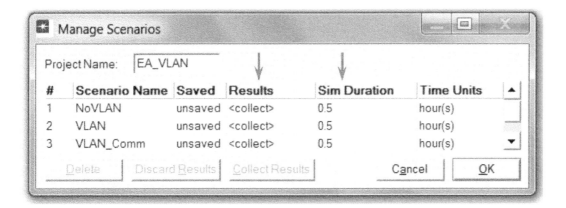

3. Click **OK** to run the three simulations. Depending on the speed of your processor, this process may take several seconds to complete.
4. After the three simulation runs complete, one for each scenario, click **Close**.

View the Results

Compare the routes:

1. Go to the **NoVLAN** scenario → Select the **Protocols** menu → **IP** → **Demands** → **Display Routes for Configured Demands** → Click **OK**.
2. Repeat the previous step for the **VLAN** and **VLAN_Comm** scenarios.
3. Expand the routes hierarchies so that your results resemble those in the following figure. The demand route that is marked with a red bullet indicates an incomplete filtered route. The demand route that is marked with a green bullet indicates a complete route. Take note of which routes are complete and which ones are incomplete. You can click on a specific route and choose **Yes** under *Display* on the right pane. You can also click on **Show All Routes** to display all routes on the project workspace.

Compare the throughput:

1. Select **Compare Results** from the **Results** menu.
2. Show the results of the following two statistics:
   a. **Object Statistics** → **Campus Network** → **ServersSwitch <-> CenterSwitch** → **point-to-point** → **throughput (bits/sec)**. (Hint: Choose the throughput direction that brings results similar to the following one.)
   b. **Object Statistics** → **Campus Network** → **ServersSwitch <-> ResearchServer** → **point-to-point** → **throughput (bits/sec)**. (Hint: Choose the throughput direction that brings results similar to the following one.)

3. Your results should resemble the following figures:

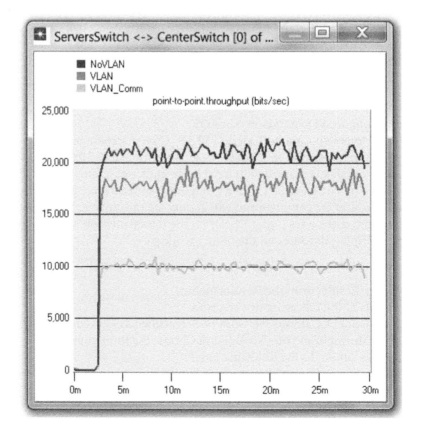

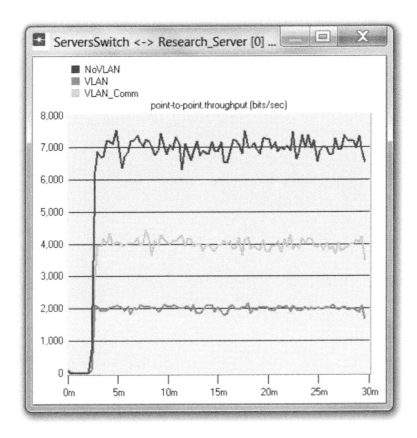

FURTHER READING

IEEE Standard for Virtual Bridged Local Area Networks (IEEE Std 802.1Q™-2005): http://
standards.ieee.org/getieee802/download/802.1Q-2005.pdf

EXERCISES

1. On the results of the Routes for Configured Demands, elaborate on each route for the
   three scenarios, explaining why each is complete or incomplete.
2. In the graph showing the throughput of the link connecting the ServerSwitch and the
   CenterSwitch, explain why it is about 21,000 bits/sec, 18,000 bits/sec, and 10,000 bits/sec
   for the NoVLAN, VLAN, and VLAN_Comm scenarios, respectively.
3. In the graph showing the throughput of the link connecting the ServerSwitch and the
   Research_Server, explain why it is about 7000 bits/sec, 2000 bits/sec, and 4000 bits/sec
   for the NoVLAN, VLAN, and VLAN_Comm scenarios, respectively.
4. Create a new scenario called **VLAN_AllComm** as a copy from the **VLAN_Comm** scenario.
   Modify the new scenario so that all professors, staff members, and students have access to
   all three servers. The only one who is prevented from accessing the servers is the hacker.
   a. Display and comment on the **Routes for Configured Demands** for the new scenario.
   b. Compare the throughput of the links as in Exercises 2 and 3.

LAB REPORT

Prepare a report that follows the guidelines explained in the Introduction Lab. The report
should include the answers to the preceding exercises as well as the graphs you generated
from the simulation scenarios. Discuss the results you obtained and compare these results
with your expectations. Mention any anomalies or unexplained behaviors.

Network Design
Planning a Network with Different Users, Hosts, and Services

OBJECTIVES

The objective of this lab is to demonstrate the basics of designing a network while considering the users, services, and locations of the hosts.

OVERVIEW

Optimizing the design of a network is a major issue. Simulations are usually used to analyze the conceptual design of the network. The initial conceptual design is usually refined several times until a final decision is made to implement the design. The objective is to have a design that maximizes the network performance, considering the cost constraints and the required services to be offered to different types of users. After the network has been implemented, network optimization should be performed periodically throughout the lifetime of the network to ensure its maximum performance and to monitor the utilization of the network resources.

In this lab, you will design a network for a company that has four departments: research, engineering, e-commerce, and sales. You will utilize a LAN model that allows you to simulate multiple clients and servers in one simulation object. This model dramatically reduces both the amount of configuration work you need to perform and the amount of memory needed to execute the simulation. You will be able to define a profile that specifies the pattern of applications used by the users of each department in the company. By the end of this lab, you will be able to study how different design decisions can affect the performance of the network.

PRE-LAB ACTIVITIES

📖 Read Chapter 3 from *Computer Networks: A Systems Approach, 5th Edition*.

💻 Go to www.net-seal.net and play the following animation:
  ○ Adding Switches

PROCEDURE
Create a New Project

1. Start **OPNET IT Guru Academic Edition** → Choose **New** from the **File** menu.
2. Select **Project** and click **OK** → Name the project **<your initials>_NetDesign**, and the scenario **SimpleNetwork** → Click **OK**.

3. In the *Startup Wizard: Initial Topology* dialog box, make sure that **Create Empty Scenario** is selected → Click **Next** → Choose **Campus** from the *Network Scale* list → Click **Next** → Choose **Miles** from the **Size** drop-down menu and assign **1** for both **X Span** and **Y Span** → Click **Next** twice → Click **OK**.

Initialize the Network

1. The *Object Palette* dialog box should now be on the top of your project space. If it is not there, open it by clicking 🖾. Make sure that the **internet_toolbox** is selected from the pull-down menu on the object palette.

Application Config is used to specify applications that will be used to configure users' profiles.

Profile Config describes the activity patterns of a user or group of users in terms of the applications used over a period of time. You must define the applications using the Application Config object before using this object.

2. Add to the project workspace the following objects from the palette: **Application Config**, **Profile Config**, and a **subnet**.

    a. To add an object from a palette, click its icon in the object palette → Move your mouse to the workspace → Left-click to place the object. Right-click when finished. The workspace should contain the shown three objects.

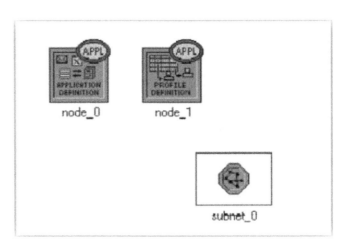

3. Close the *Object Palette* dialog box and save your project.

Configure the Services

1. Right-click on the **Application Config** node → **Edit Attributes** → Change the **name** attribute to **Applications** → Change the **Application Definitions** attribute to **Default** → Click **OK**.

2. Right-click on the **Profile Config** node → **Edit Attributes** → Change the **name** attribute to **Profiles** → Change the **Profile Configuration** attribute to **Sample Profiles** → Click **OK**.

Sample Profiles provides patterns of applications employed by users such as engineers, researchers, salespeople, and multimedia workers.

Configure a Subnet

1. Right-click on the **subnet** node → **Edit Attributes** → Change the **name** attribute to **Engineering** and click **OK**.

2. Double-click on the **Engineering** node. You get an empty workspace, indicating that the subnet contains no objects.

3. Open the object palette 🖾, and make sure it is still set to **internet_toolbox**.

4. Add the following items to the subnet workspace: **10BaseT LAN**, **ethernet16 Switch**, and a **10BaseT link** to connect the LAN with the switch → Close the palette.

5. Right-click on the **10BaseT LAN** node → **Edit Attributes** → Change the **name** attribute to **LAN** → Observe that the **Number of Workstations** attribute has a value of 10. Click in the **Value** column for the **Application: Supported Profiles** attribute, and select **Edit**. You should get a table in which you should do the following:

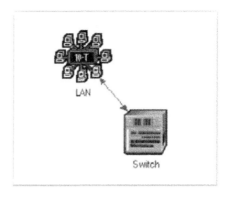

LAN

Switch

   a. Set the number of **rows** to **1**.
   b. Set the **Profile Name** to **Engineer**. *Note:* Engineer is one of the "sample" profiles provided within the **Profile Config** object → Click **OK** twice.

   The object we just created is equivalent to a 10-workstation star topology LAN. The traffic generated from the users of this LAN resembles that generated by "engineers."

6. Rename the **ethernet16 Switch** to **Switch**.
7. The subnet should look like the shown one.
8. **Save** your project.

Configure All Departments

1. Now you have completed the configuration of the Engineering department subnet. To return to the main project space, click the **Go to the higher level** 💡 button. The subnets of the other departments in the company should be similar to the engineering one except for the supported profiles.
2. Make three copies of the **Engineering** subnet we just created: Click on the **Engineering** node → From the **Edit** menu, select **Copy** → From the **Edit** menu, select **Paste** three times, placing the subnet in the workspace after each, to create the new subnets.
3. Rename (right-click on the subnet and select **Set Name**) and arrange the subnets as shown here:

45

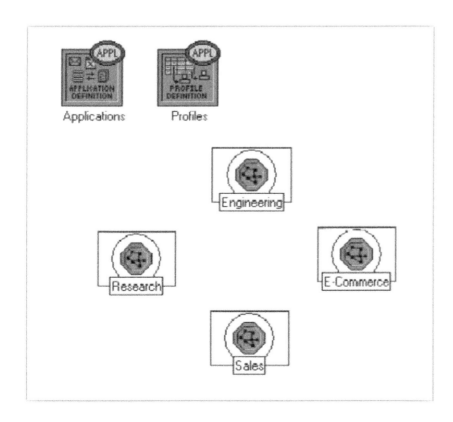

4. Double-click the **Research** node → **Edit** the attributes of its **LAN** → **Edit** the value of the **Application: Supported Profiles** attribute → Change the value of the **Profile Name** from **Engineer** to **Researcher** → Click **OK** twice → Go to the higher level by clicking the 💡 button.
5. Repeat Step 4 with the **Sales** node and assign to its **Profile Name** the profile **Sales Person**.
6. Repeat Step 4 with the **E-Commerce** node and assign to its **Profile Name** the profile **E-commerce Customer**.
7. **Save** your project.

Configure the Servers

Now we need to implement a subnet that contains the servers. The servers have to support the applications defined in the profiles we deployed. You can double-check those applications by editing the attributes of our **Profile** node. Inspect each row under the **Applications** hierarchy, which in turn is under the **Profile Configuration** hierarchy. You will see that we need servers that support the following applications: Web browsing, email, Telnet, file transfer, database, and file print.

1. Open the **Object Palette** 🖼 and add a new **subnet** → Rename the new subnet to **Servers** → Double-click the **Servers** node to enter its workspace.
2. From the **Object Palette**, add three **ethernet_servers**, one **ethernet16_switch**, and three **10BaseT** links to connect the servers with the switch.
3. Close the **Object Palette**.
4. Rename the servers and the switch as shown.

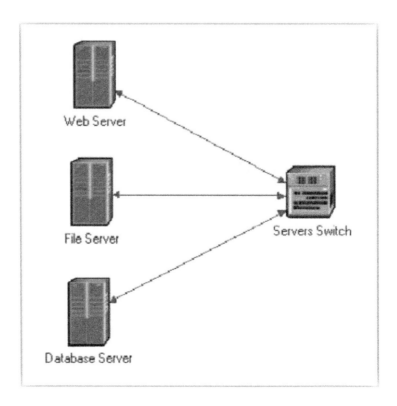

5. Right-click on each one of the preceding servers and **Edit** the value of the **Application: Supported Services** attribute.
   a. For the *Web Server*, add four rows to support the following services as shown in the figure: **Web Browsing (Light HTTP1.1)**, **Web Browsing (Heavy HTTP1.1)**, **Email (Light)**, and **Telnet Session (Light)**.

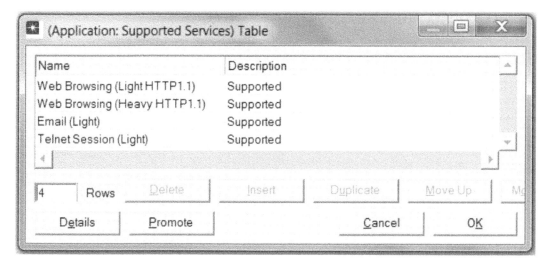

b. For the *File Server*, add two rows to support the following services: **File Transfer (Light)** and **File Print (Light)**.

c. For the *Database Server*, add one row to support the following service: **Database Access (Light)**.

6. Go back to the project space by clicking the **Go to the higher level** button.

7. **Save** your project.

Connect the Subnets

Now all subnets are ready to be connected together.

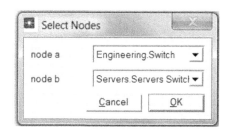

1. **Open** the **Object Palette** and add four **100BaseT** links to connect the subnets of the departments to the **Servers** subnet.

As you create each link, make sure that it is configured to connect the "switches" in both subnets to each other. Do this by choosing them from the drop-down menus as shown.

2. Close the **Object Palette** and **Save** your project.

3. Now your network should resemble the following one:

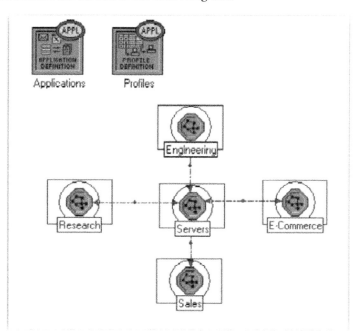

Choose the Statistics

To test the performance of our network, we will collect one of the many available statistics as follows:

1. Right-click anywhere in the project workspace and select **Choose Individual Statistics** from the pop-up menu.

2. In the *Choose Results* dialog box, choose the following statistic:

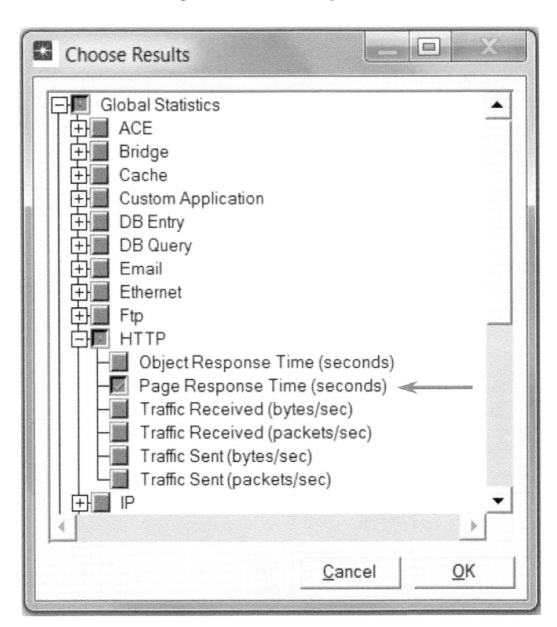

Page Response Time is the required time to retrieve the entire page.

3. Click **OK**.

Configure the Simulation

Here we need to configure the duration of the simulation:

1. Click on the **Configure/Run Simulation** button.

2. Set the duration to **30.0 minutes**.

3. Press **OK**.

48

Duplicate the Scenario

In the network we just created, we assumed that there is no background traffic already in the links. In real networks, the links usually have some existing background traffic. We will create a duplicate of the **SimpleNetwork** scenario but with background utilization in the 100BaseT links.

1. Select **Duplicate Scenario** from the **Scenarios** menu and give it the name **BusyNetwork** → Click **OK**.
2. Select all the **100BaseT** links simultaneously (click on all of them while holding the **Shift** key) → Right-click on any one of them → **Edit Attributes** → Check the **Apply Changes to Selected Objects** check box.
3. Expand the hierarchy of the **Background Utilization** attribute → Expand the **row 0** hierarchy → Assign 99 to the **background utilization (%)** as shown here:

Link utilization is the percentage of the used link bandwidth.

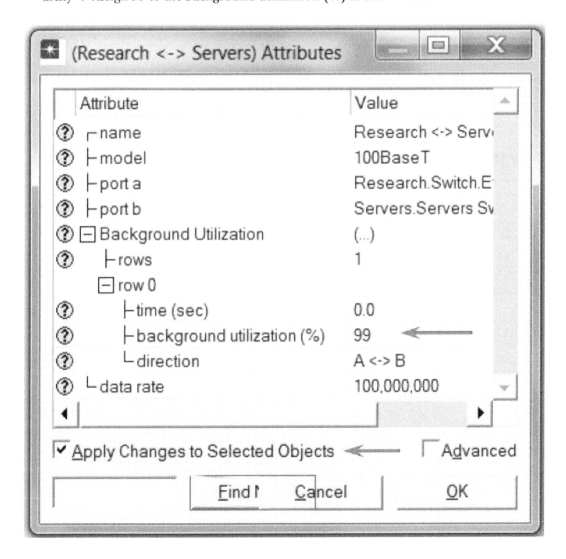

4. Click **OK**.
5. **Save** your project.

Run the Simulation

To run the simulation for both scenarios simultaneously:

1. Go to the **Scenarios** menu → Select **Manage Scenarios**.

49

2. Change the values under the **Results** column to **<collect>** (or **<recollect>**) for both scenarios. Compare to the following figure.

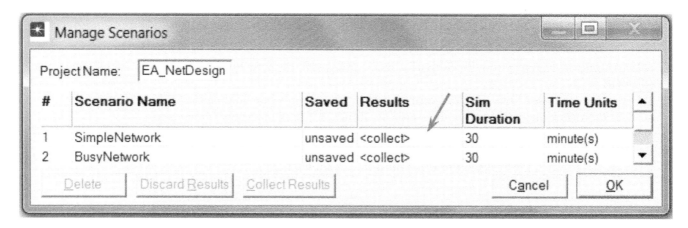

3. Click **OK** to run the two simulations. Depending on the speed of your processor, this task may take several seconds to complete.
4. After the two simulation runs complete (one for each scenario), click **Close**.
5. **Save** your project.

View the Results

To view and analyze the results:

1. Select **Compare Results** from the **Results** menu.
2. Change the drop-down menu in the lower-right part of the *Compare Results* dialog box from **As Is** to **time_average** as shown.
3. Select the **Page Response Time (seconds)** statistic and click **Show**. The resulting graph should resemble the one that follows. (*Note:* Results may vary slightly due to different node placement.)

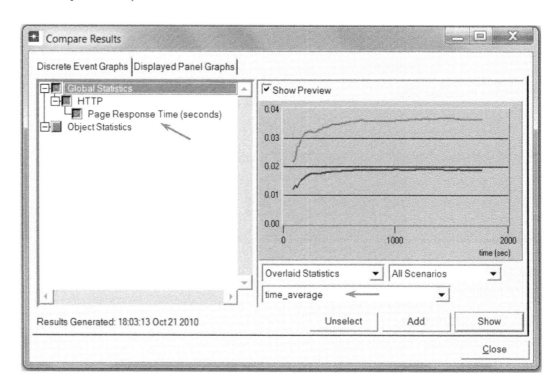

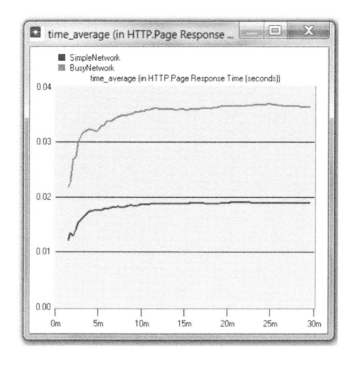

FURTHER READING

OPNET Configuring Applications and Profiles: From the **Protocols** menu, select **Applications →
Model Usage Guide → Configuring Profiles and Applications**.

EXERCISES

1. Analyze the result we obtained regarding the HTTP page response time. Collect four other statistics of your choice and rerun the simulation of the *Simple* and the *Busy* network scenarios. Get the graphs that compare the collected statistics. Comment on these results.
2. In the **BusyNetwork** scenario, study the **utilization%** of the CPUs in the servers (right-click on each server and select **Choose Individual Statistics → CPU → Utilization**).
3. Create a new scenario as a duplicate of the **BusyNetwork** scenario. Name the new scenario **Q3_OneServer**. Replace the three servers with only one server that supports all required services. Study the **utilization%** of that server's CPU. Compare this utilization with the three CPU utilizations you obtained in the previous exercise.
4. Create a new scenario as a duplicate of the **BusyNetwork** scenario. Name the new scenario **Q4_FasterNetwork.** In the **Q4_FasterNetwork** scenario, replace all **100BaseT** links in the network with **10Gbps Ethernet** links and replace all **10BaseT** links with **100BaseT** links. Study how increasing the bandwidth of the links affects the performance of the network in the new scenario (e.g., compare the HTTP page response time in the new scenario with that of the **BusyNetwork**).

LAB REPORT

Prepare a report that follows the guidelines explained in the Introduction Lab. The report should include the answers to the preceding exercises as well as the graphs you generated from the simulation scenarios. Discuss the results you obtained and compare these results with your expectations. Mention any anomalies or unexplained behaviors.

RIP: Routing Information Protocol
A Routing Protocol Based on the Distance-Vector Algorithm

OBJECTIVES

The objective of this lab is to configure and analyze the performance of the Routing Information Protocol (RIP) model.

OVERVIEW

A router in the network needs to be able to look at the destination address in the packet and then determine which one of the output ports is the best choice to get the packet to that address. The router makes this decision by consulting a forwarding table. The fundamental problem of routing is: How do routers acquire the information in their forwarding tables?

Routing algorithms are required to build the routing tables and, hence, forwarding tables. The basic problem of routing is to find the lowest-cost path between any two nodes, where the cost of a path equals the sum of the costs of all the edges that make up the path. Routing is achieved in most practical networks by running routing protocols among the nodes. The protocols provide a distributed, dynamic way to solve the problem of finding the lowest-cost path in the presence of link and node failures and changing edge costs.

One of the main classes of routing algorithms is the distance-vector algorithm. Each node constructs a vector containing the distances (costs) to all other nodes and distributes that vector to its immediate neighbors. RIP is the canonical example of a routing protocol built on the distance-vector algorithm. Routers running RIP send their advertisements regularly (e.g., every 30 s). A router also sends an update message whenever a triggered update from another router causes it to change its routing table.

The Internet Control Message Protocol (ICMP) can be utilized to analyze the performance of the created routes. It can be used to model traffic between routers without the need for running applications in an end node.

In this lab, you will set up a network that utilizes RIP as its routing protocol. You will analyze the routing tables generated in the routers, and you will observe how RIP is affected by link failures. You will also utilize the ICMP to create echo reply messages (i.e., ping) to analyze the created routes.

PRE-LAB ACTIVITIES

📖 Read Section 3.3.2 from *Computer Networks: A Systems Approach, 5th Edition.*

💻 Go to www.net-seal.net and play the following animations:
   ○ The Address Resolution Protocol (ARP)
   ○ ARP with Multiple Networks
   ○ Dynamic Host Configuration Protocol (DHCP)
   ○ Routing

PROCEDURE
Create a New Project

1. Start **OPNET IT Guru Academic Edition** → Choose **New** from the **File** menu.
2. Select **Project** and click **OK** → Name the project **<your initials>_RIP**, and the scenario **No_Failure** → Click **OK**.
3. In the *Startup Wizard: Initial Topology* dialog box, make sure that **Create Empty Scenario** is selected → Click **Next** → Select **Campus** from the *Network Scale* list → Click **Next** three times → Click **OK**.

Create and Configure the Network

Initialize the network:

1. The *Object Palette* dialog box should now be on top of your project workspace. If it is not there, open it by clicking 🗔. Make sure that the **internet_toolbox** is selected from the pull-down menu on the object palette.
2. Add to the project workspace the following objects from the palette: one **ethernet4_slip8_gtwy** router and two **100BaseT_LAN** objects.
   a. To add an object from a palette, click its icon in the object palette → Move your mouse to the workspace → Click to place the object → Right-click to stop creating objects of that type.
3. Use bidirectional **100BaseT** links to connect the objects you just added as in the following figure. Also, rename the objects as shown (right-click on the node → **Set Name**).
4. Close the *Object Palette* dialog box, and **Save** your project.

The **ethernet4_slip8_gtwy** node model represents an IP-based gateway supporting four Ethernet hub interfaces and eight serial line interfaces. IP packets arriving on any interface are routed to the appropriate output interface based on their destination IP address. The RIP or the OSPF protocols may be used to dynamically create the gateway's routing tables.

54

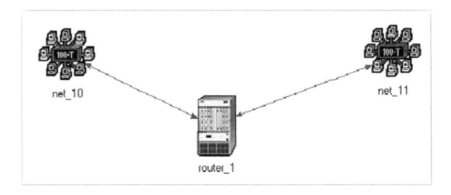

Configure the Router

1. Right-click on **router_1** → **Edit Attributes** → Expand the **IP Routing Parameters** hierarchy and set the following:
   a. **Routing Table Export = Once at End of Simulation**. This asks the router to export its routing table at the end of the simulation to the OPNET simulation log.
2. Click **OK**, and then **Save** your project.

Add the Remaining LANs

1. Highlight or select simultaneously (using **Ctrl + A**) all five objects that you currently have in the project workspace (one router, two LANs, and two links).
2. Press **Ctrl + C** to copy the selected objects, and then press **Ctrl + V** three times to paste them to generate three new copies of the objects.
3. Arrange the objects in a way similar to the following figure and rename them as shown.
4. Connect routers as shown using **PPP_DS3** links.

The **PPP_DS3** link has a data rate of 44.736 Mbps.

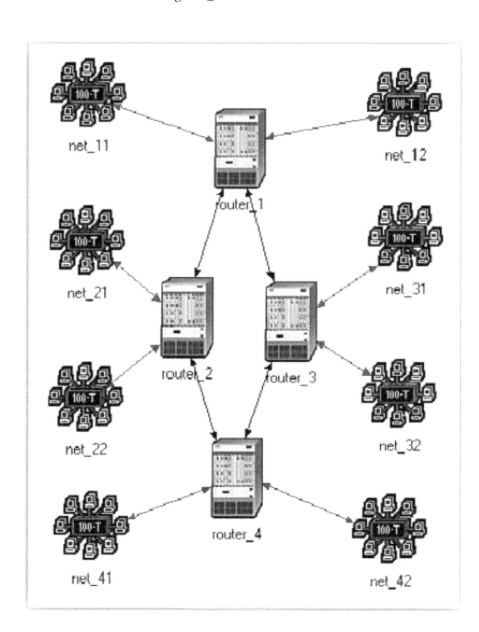

55

Choose the Statistics

To test the performance of the RIP, we will collect the following statistics:

1. Right-click anywhere in the project workspace and select **Choose Individual Statistics** from the pop-up menu.
2. In the *Choose Results* dialog box, check the following statistics:
   a. **Global Statistics → RIP → Traffic Sent (bits/sec).**

RIP traffic is the total amount of RIP update traffic (in bits) sent/ received per second by all the nodes using RIP as the routing protocol in the IP interfaces in the node.

Total Number of Updates is the number of times the routing table at this node gets updated (e.g., because of a new route addition, an existing route deletion, and/or a next hop update).

Auto Addressed means that all IP interfaces are assigned IP addresses automatically during simulation. The class of address (e.g., A, B, or C) is determined based on the number of hosts in the designed network. Subnet masks assigned to these interfaces are the default subnet masks for that class.

Export causes the autoassigned IP interface to be exported to a file (name of the file is <net_name>-ip_addresses.gdf and gets saved in the primary model directory).

56

    b. Global Statistics → RIP → Traffic Received (bits/sec).
    c. Nodes Statistics → Route Table → Total Number of Updates.
3. Click **OK**, and then **Save** your project.

Configure the Simulation

Here we need to configure some of the simulation parameters:

1. Click on 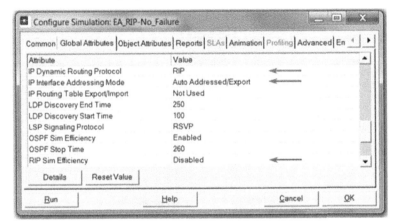 and the *Configure Simulation* window should appear.
2. Set the duration to be **10.0 minutes**.
3. Click on the **Global Attributes** tab and change the following attributes:
    a. **IP Dynamic Routing Protocol = RIP**. This sets the RIP protocol to the routing protocol of all routers in the network.
    b. **IP Interface Addressing Mode = Auto Addressed/Export**.
    c. **RIP Sim Efficiency = Disabled**. This makes RIP keep updating the routing table in case there are any changes in the network (as we will see in the second scenario).
4. Click **OK**, and then **Save** the project.

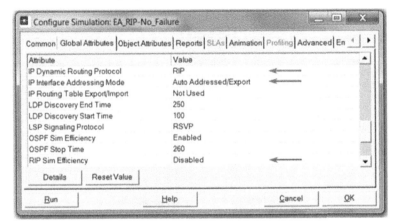

The Ping Scenario

In this scenario, we will utilize the ping model to print the list of traversed nodes while the ICMP request message is sent to the destination and the ICMP response is received from the destination. Traversed routes are logged in the simulation log file.

1. Select **Duplicate Scenario** from the **Scenarios** menu and name it **ICMP_Ping** → Click **OK**.
2. Select both **router_1** and **router_4** simultaneously (click on both of them while holding the **Shift** key) → Select the **Protocols** menu → **IP** → **Demands** → **Configure Ping Traffic on Selected Nodes**.
3. Change the **Pattern** attribute to **Record Route** as shown → Click **OK**.

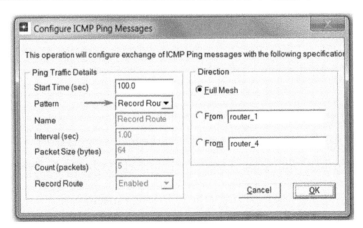

Notice that a Ping Parameter node will be added to the project space. In addition, the ping demand is created between router_1 and router_4 as a dotted line.

The Failure Scenario

The routers in the network we created will build their routing tables with no need for further updating because we didn't simulate any node or link failures. In this scenario, we will simulate failures so that we can compare the behavior of the routers in both cases.

1. Go to the **No_Failure** scenario by clicking **Ctrl + 1** → Select **Duplicate Scenario** from the **Scenarios** menu and name it **Failure** → Click **OK**.
2. Open **Object Palette** by clicking ▓. Select the **Utilities** palette from the drop-down menu → Add a **Failure Recovery** object to your workspace and name it **Failure** as shown → Close the *Object Palette* dialog box.

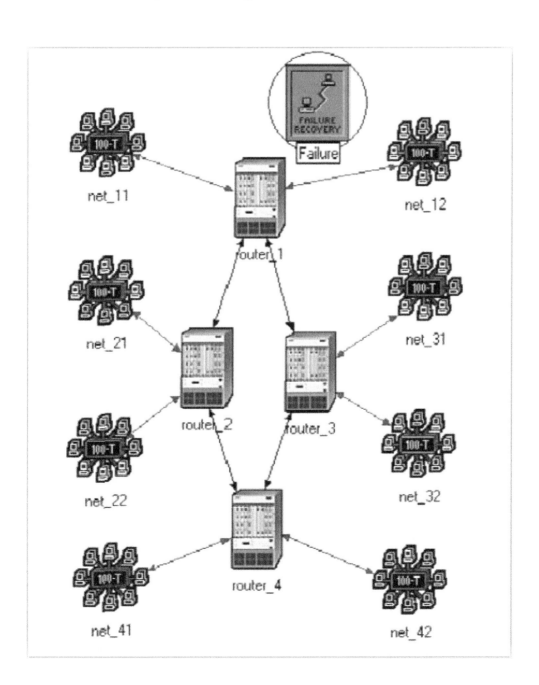

3. Right-click on the **Failure** object → **Edit Attributes** → Expand the **Link Failure/Recovery Specification** hierarchy → Set **rows** to **1** → Set the attributes of the added row, **row 0**, as follows:

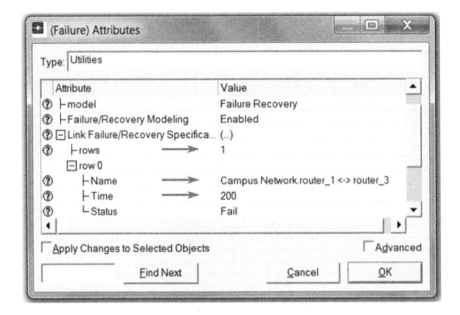

This will "fail" the link between **router_1** and **router_3** 200 s into the simulation.

4. Click **OK**, and then **Save** the project.

Run the Simulation

To run the simulation for both scenarios simultaneously:

1. Go to the **Scenarios** menu → Select **Manage Scenarios**.
2. Change all values under the **Results** column to **<collect>** (or **<recollect>**) as shown.

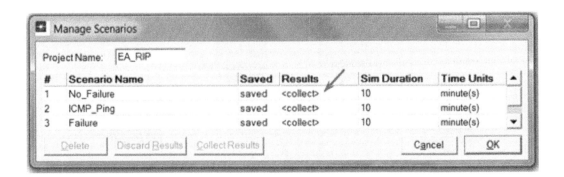

3. Click **OK** to run the three simulations. This task may take several seconds to complete.
4. After the three simulation runs complete, one for each scenario, click **Close**.

View the Results

Compare the number of updates:

1. Select **Compare Results** from the **Results** menu → From the drop-down menus select **Stacked Statistics** and **Select Scenarios** as shown.

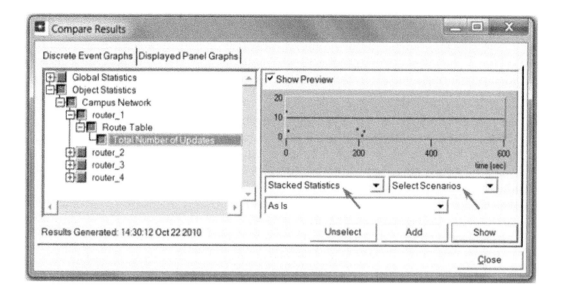

2. Select the **Total Number of Updates** statistic for **router_1** and click **Show** → Select the **NO_Failure** and **Failure** scenarios in the *Select Scenarios* dialog box.
3. You should get two graphs, one for each scenario. Right-click on each graph and select **Draw Style** → **Bar**.
4. The resulting graphs should resemble the following (you can zoom in on the graphs by clicking and dragging a box over the region of interest):

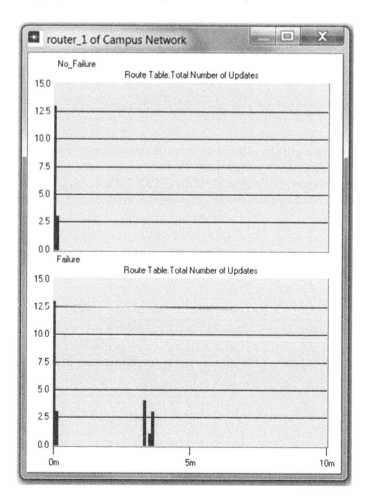

59

Obtain the IP Addresses of the Interface

Before checking the contents of the routing tables, we need to determine the IP address information for all interfaces in the current network. Recall that these IP addresses are assigned automatically during simulation, and we set the global attribute IP Interface Addressing Mode to export this information to a file.

1. From the **File** menu, select **Model Files → Refresh Model Directories**. This causes OPNET IT Guru to search the model directories and update its list of files.

2. From the **File** menu, select **Open → In** the top drop-down menu, select **Generic Data File →** Select the **<your initials>_RIP-NO_Failure-ip_addresses** file (the other file created from the Failure scenario should contain the same information) → Click **OK**.

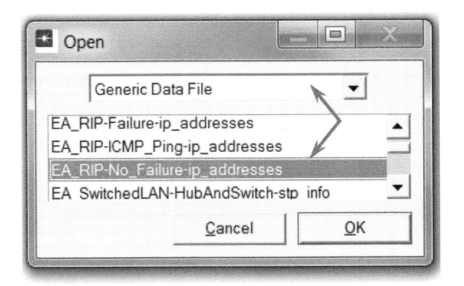

3. The following is a part of the **gdf** file content. It shows the IP addresses assigned to the interfaces of router_1 in our network. For example, the interface of router_1 that is connected to net_11 has the IP address 192.0.0.1. (*Note:* Your result may vary due to different node placement.) The subnet mask associated with that interface indicates that the address of the subnetwork to which the interface is connected is 192.0.0.0 (i.e., the logical AND of the interface IP address and the subnet mask).

```
Node Name: Campus Network.router_1
  Iface Name        Iface Index   IP Address      Subnet Mask      Connected Link
  ----------        -----------   ----------      -----------      --------------
  IF0                 0           192.0.0.1       255.255.255.0    Campus Network.router_1 <-> net_11
  IF1                 1           192.0.1.1       255.255.255.0    Campus Network.router_1 <-> net_12
  IF10                10          192.0.2.1       255.255.255.0    Campus Network.router_1 <-> router_3
  IF11                11          192.0.3.1       255.255.255.0    Campus Network.router_1 <-> router_2
  Loopback            12          192.0.4.1       255.255.255.0    Not connected to any link.
```

4. Print out the layout of the network you implemented in this lab. On this layout and from the information included in the gdf file, write down the IP addresses associated with the interfaces of the four routers as shown in the following diagram. Double-check that the addresses of each subnet agree with the addresses of the interfaces connected to it.

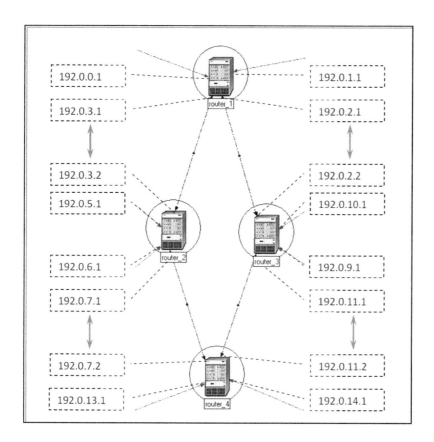

Getting the Ping Report

To check the content of the ping report for router_1:

1. Go to the **ICMP_Ping** scenario → Go to the **Results** menu → **Open Simulation Log** → Click on the field **PING REPORT for "Campus Network router_1"** as shown.

```
1    PING REPORT for "Campus Network.router_1" (192.0.4.1)
2
3    DETAILS:
4      Received  ICMP echo reply packet for a
5      request packet sent to the following node:
6
7        IP Address: 192.0.4.1
8        Node Name : Campus Network.router_1
9
10   PERFORMANCE:
11     Based on the first ICMP echo request packet
12     (i.e., a "ping" packet) sent to the above
13     node, the following metrics were computed:
14
15       1. Response Time: 0.00025 seconds
16
17       2. List of traversed IP interfaces:
18
19          IP Address      Hop Delay     Node Name
20          ----------      ---------     ---------
21            192.0.11.2    0.00000       Campus Network.router_4
22            192.0.2.2     0.00005       Campus Network.router_3
23            192.0.4.1     0.00005       Campus Network.router_1
24            192.0.2.1     0.00002       Campus Network.router_1
25            192.0.11.1    0.00005       Campus Network.router_3
26            192.0.11.2    0.00005       Campus Network.router_4
27
28     Note that the IP addresses shown above represent
29     the address of the output interface on which the
30     IP datagram was routed from the corresponding
31     nodes to the next node enroute to its destination
32     and back.
```

Compare the Routing Tables Content

To check the content of the routing tables in router_1 for the NO_Failure and Failure scenarios:

1. Press **Ctrl + 1** to go to the **NO_Failure** scenario → Go to the **Results** menu → **Open Simulation Log** → Expand the hierarchy on the left as shown in the following figure → Click on the field **COMMON ROUTE TABLE** for **router_1**.

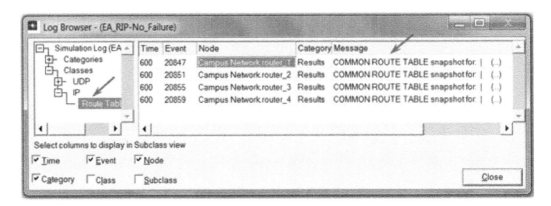

2. Carry out the previous step for the **Failure** scenario. The following are partial contents of router_1's routing table for both scenarios. (*Note:* Your results may vary because of different nodes placement.)

Routing Table of router_1 (NO_Failure scenario)

62

```
Router name: Campus Network.router_1
         at time: 600.00 seconds

ROUTE TABLE contents:

  Dest. Address     Subnet Mask       Next Hop       Interface Name    Metric     Protocol     Insertion Time
  -------------     -----------       --------       --------------    ------     --------     --------------

  192.0.0.0         255.255.255.0     192.0.0.1      IF0               0          Direct       0.000
  192.0.1.0         255.255.255.0     192.0.1.1      IF1               0          Direct       0.000
  192.0.2.0         255.255.255.0     192.0.2.1      IF10              0          Direct       0.000
  192.0.3.0         255.255.255.0     192.0.3.1      IF11              0          Direct       0.000
  192.0.4.0         255.255.255.0     192.0.4.1      Loopback          0          Direct       0.000
  192.0.5.0         255.255.255.0     192.0.3.2      IF11              1          RIP          5.000
  192.0.6.0         255.255.255.0     192.0.3.2      IF11              1          RIP          5.000
  192.0.7.0         255.255.255.0     192.0.3.2      IF11              1          RIP          5.000
  192.0.8.0         255.255.255.0     192.0.3.2      IF11              1          RIP          5.000
  192.0.9.0         255.255.255.0     192.0.2.2      IF10              1          RIP          5.000
  192.0.10.0        255.255.255.0     192.0.2.2      IF10              1          RIP          5.000
  192.0.11.0        255.255.255.0     192.0.2.2      IF10              1          RIP          5.000
  192.0.12.0        255.255.255.0     192.0.2.2      IF10              1          RIP          5.000
  192.0.13.0        255.255.255.0     192.0.3.2      IF11              2          RIP          7.310
  192.0.14.0        255.255.255.0     192.0.3.2      IF11              2          RIP          7.310
  192.0.15.0        255.255.255.0     192.0.3.2      IF11              2          RIP          7.310
```

Routing Table of router_1 (Failure scenario)

```
Router name: Campus Network.router_1
         at time: 600.00 seconds

ROUTE TABLE contents:

  Dest. Address     Subnet Mask       Next Hop       Interface Name    Metric     Protocol     Insertion Time
  -------------     -----------       --------       --------------    ------     --------     --------------

  192.0.0.0         255.255.255.0     192.0.0.1      IF0               0          Direct       0.000
  192.0.1.0         255.255.255.0     192.0.1.1      IF1               0          Direct       0.000
  192.0.2.0         255.255.255.0     192.0.2.1      IF10              0          Direct       0.000
  192.0.3.0         255.255.255.0     192.0.3.1      IF11              0          Direct       0.000
  192.0.4.0         255.255.255.0     192.0.4.1      Loopback          0          Direct       0.000
  192.0.5.0         255.255.255.0     192.0.3.2      IF11              1          RIP          5.000
  192.0.6.0         255.255.255.0     192.0.3.2      IF11              1          RIP          5.000
  192.0.7.0         255.255.255.0     192.0.3.2      IF11              1          RIP          5.000
  192.0.8.0         255.255.255.0     192.0.3.2      IF11              1          RIP          5.000
  192.0.13.0        255.255.255.0     192.0.3.2      IF11              2          RIP          7.310
  192.0.14.0        255.255.255.0     192.0.3.2      IF11              2          RIP          7.310
  192.0.15.0        255.255.255.0     192.0.3.2      IF11              2          RIP          7.310
  192.0.11.0        255.255.255.0     192.0.3.2      IF11              2          RIP          215.000
  192.0.9.0         255.255.255.0     192.0.3.2      IF11              3          RIP          216.930
  192.0.10.0        255.255.255.0     192.0.3.2      IF11              3          RIP          216.930
  192.0.12.0        255.255.255.0     192.0.3.2      IF11              3          RIP          216.930
```

FURTHER READINGS

RIP: IETF RFC number 2453 (www.ietf.org/rfc.html).

ICMP: IETF RFC number 792 (www.ietf.org/rfc.html).

EXERCISES

1. Obtain and analyze the graphs that compare the sent RIP traffic for the **Failure** and **NO_Failure** scenarios. Make sure to change the draw style for the graphs to **Bar**.
2. Describe and explain the effect of the failure of the link connecting **Router1** to **Router2** on the routing tables of **Router1**.
3. Create another scenario as a duplicate of the **Failure** scenario. Name the new scenario **Q3_Recover**. This new scenario has the link connecting **Router1** to **Router2** recover after 400 s. (Make sure to keep the failure that occurs at the 200th second.) Generate and analyze the graph that shows the effect of this recovery on the **Total Number of Updates** in the routing table of **Router1**. Check the contents of **Router1**'s routing table. Compare this table with the corresponding routing tables generated in the **NO_Failure** and **Failure** scenarios.
4. Change the Ping packet size to 5000 bytes. (*Hint:* Edit the attributes of the Ping Parameters node.) Run the simulation to generate a new Ping report. What is the effect of the new size on the ICMP packet response time?

LAB REPORT

Prepare a report that follows the guidelines explained in the Introduction Lab. The report should include the answers to the preceding exercises as well as the graphs you generated from the simulation scenarios. Discuss the results you obtained, and compare these results with your expectations. Mention any anomalies or unexplained behaviors.

OSPF: Open Shortest Path First

A Routing Protocol Based on the Link-State Algorithm

OBJECTIVES

The objective of this lab is to configure and analyze the performance of the Open Shortest Path First (OSPF) routing protocol.

OVERVIEW

In the RIP lab, we discussed a routing protocol that is the canonical example of a routing protocol built on the distance-vector algorithm. Each node constructs a vector containing the distances (costs) to all other nodes and distributes that vector to its immediate neighbors. Link-state routing is the second major class of intradomain routing protocol. The basic idea behind link-state protocols is very simple: Every node knows how to reach its directly connected neighbors, and if we make sure that the totality of this knowledge is disseminated to every node, then every node will have enough knowledge of the network to build a complete map of the network.

Once a given node has a complete map for the topology of the network, it is able to decide the best route to each destination. Calculating those routes is based on a well-known algorithm from graph theory—Dijkstra's shortest-path algorithm.

OSPF introduces another layer of hierarchy into routing by allowing a domain to be partitioned into areas. This means that a router within a domain does not necessarily need to know how to reach every network within that domain; it may be sufficient for it to know how to get to the right area. Thus, there is a reduction in the amount of information that must be transmitted to and stored in each node. In addition, OSPF allows multiple routes to the same destination to be assigned the same cost and causes traffic to be distributed evenly over those routers.

In this lab, you will set up a network that utilizes OSPF as its routing protocol. You will analyze the routing tables generated in the routers and will observe how the resulting routes are affected by assigning areas and enabling load balancing.

PRE-LAB ACTIVITIES

📖   Read Section 3.3.3 from *Computer Networks: A Systems Approach, 5th Edition.*

💻   Go to www.net-seal.net and play the following animation:
    ○ Routing

PROCEDURE

Create a New Project

1. Start **OPNET IT Guru Academic Edition** → Choose **New** from the **File** menu.
2. Select **Project** and click **OK** → Name the project **<your initials>_OSPF**, and the scenario **No_Areas** → Click **OK**.
3. In the *Startup Wizard: Initial Topology* dialog box, make sure that **Create Empty Scenario** is selected → Click **Next** → Select **Campus** from the *Network Scale* list → Click **Next** three times → Click **OK**.

Create and Configure the Network

Initialize the network:

The **slip8_gtwy** node model represents an IP-based gateway supporting up to eight serial line interfaces at a selectable data rate. The RIP or OSPF protocols may be used to automatically and dynamically create the gateway's routing tables and select routes in an adaptive manner.

The **PPP_DS3** link has a data rate of 44.736 Mbps.

1. The *Object Palette* dialog box should now be on top of your project workspace. If it is not there, open it by clicking ▨. Select the **routers** item from the pull-down menu on the top of the object palette.
   a. Add to the project workspace eight routers of type **slip8_gtwy**. To add an object from a palette, click its icon in the object palette → Move your mouse to the workspace, and click to place the object → Right-click when you are finished placing the last object.
2. Select the **internet_toolbox** item from the pull-down menu on the top of the object palette. Use the PPP_DS3 links to connect the routers. Rename the routers as shown → Close the *Object Palette*.

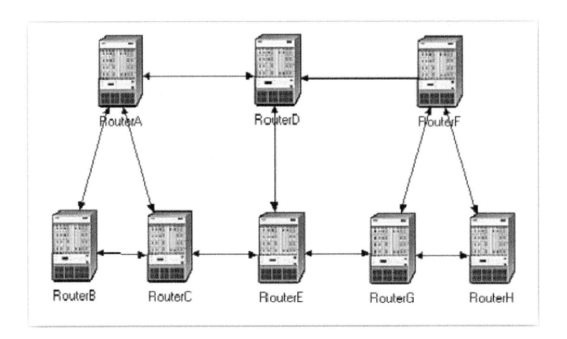

Configure the Link Costs

We need to assign link costs to match the following figure:

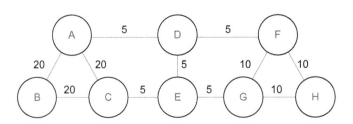

Like many popular commercial routers, OPNET router models support a parameter called a *reference bandwidth* to calculate the actual cost, as follows:

$$Cost = (Reference\ bandwidth) / (Link\ bandwidth)$$

where the default value of the *reference bandwidth* is 1,000,000 Kbps.

For example, to assign a cost of 5 to a link, assign a bandwidth of 200,000 Kbps to that link. This is not the actual bandwidth of the link in the sense of transmission speed, but merely a parameter used to configure link costs. To assign the costs to the links of our network, do the following:

1. Select all links in your network that correspond to the links with a cost of 5 in the preceding graph by shift-clicking on them.
2. Select the **Protocols** menu → **IP** → **Routing** → **Configure Interface Metric Information**.

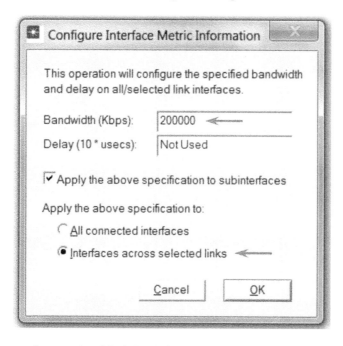

3. Assign **200000** to the **Bandwidth (Kbps)** field → Check the **Interfaces across selected links** radio button, as shown → Click **OK**.
4. Repeat for all links with a cost of 10 but assign **100000** to the **Bandwidth (Kbps)** field.
5. Repeat for all links with a cost of 20 but assign **50000** to the **Bandwidth (Kbps)** field.
6. **Save** your project.

Configure the Traffic Demands

1. Select both **RouterA** and **RouterC** by shift-clicking on them.
   a. Select the **Protocols** menu → **IP** → **Demands** → **Create Traffic Demands** → Check the **From RouterA** radio button as shown → Keep the color as **blue** → Click **Create**. Now you should see a blue dotted line representing the traffic demand between **RouterA** and **RouterC**.
2. Select both **RouterB** and **RouterH** by shift-clicking on them.
   a. Select the **Protocols** menu → **IP** → **Demands** → **Create Traffic Demands** → Check the **From RouterB** radio button → Change the color to **red** → Click **OK** → Click **Create**.

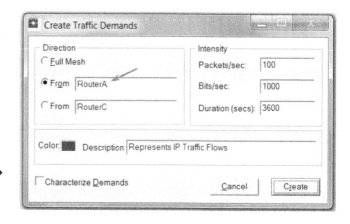

Now you can see the lines representing the traffic demands as shown.

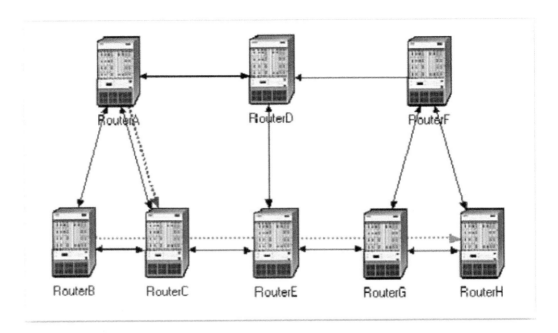

3. To hide these lines: Select the **View** menu → Select **Demand Objects** → Select **Hide All**.

Configure the Routing Protocol and Addresses

1. Select the **Protocols** menu → **IP** → **Routing** → **Configure Routing Protocols**.

2. Check the **OSPF** check box → Uncheck the **RIP** check box → Uncheck the **Visualize Routing Domains** check box, as shown:

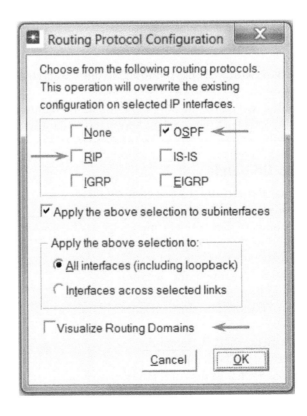

3. Click **OK**.
4. Select **RouterA** and **RouterB** only → Select the **Protocols** menu → **IP** → **Routing** → Select **Export Routing Table for Selected Routers** → Click **OK** on the *Status Confirm* dialog box.
5. Select the **Protocols** menu → **IP** → **Addressing** → Select **Auto-Assign IP Addresses**.
6. **Save** your project.

Auto-Assign IP Addresses assigns a unique IP address to connected IP interfaces whose IP address is currently set to auto assigned. It does not change the value of manually set IP addresses.

Configure the Simulation

Here we need to configure some of the simulation parameters:

1. Click on ![icon] and the *Configure Simulation* window should appear.
2. Set the duration to **10.0 minutes**.
3. Click **OK** and **Save** your project.

Duplicate the Scenario

In the network we just created, all routers belong to one level of hierarchy (i.e., one area). Also, we did not enforce load balancing for any routes. Two new scenarios will be created. The first new scenario will define two new areas in addition to the backbone area. The second one will be configured to balance the load for the traffic demands between **RouterB** and **RouterH**.

THE AREAS SCENARIO

1. Select **Duplicate Scenario** from the **Scenarios** menu, and give it the name **Areas** → Click **OK**.
2. Creating Area 0.0.0.1:
   a. Select the three links that connect **RouterA**, **RouterB**, and **RouterC** by shift-clicking on them → Select the **Protocols** menu → **OSPF** → **Configure Areas** → Assign the value **0.0.0.1** to the **Area Identifier**, as shown → Click **OK**.

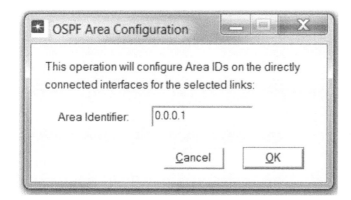

   b. Right-click on **RouterC** → **Edit Attributes** → Expand the **OSPF Parameters** hierarchy → Expand the **Loopback Interfaces** hierarchy → Expand the **row0** hierarchy → Assign **0.0.0.1** to the value of the **Area ID** attribute → Click **OK**.
3. Creating Area 0.0.0.2:
   a. Click somewhere in the project workspace to disable the selected links, and then repeat Step 2a for the three links that connect **RouterF**, **RouterG**, and **RouterH** but assign the value **0.0.0.2** to their **Area Identifier**.
4. To visualize the areas we just created, select the **Protocols** menu → **OSPF** → **Visualize Areas** → Click **OK**. The network should look like the following one with different colors assigned to each area (you may get different colors, though).

Loopback interface allows a client and a server on the same host to communicate with each other using TCP/IP.

69

Note:

- The area you did not configure is the backbone area with **Area Identifier** = 0.0.0.0.
- The figure shows the links with a thickness of 3.

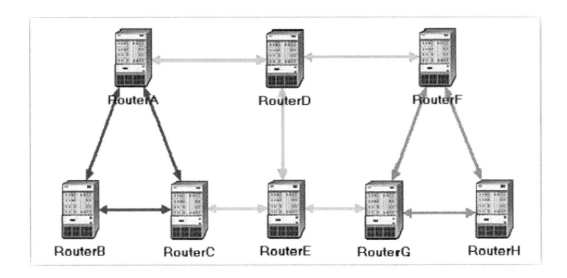

THE BALANCED SCENARIO

1. Under the **Scenarios** menu, **Switch to Scenario** → Select **No_Areas**.
2. Select **Duplicate Scenario** from the **Scenarios** menu and give it the name **Balanced** → Click **OK**.
3. In the new scenario, select both **RouterB** and **RouterH** by shift-clicking on them.
4. Select the **Protocols** menu → **IP** → **Routing** → **Configure Load Balancing Options** → Make sure that the option is **Packet-Based** and the radio button **Selected Routers** is selected as shown → Click **OK**.

OPNET provides two types of IP load balancing:

With **Destination Based**, load balancing is done on a per-destination basis. The route chosen from the source router to the destination network is the same for all packets.

With **Packet Based**, load balancing is done on a per-packet basis. The route chosen from the source router to the destination network is redetermined for every individual packet.

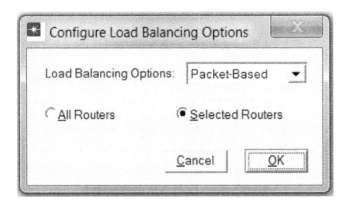

5. **Save** your project.

Run the Simulation

To run the simulation for the three scenarios simultaneously:

1. Go to the **Scenarios** menu → Select **Manage Scenarios**.
2. Click on the row of each scenario, and click the **Collect Results** button. This should change the values under the **Results** column to **<collect>** as shown.

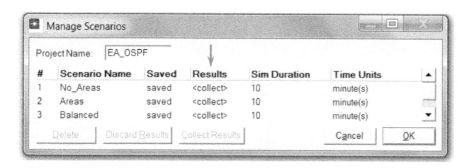

3. Click **OK** to run the three simulations. Depending on the speed of your processor, this task may take several seconds to complete.

4. After the three simulation runs complete, one for each scenario, click **Close**, and then **save** your project.

View the Results

THE NO_AREAS SCENARIO

1. Go back to the **No_Areas** scenario.

2. To display the route for the traffic demand between **RouterA** and **RouterC**: Select the **Protocols** menu → **IP** → **Demands** → **Display Routes for Configured Demands** → Expand the hierarchies as shown and select **RouterA** → **RouterC** → Go to the **Display** column and pick **Yes** → Click **Close**.

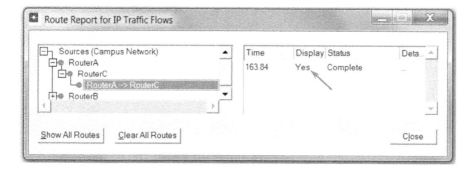

3. The resulting route will appear on the network as shown:

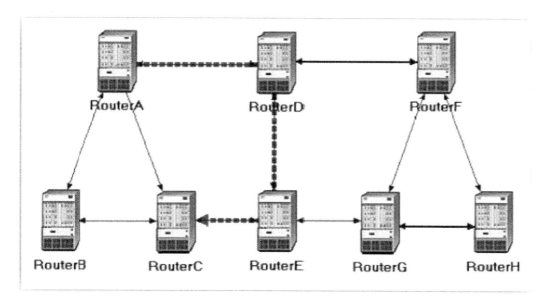

4. Repeat Step 2 to show the route for the traffic demand between **RouterB** and **RouterH**. The route is as shown in the following diagram. (*Note:* Depending on the order in which you created the network topology, the other "equal-cost" path can be used, that is, the *RouterB–RouterA–RouterD–RouterF–RouterH* path).

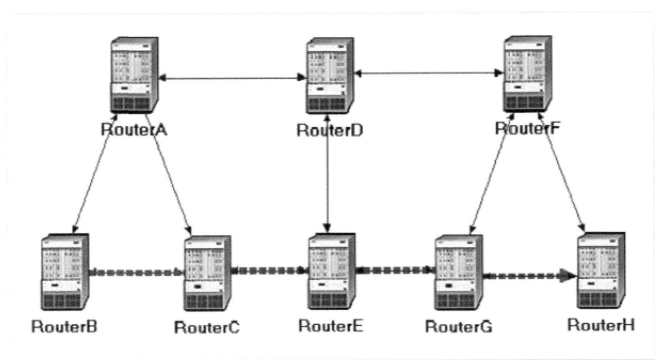

THE AREAS SCENARIO

1. Go to **Areas** scenario.
2. Display the route for the traffic demand between **RouterA** and **RouterC**. The route is as shown here:

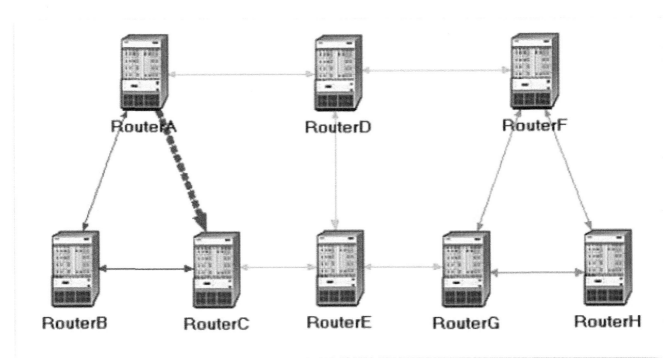

THE BALANCED SCENARIO

1. Go to scenario **Balanced**.
2. Display the route for the traffic demand between **RouterB** and **RouterH**. The route is as shown here:

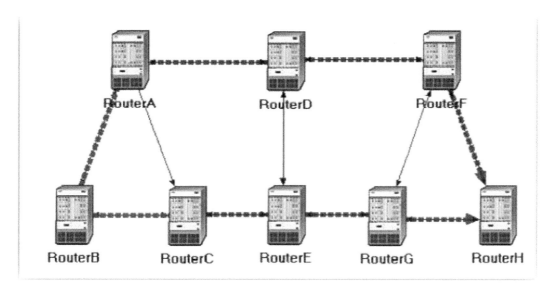

3. **Save** your project.

FURTHER READINGS

OPNET OSPF Model Description: From the **Protocols** menu, select **OSPF → Model Usage Guide**.

OSPF: IETF RFC number 2328 (www.ietf.org/rfc.html).

73

EXERCISES

1. Explain why, for the same pair of routers, the **Areas** and **Balanced** scenarios result in different routes than those observed in the **No_Areas** scenario.
2. Using the simulation log, examine the generated routing table in **RouterA** for each one of the three scenarios. Explain the values assigned to the *Metric* column of each route.

Hints:

- Refer to the "View Results" section in Lab 6 for information about examining the routing tables. You will need to set the global attribute **IP Interface Addressing Mode** to the value **Auto Addressed/Export** and rerun the simulation.
- To determine the IP address information for all interfaces, you need to open the *Generic Data File* that contains the IP addresses associated with the scenarios.

3. OPNET allows you to examine the link-state database that is used by each router to build the directed graph of the network. Examine this database for **RouterA** in the **No_Areas** scenario. Show how **RouterA** utilizes this database to create a map for the topology of the network, and draw this map. (This is the map that the router will use later to create its routing table.)

Note: A stub network only carries local traffic (i.e., packets to and from local hosts). Even if it has paths to more than one other network, it does not carry traffic for other networks (RFC 1983).

Hints:

- To export the link-state database of a router, **Edit** the attributes of the router, and set the **Link State Database Export** parameter (one of the **OSPF Parameters**, under **Processes**) to **Once at End of Simulation**.

- You will need to set the global attribute **IP Interface Addressing Mode** to the value **Auto Addressed/Export**. This will allow you to check the automatically assigned IP addresses to the interfaces of the network. (Refer to the notes of Exercise 2.)
- After rerunning the simulation, you can check the link-state database by opening the simulation log (from the **Results** menu). The link-state database is available in **Classes → OSPF → LSDB_Export**.

4. Create another scenario as a duplicate of the **No_Areas** scenario. Name the new scenario **Q4_No_Areas_Failure**. In this new scenario, simulate a failure of the link connecting **RouterD** and **RotuerE**. Have this failure start after 100 s. Rerun the simulation. Show how that link failure affects the content of the link-state database and routing table of **RouterA**. (You will need to disable the global attribute **OSPF Sim Efficiency**. This will allow OSPF to update the routing table if there is any change in the network.)

5. For both **No_Areas** and **Q4_No_Areas_Failure** scenarios, collect the **Traffic Sent (bits/ sec)** statistic (one of the **Global Statistics** under **OSPF**). Rerun the simulation for these two scenarios and obtain the graph that compares the OSPF's **Traffic Sent (bits/sec)** in both scenarios. Comment on the obtained graph.

LAB REPORT

Prepare a report that follows the guidelines explained in the Introduction Lab. The report should include the answers to the preceding exercises as well as the graphs you generated from the simulation scenarios. Discuss the results you obtained and compare these results with your expectations. Mention any anomalies or unexplained behaviors.

BGP: Border Gateway Protocol
An Interdomain Routing Protocol

OBJECTIVES

The objective of this lab is to simulate and study the basic features of an interdomain routing protocol called Border Gateway Protocol (BGP).

OVERVIEW

The Internet is organized as a set of routing domains. Each routing domain is called an *autonomous system* (AS). Each AS is controlled by a single administrative entity (e.g., an AS of a single service provider). Each AS has a unique 16-bit identification number. This number is assigned by a central authority. An AS uses its own intradomain routing protocol (e.g., RIP or OSPF). An AS establishes routes with other ASs through interdomain routing protocols. The Border Gateway Protocol (BGP) is one of the well-known interdomain routing protocols.

The main goal of BGP is to find any path to the destination that is loop-free. This is different from the common goal of intradomain routing protocols, which is to find an optimal route to the destination based on a specific link metric. The routers that connect different ASs are called *border gateways*. The task of the border gateways is to forward packets between ASs. Each AS has at least one BGP speaker. BGP speakers exchange reachability information among ASs.

BGP advertises the complete path to the destination AS as an enumerated list. In this way, routing loops can be avoided. A BGP speaker can also apply some policies such as balancing the load over the neighboring ASs. If a BGP speaker has a choice of several different routes to a destination, it will advertise the best one according to its own local policies. BGP is defined to run on top of TCP, and hence BGP speakers do not need to worry about acknowledging received information or retransmission of sent information.

In this lab, you will set up a network with three different ASs. RIP will be used as the intradomain routing protocol and BGP as the interdomain routing protocol. You will analyze the routing tables generated in the routers as well as the effect of applying a simple policy.

PRE-LAB ACTIVITIES

    Read Section 4.1.2 from *Computer Networks: A Systems Approach, 5th Edition.*

    Go to www.net-seal.net and play the following animation:
       o IP Subnets

PROCEDURE

Create a New Project

1. Start **OPNET IT Guru Academic Edition** → Choose **New** from the **File** menu.
2. Select **Project** and click **OK** → Name the project **<your initials>_BGP**, and the scenario **No_BGP** → Click **OK**.
3. In the *Startup Wizard: Initial Topology* dialog box, make sure that **Create Empty Scenario** is selected → Click **Next** → Select **Enterprise** from the *Network Scale* list → Click **Next** four times → Click **OK**.

Create and Configure the Network

The **ethernet4_slip8_gtwy** node model represents an IP-based gateway supporting four Ethernet hub interfaces and eight serial line interfaces. IP packets arriving on any interface are routed to the appropriate output interface based on their destination IP address.

1. The *Object Palette* dialog box should now be on top of your project workspace. If it is not there, open it by clicking ⊞. Make sure that the **internet_toolbox** is selected from the pull-down menu on the object palette.
2. Add to the project workspace the following objects from the palette: six **ethernet4_slip8_gtwy** routers and two **100BaseT_LAN** objects.
   a. To add an object from a palette, click its icon in the object palette → Move your mouse to the workspace → Click to place the object → Right-click to stop creating objects of that type.
3. Use bidirectional **PPP_DS3** links to connect the routers you just added, as shown in the following figure. Rename the objects as shown (right-click on the node → **Set Name**).
4. Use a bidirectional **100BaseT** link to connect **LAN_West** to **Router1** and another **100BaseT** link to connect **LAN_East** to **Router6** as shown.
5. Close the *Object Palette* dialog box → **Save** your project.

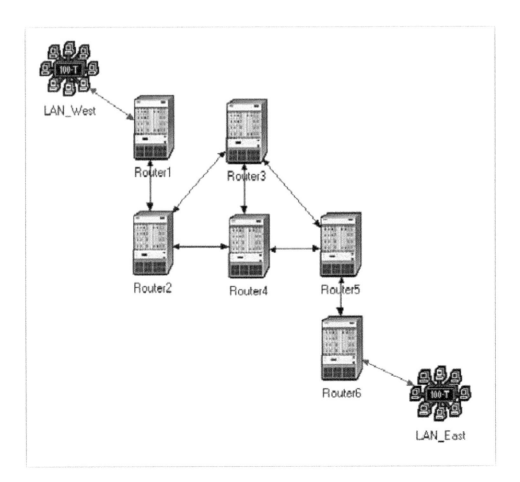

Routers Configuration

1. Right-click on any router → Click **Select Similar Nodes** (make sure that all routers are selected) → Right-click on any router → **Edit Attributes** → Check the **Apply Changes to Selected Objects** check box.
2. Expand the **BGP Parameters** hierarchy and set the following:
   a. **Redistribution** → **Routing Protocols** → **RIP** → **Redistribute w/ Default** as shown.

Redistribute w/ Default allows a router to have a route to a destination that belongs to another autonomous system.

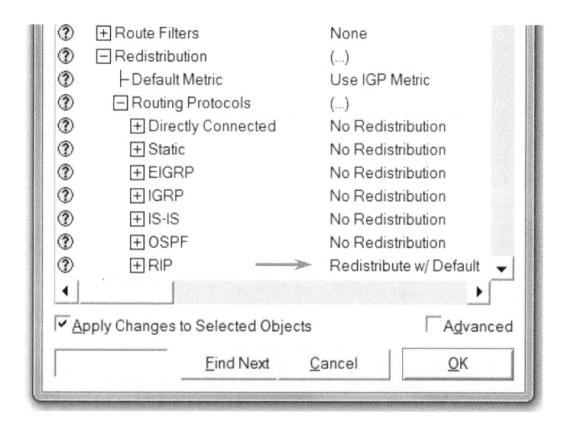

3. Expand the **IP Routing Parameters** hierarchy and set the following:
   a. **Routing Table Export = Once at End of Simulation**. This asks the router to export its routing table at the end of the simulation to the *simulation log*.
4. Expand the **RIP Parameters** hierarchy and set the following:
   a. **Redistribution** → **Routing Protocols** → **Directly Connected** → **Redistribute w/ Default**.
5. Click **OK**, and then **Save** your project.

Application Configuration

1. Right-click on **LAN_West** → **Edit Attributes** → Assign **All** to **Application: Supported Services** → Assign **West_Server** to the **LAN Server Name** attribute as shown → Click **OK**.

Notice that two objects for *Applications* and *Profiles* will be added automatically to the project.

2. Right-click on **LAN_East** → **Edit Attributes**:
   a. Expand the **Application: Supported Profiles** hierarchy → Set **rows** to 1 → Expand the **row 0** hierarchy → Set **Profile Name** to **E-commerce Customer**.

Application: Destination Preferences provides mappings between symbolic destination names specified in the Application Definition or Task Definition objects and real names specified in Server Name or Client Name on each node.

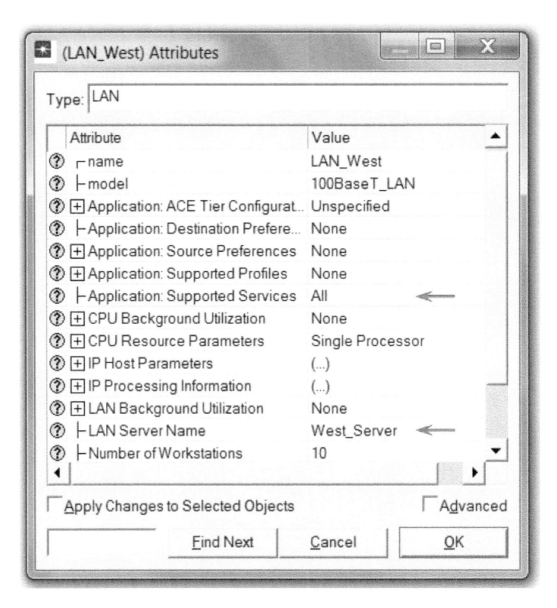

b. Edit the **Application: Destination Preferences** attribute as follows: Set **rows** to **1** →
Set **Symbolic Name** to **HTTP Server** → Edit **Actual Name** → Set **rows** to **1** → In the
new row, assign **West_ Server** to the **Name** column.

3. Click **OK** three times, and **Save** your project.

Auto Addressed means
that all IP interfaces are
assigned IP addresses
automatically during
simulation. The class of
address (e.g., A, B, or C)
is determined based on
the number of hosts in
the designed network.
Subnet masks assigned
to these interfaces are
the default subnet masks
for that class.

Configure the Simulation

Here, we need to configure some of the simulation parameters:

1. Click on 🗙 and the *Configure Simulation* window should appear.

2. Set the duration to **10.0 minutes**.

3. Click on the **Global Attributes** tab and make sure that the following attributes are
assigned as follows:

a. **IP Interface Addressing Mode = Auto Addressed/Export.**

b. **IP Routing Table Export/Import = Export.**

c. **RIP Sim Efficiency = Disabled.** If this attribute is enabled, RIP will stop after the "RIP
Stop Time." But we need the RIP to keep updating the routing table in case there is any
change in the network.

4. Click **OK**, and then **Save** the project.

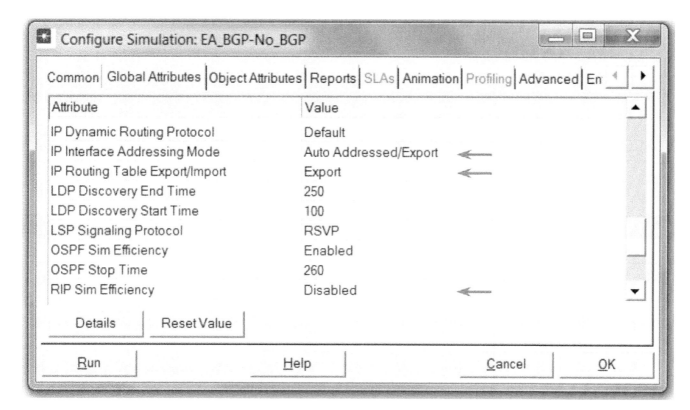

Export causes the autoassigned IP interface to be exported to a file (name of the file is <net_name>-ip_addresses.gdf and it gets saved in the primary model directory).

Choose the Statistics

1. Right-click on **LAN_East** and select **Choose Individual Statistics** → From the **Client HTTP** hierarchy choose the **Traffic Received (bytes/sec)** statistic → Click **OK**.

2. Right-click on the link that connects **Router2** to **Router3** and select **Choose Individual Statistics** from the pop-up menu → From the **point-to-point** hierarchy choose the "**Throughput (bits/sec) -->**" statistic → Click **OK**.

Note: If the name of the link is "Router3 <-> Router2," then you will need to choose the "**Throughput (bits/sec) <--**" statistic instead.

3. Right-click on the link that connects **Router2** to **Router4** and select **Choose Individual Statistics** from the pop-up menu → From the **point-to-point** hierarchy choose the "**Throughput (bits/sec) -->**" statistic → Click **OK**.

Note: If the name of the link is "Router4 <-> Router2," then you will need to choose the "**Throughput (bits/sec) <--**" statistic instead.

Router Interfaces and IP Addresses

Before setting up the routers to use BGP, we need to get the information of the routers' interfaces along with the IP addresses associated to these interfaces. Recall that these IP addresses are assigned automatically during simulation, and we set the global attribute **IP Interface Addressing Mode** to export this information to a file.

1. First, we need to run the simulation. Click on 🖳 and the *Configure Simulation* window should appear → Click on **Run**.

2. After the simulation run completes, click **Close**.

3. From the **File** menu choose **Model Files** → **Refresh Model Directories**. This causes OPNET IT Guru to search the model directories and update its list of files.
4. From the **File** menu choose **Open** → From the drop-down menu choose **Generic Data File** → Select the **<<your initials>_BGP-No_BGP -ip_addresses** file → Click **OK**.

The file that contains all the information about router interfaces and their IP addresses will open. Table 8.1 shows the interface number and IP addresses between the six routers in our projects. For example, Router1 is connected to Router2 through interface (IF) 11, which is assigned 192.0.1.1 as its IP address. A router is connected to itself by a Loopback interface as shown. Create a similar table for your project, but note that your result may vary due to different node placement.

TABLE 8.1 Interfaces That Connect the Routers and Their Assigned IP Addresses						
Routers	1	2	3	4	5	6
1	IF: 12 IP: 192.0.2.1	IF: 10 IP: 192.0.1.1				
2	IF: 10 IP: 192.0.1.2	IF: 12 IP: 192.0.5.1	IF: 11 IP: 192.0.4.1	IF: 4 IP: 192.0.3.1		
3		IF: 10 IP: 192.0.4.2	IF: 12 IP: 192.0.8.1	IF: 4 IP: 192.0.6.1	IF: 11 IP: 192.0.7.1	
4		IF: 10 IP: 192.0.3.2	IF: 4 IP: 192.0.6.2	IF: 12 IP: 192.0.10.1	IF: 11 IP: 192.0.9.1	
5			IF: 11 IP: 192.0.7.2	IF: 10 IP: 192.0.9.2	IF: 12 IP: 192.0.12.1	IF: 4 IP: 192.0.11.1
6					IF: 10 IP: 192.0.11.2	IF: 12 IP: 192.0.14.1

Creating the BGP Scenario

In the network we just created, all routers belong to the same autonomous system. We will divide the network into three autonomous systems and utilize BGP to route packets among these systems.

1. Select **Duplicate Scenario** from the **Scenarios** menu and name it **BGP_Simple** → Click **OK**.
2. Highlight or select simultaneously (using shift and left-click) **Router1** and **Router2** → Right-click on **Router1** → **Edit Attributes** → Check the **Apply Changes to Selected Objects** check box.
3. Expand the **IP Routing Parameters** hierarchy and set the **Autonomous System Number** to **12** → Click **OK**.
4. Repeat Steps 2 and 3 for routers **Router3** and **Router4**. Assign their **Autonomous System Number** to **34**.
5. Repeat Steps 2 and 3 for routers **Router5** and **Router6**. Assign their **Autonomous System Number** to **56**.

The following figure shows the created autonomous systems. The figure also shows the interfaces that connect routers across different autonomous systems. There interfaces are taken from Table 8.1. (*Note:* the interface numbers in your project may vary.)

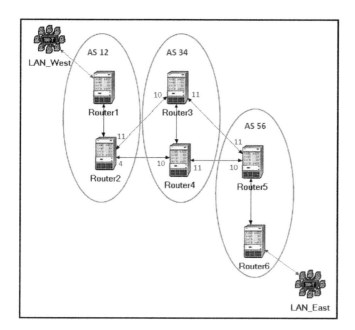

6. The next step is to disable the RIP protocol on the interfaces shown in the previous figure (i.e., Router2: IF4 and IF11, Router3: IF10 and IF11, Router4: IF10 and IF11, Router5: IF10 and IF11).

Note: Make sure to apply the next step on the interfaces in your simulation because they might be different from the preceding interfaces.

7. Right-click on **Router2** → **Edit Attributes** → Expand the **IP Routing Parameters** hierarchy → Expand the **Interface Information** hierarchy → Expand **row 4** hierarchy → Click on the values of the **Routing Protocol(s)** attribute → Disable **RIP** as shown → Click **OK** twice.

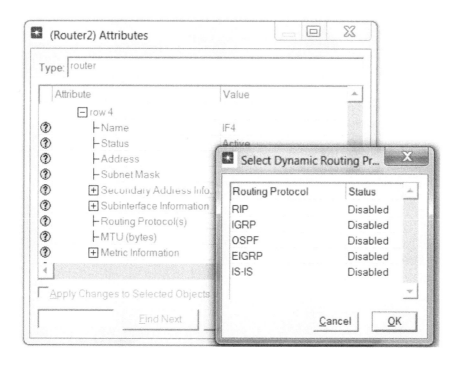

81

8. Repeat Step 7 for all other interfaces that connect routers across autonomous systems (i.e., all the remaining seven interdomain interfaces listed in Step 6).
9. **Save** your project.

Configuring the BGP Neighbor Information

If you try to run the simulation of the BGP_Simple scenario, you will receive hundreds of errors! This is because there is no routing protocol running between the interdomain routers. Therefore, no routing tables are created to deliver packets among autonomous systems. The solution is to utilize BGP by defining the neighbors of interdomain routers. Table 8.2 shows the neighbors of the routers that will run BGP. Neighbors are defined by their interface IP addresses and the AS numbers. For each router in Table 8.2, carry out the following step:

1. Right-click on the router → **Edit Attributes** → Expand the **BGP Parameters** hierarchy → Expand the **Neighbor Information** hierarchy → Assign to the **rows** attribute the value **1** for **Router1** and **Router6**. For all other routers, assign the value **3** to the **rows** attribute → Utilize Table 8.2 to assign the corresponding values to the **IP Address**, **Remote AS**, and **Update Source** attributes for each of the added rows.

Note: The values to be assigned to the IP Address attribute have to match the values you collected in your Table 8.1.

IBGP stands for Internal BGP, where BGP runs between two routers belonging to the same autonomous system. When a BGP speaker receives an update from an IBGP neighbor, the speaker will not redistribute the route advertisement to its other IBGP peers. To make sure that the routing information is consistently distributed throughout the network, each BGP speaker should maintain an IBGP connection to all the BGP speakers in its own autonomous system.

EBGP stand is for external BGP.

IP Address here is the IP address of the neighbor. The node should have knowledge of a valid route to reach this address. For IBGP connections, it is recommended that a Loopback interface address of the neighbor be used. For EBGP connections, a physical interface address that is within one IP hop is used.

Remote AS specifies the autonomous system number of the neighbor.

TABLE 8.2 Neighbors' Info for Interdomain Routers

| Routers | BGP Parameters ⇒ Neighbor Information | | |
	row 0	*row 1*	*row 2*
Router1	IP Address: 192.0.5.1 Remote AS: 12 Update Source: Loopback		
Router2	IP Address: 192.0.4.2 Remote AS: 34 Update Source: Not Used	IP Address: 192.0.3.2 Remote AS: 34 Update Source: Not Used	IP Address: 192.0.2.1 Remote AS: 12 Update Source: Loopback
Router3	IP Address: 192.0.4.1 Remote AS: 12 Update Source: Not Used	IP Address: 192.0.7.2 Remote AS: 56 Update Source: Not Used	IP Address: 192.0.10.1 Remote AS: 34 Update Source: Loopback
Router4	IP Address: 192.0.3.1 Remote AS: 12 Update Source: Not Used	IP Address: 192.0.9.2 Remote AS: 56 Update Source: Not Used	IP Address: 192.0.8.1 Remote AS: 34 Update Source: Loopback
Router5	IP Address: 192.0.7.1 Remote AS: 34 Update Source: Not Used	IP Address: 192.0.9.1 Remote AS: 34 Update Source: Not Used	IP Address: 192.0.14.1 Remote AS: 56 Update Source: Loopback
Router6	IP Address: 192.0.12.1 Remote AS: 56 Update Source: Loopback		

Creating the BGP with Policy Scenario

BGP allows for routing policies that can be enforced using route maps. We will utilize this feature to configure Router2 to redirect its load on the two egress links of its autonomous system.

1. Make sure that your project is in the **BGP_Simple** scenario. Select **Duplicate Scenario** from the **Scenarios** menu and name it **BGP_Policy** → Click **OK**.

2. Right-click on **Router2** → **Edit Attributes** → Expand the **IP Routing Parameters** hierarchy → Expand the **Route Map Configuration** hierarchy → Set the attributes as shown in the following figure.

The purpose of the created route map is to reduce the degree of preference of the "route to AS 56" to the value 10. (*Note:* The normal value is 99, which is calculated as 100 – number of ASs that should be crossed to reach the destination.)

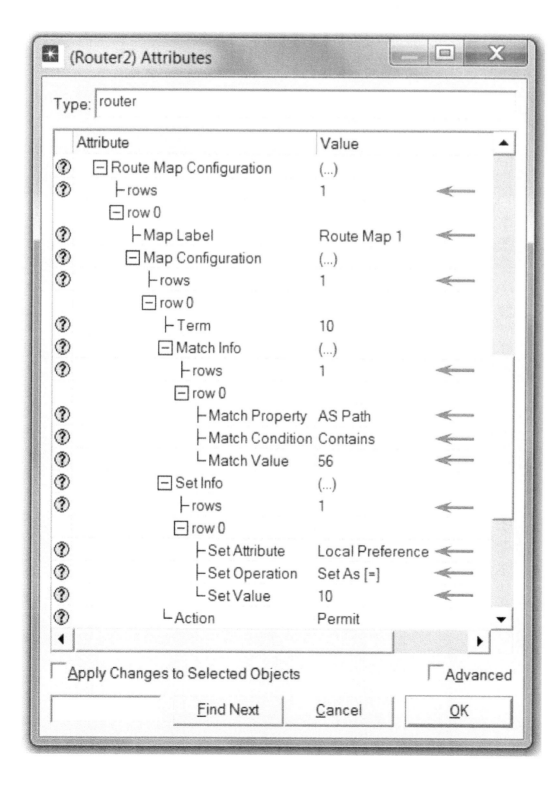

The next step is to assign the preceding route map to the link connecting Router2 to Router3. This way traffic from Router2 to AS 56 will be preferred to go through Router4 instead.

3. Right-click on **Router2** → **Edit Attributes** → Expand the **BGP Parameters** hierarchy → Expand the **Neighbor Information** hierarchy → Expand the row that has the IP address of Router3 interface (it is row 0 in my project) → Expand the **Routing Policies** hierarchy → Set its attribute as shown in the following figure.

4. Click **OK**, and **Save** your project.

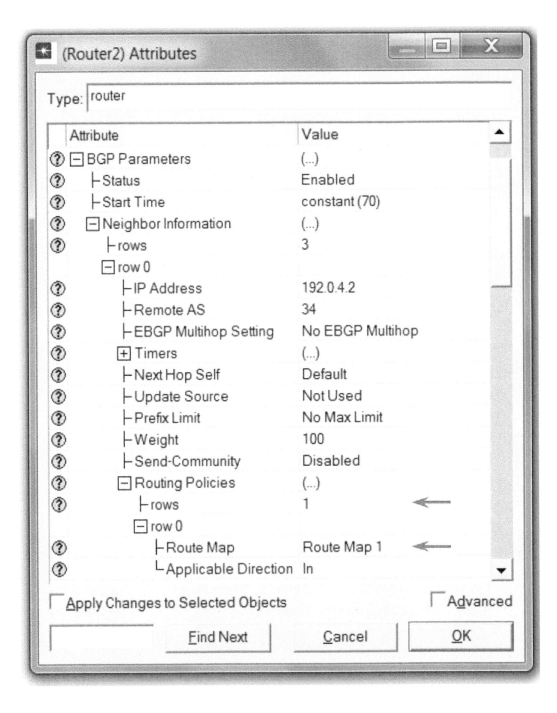

Run the Simulation

To run the simulation for the three scenarios simultaneously:

1. Go to the **Scenarios** menu → Select **Manage Scenarios**.
2. Change the values under the **Results** column to **<collect>** (or **<recollect>**) for the three scenarios. Compare with the following figure.

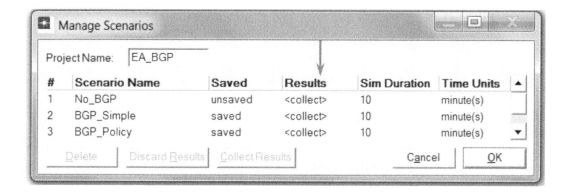

3. Click **OK** to run the three simulations.
4. After the three simulation runs complete, one for each scenario, click **Close** → **Save** your project.

View the Results

Compare the routing tables content:

1. To check the content of the routing tables in **Router2** for **No_BGP** scenario:
   a. Click **Ctrl + 1** → Go to the **Results** menu → **Open Simulation Log** → Expand the hierarchy on the left as shown in the following figure → Click on the field **COMMON ROUTE TABLE** in the row that corresponds to Router2.

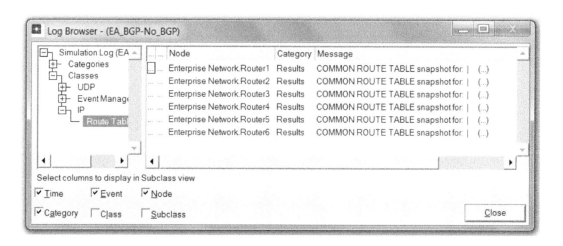

2. Carry out the previous step for scenario **BGP_Simple** by clicking **Ctrl + 2** at the beginning. The following are partial contents of **Router2**'s routing table for both scenarios. (*Note:* Your results may vary due to different node placement.)

Routing table of **Router2** for the **No_BGP** scenario:

Dest. Address	Subnet Mask	Next Hop	Interface Name	Metric	Protocol
192.0.3.0	255.255.255.0	192.0.3.1	IF4	0	Direct
192.0.1.0	255.255.255.0	192.0.1.2	IF10	0	Direct
192.0.4.0	255.255.255.0	192.0.4.1	IF11	0	Direct
192.0.5.0	255.255.255.0	192.0.5.1	Loopback	0	Direct
192.0.6.0	255.255.255.0	192.0.3.2	IF4	1	RIP
192.0.9.0	255.255.255.0	192.0.3.2	IF4	1	RIP
192.0.10.0	255.255.255.0	192.0.3.2	IF4	1	RIP
192.0.0.0	255.255.255.0	192.0.1.1	IF10	1	RIP
192.0.2.0	255.255.255.0	192.0.1.1	IF10	1	RIP
192.0.7.0	255.255.255.0	192.0.4.2	IF11	1	RIP
192.0.8.0	255.255.255.0	192.0.4.2	IF11	1	RIP
192.0.11.0	255.255.255.0	192.0.3.2	IF4	2	RIP
192.0.12.0	255.255.255.0	192.0.3.2	IF4	2	RIP
192.0.13.0	255.255.255.0	192.0.3.2	IF4	3	RIP
192.0.14.0	255.255.255.0	192.0.3.2	IF4	3	RIP

Routing table of **Router2** for the **BGP_Simple** scenario:

Dest. Address	Subnet Mask	Next Hop	Interface Name	Metric	Protocol
192.0.1.0	255.255.255.0	192.0.1.2	IF10	0	Direct
192.0.5.0	255.255.255.0	192.0.5.1	Loopback	0	Direct
192.0.3.0	255.255.255.0	192.0.3.1	IF4	0	Direct
192.0.4.0	255.255.255.0	192.0.4.1	IF11	0	Direct
192.0.0.0	255.255.255.0	192.0.1.1	IF10	1	RIP
192.0.2.0	255.255.255.0	192.0.1.1	IF10	1	RIP
192.0.10.0	255.255.255.0	192.0.3.2	IF4	0	BGP
192.0.6.0	255.255.255.0	192.0.4.2	IF11	0	BGP
192.0.8.0	255.255.255.0	192.0.4.2	IF11	0	BGP
192.0.9.0	255.255.255.0	192.0.4.2	IF11	2	BGP
192.0.7.0	255.255.255.0	192.0.4.2	IF11	2	BGP
192.0.11.0	255.255.255.0	192.0.4.2	IF11	0	BGP
192.0.12.0	255.255.255.0	192.0.4.2	IF11	0	BGP
192.0.13.0	255.255.255.0	192.0.4.2	IF11	0	BGP
192.0.14.0	255.255.255.0	192.0.4.2	IF11	0	BGP

Compare the load in the network:

1. Select **Compare Results** from the **Results** menu.
2. Change the drop-down menu in the right-lower part of the *Compare Results* dialog box from **As Is** to **time_average** as shown.

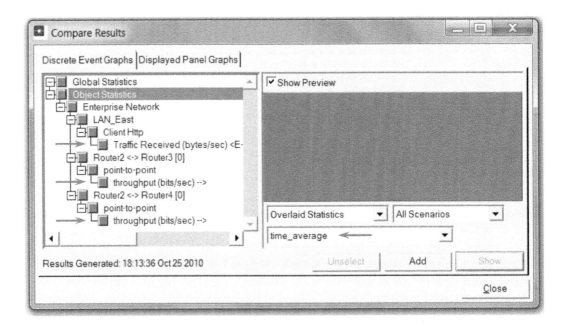

3. Select and show the graphs of the statistics shown previously: **Traffic Received** in LAN_ East, **throughput in the Router2-Router3** link, and **throughput in the Router2-Router4** link. The resulting graphs should resemble the graphs that follow.

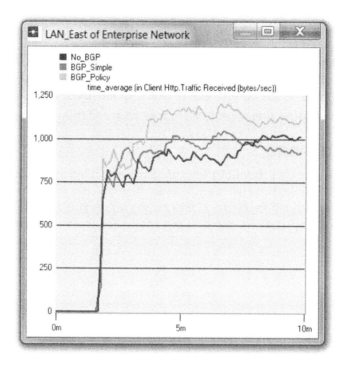

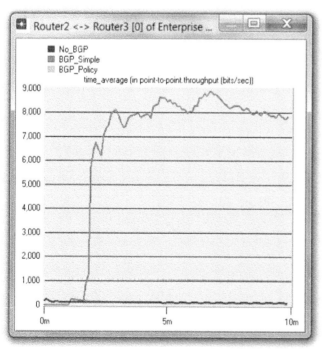

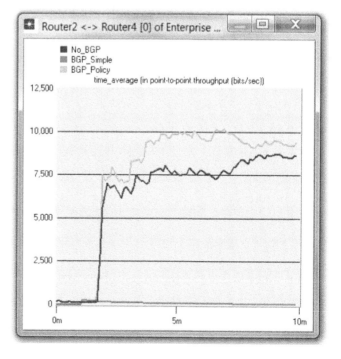

FURTHER READINGS

A Border Gateway Protocol 4 (BGP-4): IETF RFC number 1771 (www.ietf.org/rfc.html).

Application of the Border Gateway Protocol in the Internet: IETF RFC number 1772 (www.ietf.org/rfc.html).

BGP-4 Protocol Analysis: IETF RFC number 1774 (www.ietf.org/rfc.html).

EXERCISES

1. Obtain and analyze the routing table for **Router5** in the project before and after applying BGP.
2. Analyze the graphs that show the throughput in both the Router2–Router3 link and Router2–Router4 link. Explain the effect of applying the routing policy on these throughputs.
3. Create another scenario as a duplicate of the **BGP_Simple** scenario. Name the new scenario **BGP_OSPF_RIP**. In this new scenario change the intradomain routing protocol in **AS 56** to **OSPF** instead of **RIP**. Run the new scenario and check the contents of **Router5**'s routing table. Analyze the content of this table.

LAB REPORT

Prepare a report that follows the guidelines explained in the Introduction Lab. The report should include the answers to the preceding exercises as well as the graphs you generated from the simulation scenarios. Discuss the results you obtained and compare these results with your expectations. Mention any anomalies or unexplained behaviors.

Mobile Wireless Network
A Wireless Local Area Network with Mobile Stations

OBJECTIVES

This lab simulates mobility in wireless local area networks. We'll study the effect of mobility on the TCP performance. In addition, the lab examines how the request to send (RTS) and clear to send (CTS) frames are utilized in avoiding the hidden node problem usually induced by mobility in WLANs.

OVERVIEW

One of the requirements of the IEEE 802.11 standard is to handle mobile stations in wireless local area networks (WLANs). Mobile stations are defined as the stations that access the LAN while in motion. IEEE 802.11 handles station mobility within the MAC sublayer, and hence such mobility is hidden from the higher layers in the network. However, the disconnection and reconnection events induced by mobility in a WLAN significantly affect the performance of higher-layer protocols such as TCP. For example, TCP interprets disconnection due to mobility as congestion, and hence, it multiplicatively decreases its congestion window size. After reconnection, TCP takes an unnecessarily longer time to recover the congestion window to a size that matches the available bandwidth.

IEEE 802.11 utilizes the request to send (RTS) and clear to send (CTS) frames in various circumstances to further minimize collisions. RTS and CTS are especially useful in solving the hidden node problem in WLANs that have mobile stations. Exchanging the RTS and CTS between the sender and the receiver informs nearby stations that a transmission is about to begin. Duration information in RTS/CTS frames are used to set the network allocation vector (NAV) in all stations that are within the reception range of the RTS/CTS frames. This way, the problem of a hidden sender can be solved because any station that sees the CTS frame knows that it is close to the receiver and, therefore, cannot transmit for the period of time indicated in the NAV. If transmitted data frames are short, sending RTS/CTS frames is not recommended, since it adds overhead inefficiency. Therefore, a threshold is defined to use RTS/CTS only on frames longer than a specified length.

In this lab, we will simulate a wireless LAN with mobile workstations and server. The workstations will run an FTP application to upload files to the server. We will study the effect of node mobility on the performance of the TCP connection for the FTP session. We will also study the role of the RTS and CTS frames in avoiding the hidden node problem usually induced by mobility in wireless LANs.

PRE-LAB ACTIVITIES

📖 Read Section 4.4 from *Computer Networks: A Systems Approach, 5th Edition.*

💻 Go to www.net-seal.net and play the following animation:
  o Wireless Network and Multiple Access with Collision Avoidance

PROCEDURE

Create a New Project

1. Start **OPNET IT Guru Academic Edition** → Choose **New** from the **File** menu.
2. Select **Project** and click **OK** → Name the project **<your initials>_MobileWLAN**, and the scenario **Mobile_noRTSCTS** →Click **OK**.
3. In the *Startup Wizard: Initial Topology* dialog box, make sure that **Create Empty Scenario** is selected → Click **Next** → Select **Campus** from the *Network Scale* list → Click **Next** → Make sure that Kilometer is the unit chosen for the **Size** and then assign **2** and **1** to the **X Span** and **Y Span**, respectively → Click **Next** twice → Click **OK**.

Create and Configure the Network

Initialize the network:

1. The *Object Palette* dialog box should now be on the top of your project space. If it is not there, open it by clicking 🔲 → Select **wireless_lan** from the pull-down menu on the object palette.
2. Add the following objects from the palette to the project workspace: **Application Config**, **Profile Config**, two **wlan_wkstn (mob)**, and one **wlan_server (mob)**.
   a. To add an object from a palette, click its icon in the object palette → Move your mouse to the workspace → Click to drop the object in the desired location → Right-click to finish creating objects of that type.
3. **Close** the palette.
4. Arrange and rename the objects you added as shown:

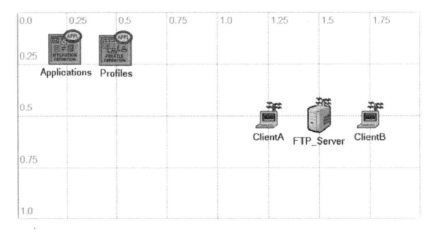

5. Position the workstations and the server according to the x and y positions shown in the following table:
   a. To position an object: Right-click on the object → **Advanced Edit Attributes** → Edit the **x position** and **y position** attributes.

Node	x position	y position
Client A	1.25	0.5
FTP_Server	1.5	0.5
Client B	1.75	0.5

Configure the applications:

1. Right-click on the **Applications** node → **Edit Attributes** → Expand the **Application Definitions** attribute and set **rows** to 1 → Expand the new row → Name the row **FTP_Application**.

    a. Expand the **Description** hierarchy → Edit the **FTP** row as shown (you will need to set the **Special Value** to **Not Used** while editing the shown attributes).

0% for the Command Mix (Get/Total) attribute means all the FTP sessions will be only "Send" from the clients to the server.

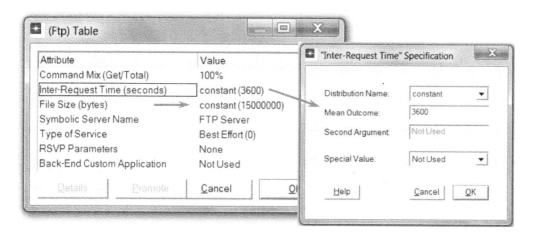

2. Click **OK** twice, and then **Save** your project.

Configure the profiles:

1. Right-click on the **Profiles** node → **Edit Attributes** → Expand the **Profile Configuration** attribute and set **rows** to 1 → Name and set the attributes of **row 0** as shown → Click **OK**.

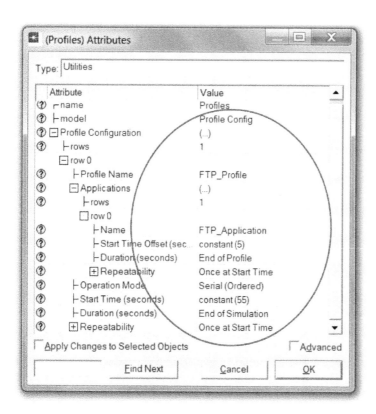

Configure the applications in the server and clients:

1. Right-click on the **FTP_Server** node → **Edit Attributes**.
   a. Edit the **Server Address** attribute → Assign the value **FTP_Server** to it.
   b. Edit **Application: Supported Services** → Set **rows** to **1** → Set **Name** to **FTP_Application** → Click **OK** twice.

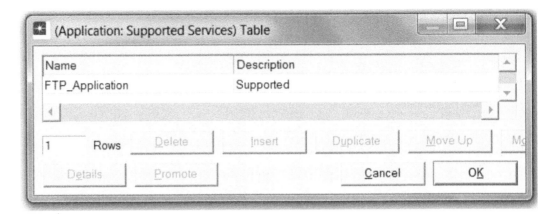

2. Select both **ClientA** and **ClientB** in the network simultaneously → Right-click on one of them → **Edit Attributes** → Check the **Apply Changes to Selected Objects** check box:
   a. Expand the **Application: Supported Profiles** hierarchy → Set **rows** to **1** → Set **Profile Name** to FTP_Profile.
   b. Edit the **Application: Destination Preferences** attribute as follows: Set **rows** to **1** → Set **Symbolic Name** to FTP Server → Edit **Actual Name** → Set **rows** to **1** → In the new row, assign **FTP_Server** to the **Name** column as shown → Click **OK**.

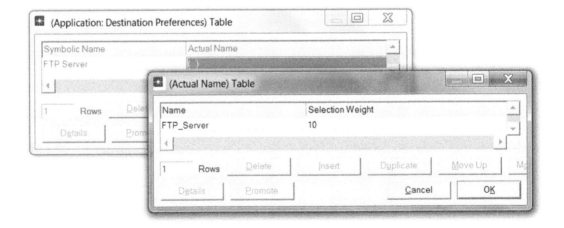

Configure the trajectory:

The **trajectory** attribute specifies the name of an ASCII trajectory file that specifies the times and locations that a mobile node will pass through as the simulation progresses.

1. Right-click on **ClientA** → **Edit Attributes** → Assign **trajectory_1** to the **trajectory** attribute → Click **OK**.
2. A green trajectory will appear on the project workspace. Right-click on that trajectory and select **Edit Trajectory** → In the *Edit Trajectory Information* dialog box, name the trajectory **<your initials>_left_trajectory** → Click **OK**.
3. From the **Edit** menu, choose **Preferences**. Check the value of the **mod_dirs** attribute. The first directory in the list is where a trajectory file with the name *<your initials>_left_trajectory.trj* is saved. Edit that file using any text editor (e.g., Notepad). Replace all the contents of the file with the info shown in the following figure and then save.

```
Version: 2
Position_Unit: Kilometers
Altitude_Unit: Meters
Coordinate_Method: relative
Altitude_Method: absolute
locale: English_United States.1252
Coordinate_Count: 6
# X Position      Y Position       Altitude          Traverse Time      Wait Time
0                ,0               ,0                ,0h0m0.00s          ,0h2m0.00s
-0.75            ,0               ,0                ,0h0m20.97s         ,0h1m0.00s
-0.75            ,0.02            ,0                ,0h0m2.24s          ,0h0m0.00s
-1               ,0.02            ,0                ,0h0m6.99s          ,0h0m0.00s
-1               ,0.04            ,0                ,0h0m2.24s          ,0h0m30.00s
0                ,0.04            ,0                ,0h0m27.96s         ,0h0m0.00s
```

4. Right-click on **ClientA** → **Edit Attributes** → Assign **<your initials>_left_trajectory** to the trajectory attribute → Click **OK**.

5. The new trajectory should look exactly like the following one. Right-click on the trajectory and select **Edit Trajectory**.

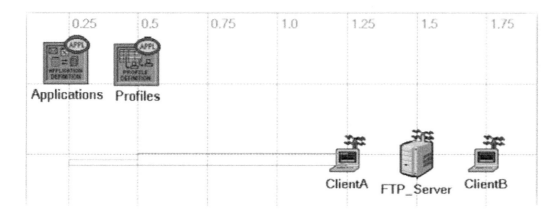

6. In the *Edit Trajectory Information* dialog box, verify that the trajectory info matches the values shown in the following figure:

Note: The trajectory makes ClientA start moving after 2 min from the beginning of the simulation. ClientA waits at X Pos 0.5 for 1 min and at X Pos 0.25 for 20 s.

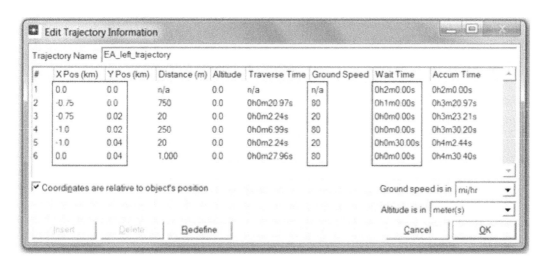

7. Click **OK** twice, and then **Save** your project.

Configure the Simulation

Here, we will configure the simulation parameters:

The **Seed** attribute is an integer that is used by the simulation's random number generator. Its default value is 128.

1. Click on ![icon] and the *Configure Simulation* window should appear.
2. Assign **10.0 minutes** to the **Duration** attribute.
3. Assign **256** to the **Seed** attribute.
4. Click **OK**, and then **Save** your project.

Choose the Statistics

To test the performance of our mobile wireless network, we will collect some of the available statistics as follows:

1. Right-click anywhere in the project workspace, and select **Choose Individual Statistics** from the pop-up menu.
2. In the *Choose Results* dialog box, expand the **Node Statistics** hierarchy → Choose the following three statistics:
   i. **Congestion Window Size (bytes)** under **TCP Connection**.
   ii. **Traffic Received (bytes)** under **TCP Connection**.
   iii. **Load (bits/sec)** under **Wireless Lan**.
3. Right-click on the **Congestion Window Size (bytes)** statistic → Choose **Change Collection Mode** → In the dialog box, check **Advanced** → From the drop-down menu, assign **all values** to **Capture mode** as shown → Click **OK**.

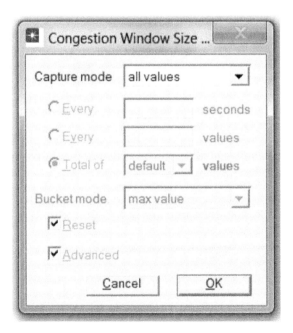

4. Right-click on the **Traffic Received (bytes)** statistic → Choose **Change Collection Mode** → In the dialog box, check **Advanced** → From the drop-down menu, assign **all values** to **Capture mode**.
5. Click **OK** twice, and then **Save** your project.

Duplicate the Scenario

We will create one more scenario to utilize the RTS and CTS frames to study their effect on minimizing collisions.

1. Select **Duplicate Scenario** from the **Scenarios** menu and give it the name **Mobile_ RTSCTS** → Click **OK**.

2. Select **ClientA**, **FTP_server**, and **ClientB** simultaneously → Right-click on any one of them → **Edit Attributes** → Check the **Apply Changes to Selected Objects** check box.
3. Expand the hierarchy of the **Wireless LAN Parameters** attribute → Assign the value **256** to the **Rts Threshold (bytes)** attribute.
4. Click **OK**, and then **Save** your project.

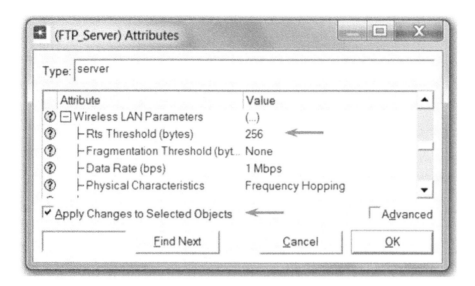

Run the Simulation

To run the simulation for both scenarios simultaneously:

1. Go to the **Scenarios** menu → Select **Manage Scenarios**.
2. Click on the row of each scenario, and click the **Collect Results** button. This should change the values under the Results column to <collect> as shown.

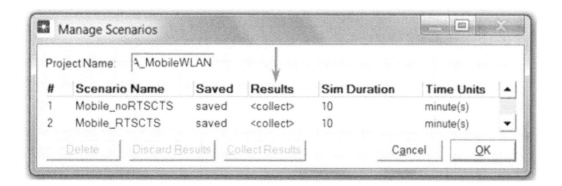

3. Click **OK** to run both simulations. Depending on the speed of your processor, this task may take several seconds to complete.
4. After the simulation of both scenarios completes, click **Close** and **Save** your project.

View the Results

Do the following to view and analyze the results. (*Note:* Actual results will vary slightly based on the actual node positioning in the project.)

1. Select **Compare Results** from the **Result** menu.
2. Select the **Congestion Window Size (bytes)** <Conn 1... statistic for the **FTP_Server** from the **TCP Connection** hierarchy as shown.

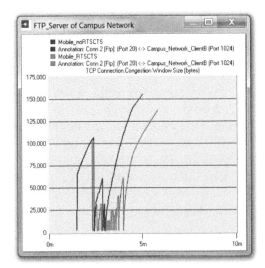

3. Click **Show** to show the result in a new panel.
4. Repeat the preceding steps for the following statistics:
   a. **FTP Server → TCP Connection → Congestion Window Size (bytes) <Conn 2...;**
   b. **ClientA → Wireless Lan → Load (bits/sec);** and
   c. **ClientB → Wireless Lan → Load (bits/sec).**

The resulting graphs should resemble the following graphs.

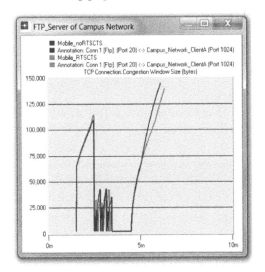

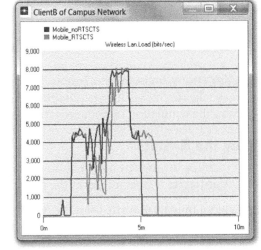

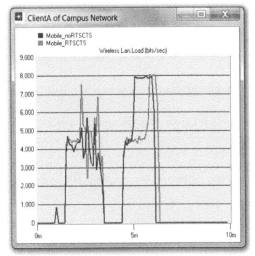

5. Go back to the *Compare Results* dialog box → Expand the **TCP Connection** hierarchy for the **ClientA** → Select the **Traffic Received (bytes)** statistic → Select **sample_sum** to replace **As Is** as shown in the following figure → Click **Show**.
6. Repeat the above step for the **Traffic Received (bytes)** by **ClientB**.
7. The resulting graphs should resemble the following graphs.

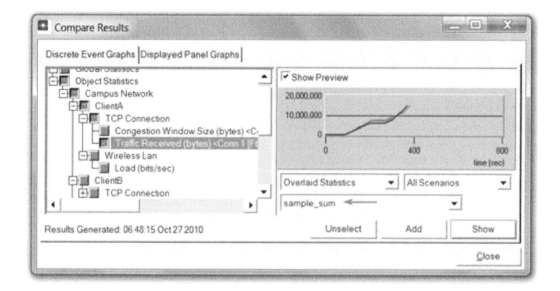

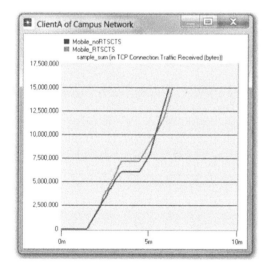
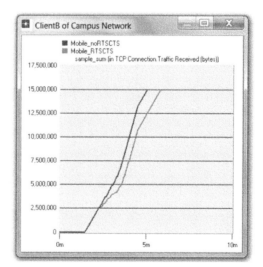

97

FURTHER READINGS

ANSI/IEEE Standard 802.11, 1999 Edition: Wireless LAN Medium Access Control (MAC) and Physical Layer (PHY) Specifications.

Transmission Control Protocol: IETF RFC number 793 (www.ietf.org/rfc.html).

EXERCISES

1. Explain how **Load** and **Congestion Window Size** are affected by the mobility of **ClientA**.
2. Explain how enabling RTS/CTS helps in avoiding the hidden node problem and hence explain the effect of RTS/CTS frames on the network performance.

3. The graphs show that the server terminates the FTP session with ClientA earlier if RTS/CTS is enabled. However, the server terminates the FTP session with ClientB later if RTS/CTS is enabled. Explain why.

4. Create a new scenario as a duplicate of the **Mobile_noRTSCTS** scenario. Name the new scenario **twoMobiles_noRTSCTS**. Create a second new scenario as a duplicate of the **Mobile_RTSCTS** scenario. Name the second new scenario **twoMobiles_RTSCTS**. In both new scenarios, edit the attribute of the **FTP_Server**, and assign **<your initials>_ left_trajectory** to its **trajectory** attribute. Run the simulation for all scenarios and create the graphs for the **Load (bits/sec)**, **Congestion Window Size (bytes)**, and **Traffic Received (bytes)** statistic results, as we did in this lab. Analyze the graphs explaining the effect of the server mobility on the network performance.

LAB REPORT

Prepare a report that follows the guidelines explained in the Introduction Lab. The report should include the answers to the preceding exercises as well as the graphs you generated from the simulation scenarios. Discuss the results you obtained and compare these results with your expectations. Mention any anomalies or unexplained behaviors.

TCP: Transmission Control Protocol
A Reliable, Connection-Oriented, Byte-Stream Service

OBJECTIVES

This lab is designed to demonstrate the congestion control algorithms implemented by the Transmission Control Protocol (TCP). The lab provides a number of scenarios to simulate these algorithms. You will compare the performance of the algorithms through the analysis of the simulation results.

OVERVIEW

The Internet's TCP guarantees the reliable, in-order delivery of a stream of bytes. It includes a flow-control mechanism for the byte streams that allows the receiver to limit how much data the sender can transmit at a given time. In addition, TCP implements a highly tuned congestion-control mechanism. The idea of this mechanism is to throttle the rate at which TCP sends data, to keep the sender from overloading the network.

The idea of TCP congestion control is for each source to determine how much capacity is available in the network so that it knows how many packets it can safely have in transit. It maintains a state variable for each connection, called the congestion window, which is used by the source to limit how much data the source is allowed to have in transit at a given time. TCP uses a mechanism called additive increase/multiplicative decrease. With this feature, TCP decreases the congestion window when the level of congestion goes up and increases the congestion window when the level of congestion goes down. TCP interprets timeouts as a sign of congestion. Each time a timeout occurs, the source sets the congestion window to half of its previous value. This halving corresponds to the multiplicative decrease part of the mechanism. The congestion window is not allowed to fall below the size of a single packet (the TCP maximum segment size, or MSS). Every time the source successfully sends a congestion window worth of packets, it adds the equivalent of one packet to the congestion window; this is the additive increase part of the mechanism.

TCP uses a mechanism called slow start to increase the congestion window "rapidly" from a cold start in TCP connections. It increases the congestion window exponentially rather than linearly. Finally, TCP utilizes a mechanism called fast retransmit and fast recovery. Fast retransmit is a heuristic that sometimes triggers the retransmission of a dropped packet sooner than the regular timeout mechanism.

In this lab, you will set up a network that utilizes TCP as its end-to-end transmission protocol, and you will analyze the size of the congestion window with different mechanisms.

PRE-LAB ACTIVITIES

📖 Read Section 5.2 from *Computer Networks: A Systems Approach, 5th Edition*.

💻 Go to www.net-seal.net and play the following animations:
- ○ TCP Connections
- ○ TCP Multiplexing
- ○ TCP Buffering and Sequencing
- ○ User Datagram Protocol (UDP)

PROCEDURE

Create a New Project

1. Start **OPNET IT Guru Academic Edition** → Choose **New** from the **File** menu.
2. Select **Project** and click **OK** → Name the project **<your initials>_TCP**, and the scenario **No_Drop** → Click **OK**.
3. In the *Startup Wizard: Initial Topology* dialog box, make sure that **Create Empty Scenario** is selected → Click **Next** → Select **Choose From Maps** from the *Network Scale* list → Click **Next** → Choose **USA** from the Map List → Click **Next** twice → Click **OK**.

Create and Configure the Network

Initialize the network:

1. The *Object Palette* dialog box should now be on the top of your project space. If it is not there, open it by clicking 🖼. Make sure that the **internet_toolbox** item is selected from the pull-down menu on the object palette.
2. Add to the project workspace the following objects from the palette: **Application Config**, **Profile Config**, an **ip32_Cloud**, and two subnets.
   a. To add an object from a palette, click its icon in the object palette → Move your mouse to the workspace → Click to drop the object in the desired location → Right-click to finish creating objects of that type.
3. **Close** the palette.
4. **Rename** the objects you added as shown.
5. **Save** your project.

The **ip32_cloud** node model represents an IP cloud supporting up to 32 serial line interfaces at a selectable data rate through which IP traffic can be modeled. IP packets arriving on any cloud interface are routed to the appropriate output interface based on their destination IP address. The RIP or OSPF protocol may be used to automatically and dynamically create the cloud's routing tables and select routes in an adaptive manner. This cloud requires a fixed amount of time to route each packet, as determined by the **Packet Latency** attribute of the node.

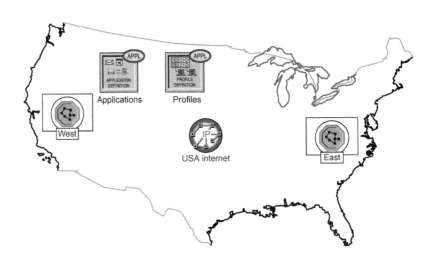

Configure the applications:

1. Right-click on the **Applications** node → **Edit Attributes** → Expand the **Application Definitions** attribute and set **rows** to **1** → Expand the new row → Name the row **FTP_Application**.

   a. Expand the **Description** hierarchy → Edit the **FTP** row as shown (first, you will need to set the **Special Value** to **Not Used** while editing the attributes shown):

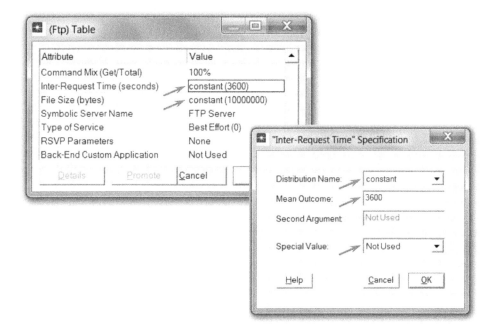

101

2. Click **OK** twice, and **Save** your project.

Configure the profiles:

1. Right-click on the **Profiles** node → **Edit Attributes** → Expand the **Profile Configuration** attribute and set **rows** to **1**.

   a. Name and set the attributes of **row 0** as shown → Click **OK**.

Configure the West subnet:

1. Double-click on the **West** subnet node. You get an empty workspace, indicating that the subnet contains no objects.
2. Open the Object palette 🔲 and make sure that the **internet_toolbox** item is selected from the pull-down menu.
3. Add the following items to the subnet workspace: one **ethernet_server**, one **ethernet4_slip8_gtwy** router, and connect them with a bidirectional **100_BaseT** link → **Close** the palette → **Rename** the objects as shown.

The **ethernet4_slip8_gtwy** node model represents an IP-based gateway supporting four Ethernet hub interfaces and eight serial line interfaces.

Server_West   Router_West

4. Right-click on the **Server_West** node → **Edit Attributes**:
   a. Edit **Application: Supported Services** → Set **rows** to **1** → Set **Name** to **FTP_Application** → Click **OK**.
   b. Edit the value of the **Server Address** attribute and write down **Server_West**.
   c. Expand the **TCP Parameters** hierarchy → Set both **Fast Retransmit** and **Fast Recovery** to **Disabled**.
5. Click **OK**, and **Save** your project.

Now, you have completed the configuration of the West subnet. To go back to the top level of the project and click the **Go to next higher level** 🔼 button.

Configure the East subnet:

1. Double-click on the **East** subnet node. You get an empty workspace, indicating that the subnet contains no objects.
2. **Open** the Object palette 🔲 and make sure that the **internet_toolbox** item is selected from the pull-down menu.
3. Add the following items to the subnet workspace: one **ethernet_wkstn**, one **ethernet4_slip8_gtwy** router, and connect them with a bidirectional **100_BaseT** link → **Close** the palette → Rename the objects as shown.

Client_East

Router_East

4. Right-click on the **Client_East** node → **Edit Attributes**:
   a. Expand the **Application: Supported Profiles** hierarchy → Set **rows** to **1** → Expand the **row 0** hierarchy → Set **Profile Name** to **FTP_Profile**.
   b. Assign **Client_East** to the **Client Address** attributes.
   c. Edit the **Application: Destination Preferences** attribute as follows:
   d. Set **rows** to **1** → Set **Symbolic Name** to **FTP Server** → Edit **Actual Name** → Set **rows** to **1** → In the new row, assign **Server_West** to the **Name** column.
5. Click **OK** three times, and then **Save** your project.

You have now completed the configuration of the **East** subnet. To go back to the project space, click the **Go to next higher level** 🔼 button.

Connect the subnets to the IP Cloud:

1. Open the Object palette ▓.
2. Using two **PPP_DS3** bidirectional links, connect the **East** subnet to the **IP Cloud** and the **West** subnet to the **IP Cloud**.
3. A pop-up dialog box will appear, asking you with what to connect the subnet to the IP Cloud with. Make sure to select the **routers.**
4. Close the palette.

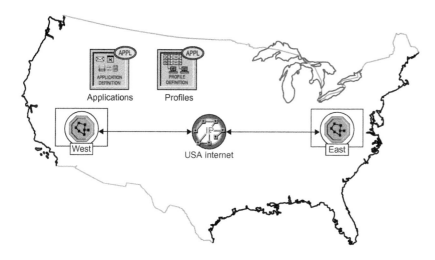

Choose the Statistics

1. Right-click on **Server_West** in the **West** subnet, and select **Choose Individual Statistics** from the pop-up menu.
2. In the *Choose Results* dialog box, choose the following statistic:
   a. **TCP Connection → Congestion Window Size (bytes)** and **Sent Segment Sequence Number**.

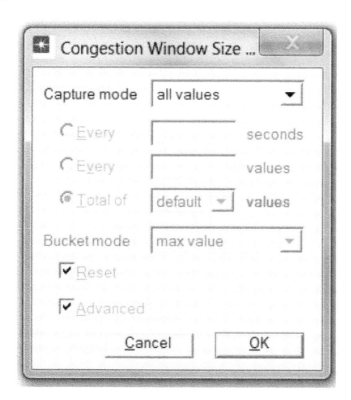

OPNET provides the following capture modes:

All values: This mode collects every data point from a statistic.

Sample: This mode collects the data according to a user-specified time interval or sample count. For example, if the time interval is 10, data is sampled and recorded every 10th second. If the sample count is 10, every 10th data point is recorded. All other data points are discarded.

Bucket: This mode collects all of the points over the time interval or sample count into a "data bucket" and generates a result from each bucket. This is the default mode.

103

b. Right-click on the **Congestion Window Size (bytes)** statistic → Choose **Change Collection Mode** → In the dialog box, check **Advanced** → From the drop-down menu, assign **all values** to **Capture mode** as shown → Click **OK**.

c. Right-click on the **Sent Segment Sequence Number** statistic → Choose **Change Collection Mode** → In the dialog box, check **Advanced** → From the drop-down menu, assign all values to Capture mode.

3. Click **OK** twice, and **Save** your project.

4. Click the **Go to next higher level** 🔍 button.

Configure the Simulation

Here we need to configure the duration of the simulation:

1. Click on 🖥 and the *Configure Simulation* window should appear.

2. Set the duration to **10.0 minutes** → Click **OK**.

Duplicate the Scenario

With **fast retransmit**, TCP performs a retransmission of what appears to be the missing segment, without waiting for a retransmission timer to expire.

After fast retransmit sends what appears to be the missing segment, congestion avoidance but not slow start is performed. This is the **fast recovery** algorithm.

The fast retransmit and fast recovery algorithms are usually implemented together (RFC 2001).

104

In the network we just created, we assumed a perfect network with no discarded packets. Also, we disabled the fast retransmit and fast recovery techniques in TCP. To analyze the effects of discarded packets and those congestion-control techniques, we will create two additional scenarios.

1. Select **Duplicate Scenario** from the **Scenarios** menu, and give it the name **Drop_NoFast** → Click **OK**.

a. In the new scenario, right-click on the **IP Cloud** → **Edit Attributes** → Assign **0.05%** to the **Packet Discard Ratio** attribute → Click **OK**, and **Save** your project.

2. While you are still in the **Drop_NoFast** scenario, select **Duplicate Scenario** from the **Scenarios** menu, and give it the name **Drop_Fast**.

a. In the **Drop_Fast** scenario, right-click on **Server_ West**, which is inside the **West** subnet → **Edit Attributes** → Expand the **TCP Parameters** hierarchy → **Enable** the **Fast Retransmit** attribute → Assign **Reno** to the **Fast Recovery** attribute.

3. Click **OK**, and **Save** your project.

Run the Simulation

To run the simulation for the three scenarios simultaneously:

1. Go to the **Scenarios** menu → Select **Manage Scenarios**.

2. Change the values under the **Results** column to **<collect>** (or **<recollect>**) for the three scenarios. Compare with the following figure.

3. Click **OK** to run the three simulations. Depending on the speed of your processor, this task may take several seconds to complete.

4. After the simulation runs complete, click **Close** → **Save** your project.

View the Results

To switch to a scenario, choose **Switch to Scenario** from the **Scenarios** menu or just press **Ctrl + <scenario number>**.

To view and analyze the results:

1. Switch to the **Drop_NoFast** scenario (the second one) and choose **View Results** from the **Results** menu.

2. Fully expand the **Object Statistics** hierarchy and select the following two results: **Congestion Window Size (bytes)** and **Sent Segment Sequence Number**.

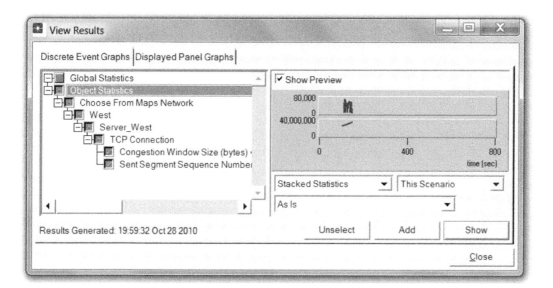

3. Click **Show**. The resulting graphs should resemble the ones that follow.

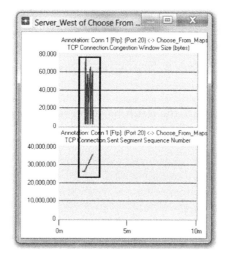

4. To zoom in on the details in the graph, click and drag your mouse to draw a rectangle, as shown in the preceding figure.

The graph should be redrawn to resemble the following one:

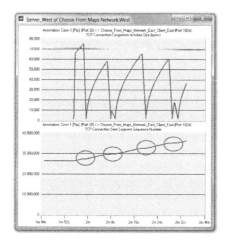

Notice the **Segment Sequence Number** is almost flat with every drop in the congestion window.

5. Close the *View Results* dialog box and select **Compare Results** from the **Result** menu.
6. Fully expand the **Object Statistics** hierarchy as shown and select the following result: **Sent Segment Sequence Number**.

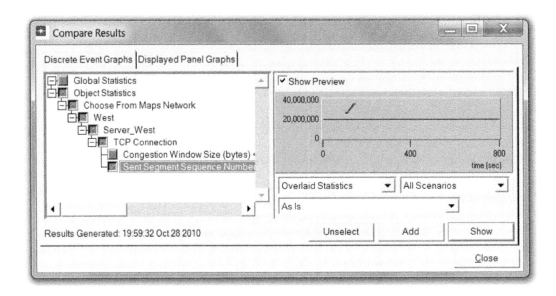

7. Click **Show**. After you zoom in, the resulting graph should resemble the one shown here.

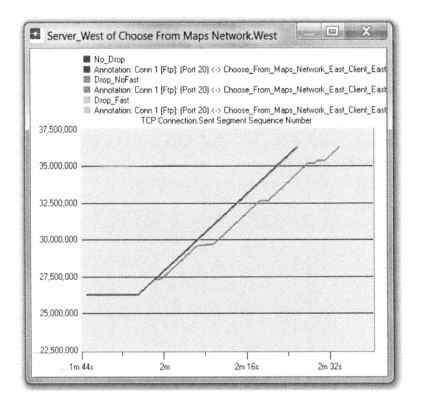

FURTHER READINGS

OPNET TCP Model Description: From the **Protocols** menu, select **TCP** → **Model Usage Guide**.

Transmission Control Protocol: IETF RFC number 793 (www.ietf.org/rfc.html).

EXERCISES

1. Why does the **Segment Sequence Number** remain unchanged (indicated by a horizontal line in the graphs) with every drop in the congestion window?
2. Analyze the graph that compares the **Segment Sequence** numbers of the three scenarios. Why does the **Drop_NoFast** scenario have the slowest growth in sequence numbers?
3. In the **Drop_NoFast** scenario, obtain the overlaid graph that compares **Sent Segment Sequence Number** with **Received Segment ACK Number** for **Server_West**. Explain the graph. *Hint:* Make sure to assign **all values** to the **Capture mode** of the **Received Segment ACK Number** statistic.
4. Create another scenario as a duplicate of the **Drop_Fast** scenario. Name the new scenario **Q4_Drop_Fast_Buffer**. In the new scenario, edit the attributes of the **Client_East** node and assign **65535** to its **Receiver Buffer (bytes)** attribute (one of the **TCP Parameters**). Generate a graph that shows how the **Congestion Window Size (bytes)** of **Server_West** gets affected by the increase in the receiver buffer. (Compare the congestion window size graph from the **Drop_Fast** scenario with the corresponding graph from the **Q4_Drop_Fast_Buffer** scenario.)

LAB REPORT

Prepare a report that follows the guidelines explained in the Introduction Lab. The report should include the answers to the preceding exercises as well as the graphs you generated from the simulation scenarios. Discuss the results you obtained and compare these results with your expectations. Mention any anomalies or unexplained behaviors.

Queuing Disciplines
Order of Packet Transmission and Dropping

OBJECTIVES

The objective of this lab is to examine the effect of various queuing disciplines on packet delivery and delay for different services.

OVERVIEW

As part of the resource allocation mechanisms, each router must implement some queuing discipline that governs how packets are buffered while waiting to be transmitted. Various queuing disciplines can be used to control which packets get transmitted (bandwidth allocation) and which packets get dropped (limited buffer space). The queuing discipline also affects the latency experienced by a packet, by determining how long a packet waits to be transmitted. Examples of the common queuing disciplines are first-in/first-out (FIFO) queuing, priority queuing (PQ), and weighted-fair queuing (WFQ).

The idea of FIFO queuing is that the first packet that arrives at a router is the first packet to be transmitted. Given that the amount of buffer space at each router is finite, if a packet arrives and the queue (buffer space) is full, then the router discards (drops) that packet. This is done without regard to which flow the packet belongs to or how important the packet is.

PQ is a simple variation of the basic FIFO queuing. The idea is to mark each packet with a priority; the mark could be carried, for example, in the IP Type of Service (ToS) field. The routers then implement multiple FIFO queues, one for each priority class. Within each priority, packets are still managed in a FIFO manner. This queuing discipline allows high-priority packets to cut to the front of the line.

The idea of the fair queuing (FQ) discipline is to maintain a separate queue for each flow currently being handled by the router. The router then services these queues in a round-robin manner. WFQ allows a weight to be assigned to each flow (queue). This weight effectively controls the percentage allocated to each flow from the link's bandwidth. We could use ToS bits in the IP header to identify that weight.

In this lab, you will set up a network that carries three applications: File Transfer Protocol (FTP), video, and Voice over IP (VoIP). You will study how the choice of the queuing discipline in the routers can affect performance of the applications and utilization of the network resources.

PRE-LAB ACTIVITIES

📖 Read Section 6.2 from *Computer Networks: A Systems Approach, 5th Edition*.

🖳 Go to www.net-seal.net and play the following animations:
   ○ Switch Congestion
   ○ IP Fragmentation

PROCEDURE
Create a New Project

1. Start **OPNET IT Guru Academic Edition** → Choose **New** from the **File** menu.
2. Select **Project** and click **OK** → Name the project **<your initials>_Queues**, and the scenario **FIFO** → Click **OK**.
3. In the *Startup Wizard: Initial Topology* dialog box, make sure that **Create Empty Scenario** is selected → Click **Next** → Select **Campus** from the *Network Scale* list → Click **Next** three times → Click **OK**.

Create and Configure the Network

The **QoS Attribute Config** node defines attribute configuration details for protocols supported at the IP layer. These specifications can be referenced by the individual nodes using symbolic names. It defines different queuing profiles such as FIFO, WFQ, priority queuing, custom queuing, MWRR, MDRR, and DWRR.

110

Initialize the network:

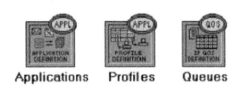

Applications   Profiles   Queues

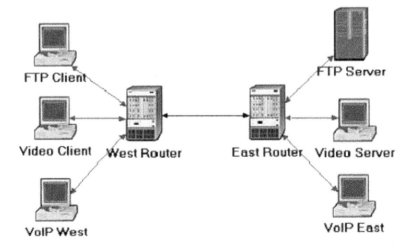

FTP Client

FTP Server

Video Client   West Router   East Router   Video Server

VoIP West   VoIP East

1. The *Object Palette* dialog box should be now on the top of your project space. If it is not there, open it by clicking 🖳. Make sure that the **internet_toolbox** item is selected from the pull-down menu on the object palette.
2. Add to the project workspace the following objects from the palette: **Application Config, Profile Config, QoS Attribute Config, five ethernet_wkstn, one ethernet_server**, and **two ethernet4_slip8_gtwy** routers.
3. Connect both routers together with a bidirectional **PPP_DS1** link.
4. Connect the workstations and the server to the routers using bidirectional **10Base_T** links, as shown.
5. Rename the objects you added as shown, and **Save** your project.

Configure the applications:

1. Right-click on the **Applications** node → **Edit Attributes** → Expand the **Application Definitions** hierarchy → **Set rows** to 3 → Name the rows: **FTP Application, Video Application**, and **VoIP Application**.

   a. Go to the **FTP Application** row → Expand the **Description** hierarchy → Assign **High Load** to **Ftp** → Click on the **High Load** value and choose **Edit** from the drop-down menu → Assign **Constant(10)** to **Inter-Request Time** → Assign **Constant(1000000)** to **File Size**. Keep the Type of Service (ToS) as Best Effort (0).

Type of Service (ToS) is assigned to the IP packets. It represents a session attribute that allows packets to be provided for the appropriate service in the IP queues.

Best-effort delivery means that delivery of a packet is attempted but is not guaranteed.

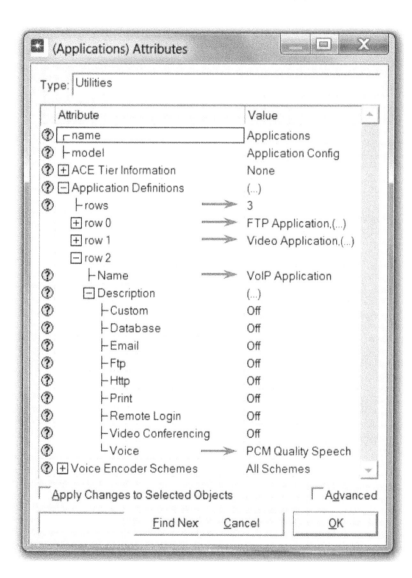

111

   b. Go to the **Video Application** row → Expand the **Description** hierarchy → Assign **Low Resolution Video** to **Video Conferencing** → Click on the **Low Resolution Video** value and choose **Edit** → Edit the value of the **Type of Service field** (the Configure TOS/DSCP window appears) → From the drop-down menu, assign **Streaming Multimedia (4)** to ToS → Click **OK** twice.

   c. Go to the **VoIP Application** row → Expand the **Description** hierarchy → Assign **PCM Quality Speech** to **Voice**. If you edit it, you can see that the ToS assigned to it is Interactive Voice (6).

2. Click **OK**, and then **Save** your project.

PCM (Pulse Code Modulation) is a procedure used to digitize speech before transmitting it over the network.

Configure the profiles:

1. Right-click on the **Profiles** node → **Edit Attributes** → Expand the **Profile Configuration** hierarchy → Set **rows** to 3.
2. Name and set the attributes of row 0 as shown:

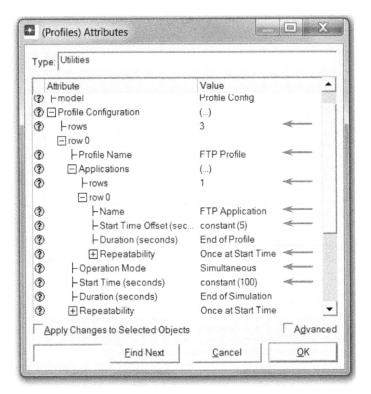

3. Name and set the attributes of row 1 as shown:

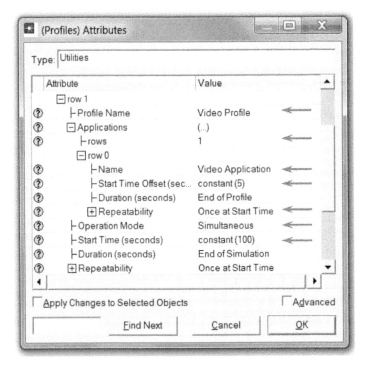

4. Name and set the attributes of row 2 as shown:

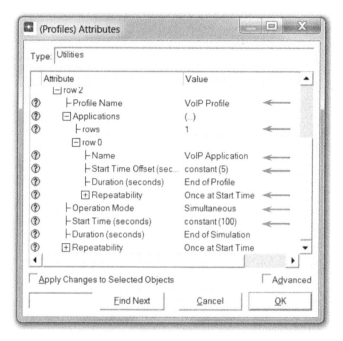

5. Click **OK**, and then **Save** your project.

Configure the queues:

We will keep the default queuing profiles that are defined in our **Queues** object. It is recommended that you check out the configuration of the FIFO, PQ, and WFQ profiles.

Configure the workstations and servers:

1. Right-click on the **FTP Client** → **Edit Attributes** → Expand the **Application: Supported Profiles** hierarchy → Set **rows** to **1** → Set **Profile Name** to **FTP Profile** → Click **OK**.

2. Right-click on the **Video Client** → **Edit Attributes** → Expand the **Application: Supported Profiles** hierarchy → Set **rows** to **1** → Set **Profile Name** to **Video Profile** → Click **OK**.

3. Right-click on the **VoIP West** → **Edit Attributes**.
   a. Expand the **Application: Supported Profiles** hierarchy → Set **rows** to **1** → Set **Profile Name** to **VoIP Profile**.
   b. Edit the **Application: Supported Services** value → Set **rows** to **1** → Set **Service Name** to **VoIP Application** → Click **OK** twice.

4. Right-click on the **VoIP East** → **Edit Attributes**.
   a. Expand the **Application: Supported Profiles** hierarchy → Set **rows** to **1** → Set **Profile Name** to **VoIP Profile**.
   b. Edit the **Application: Supported Services** value → Set **rows** to **1** → Set **Service Name** to **VoIP Application** → Click **OK** twice.

5. Right-click on the **FTP Server** → **Edit Attributes** → Edit the **Application: Supported Services** value → Set **rows** to **1** → Set **Service Name** to **FTP Application** → Click **OK** twice.

6. Right-click on the **Video Server** → **Edit Attributes** → Edit the **Application: Supported Services** value → Set **rows** to **1** → Set **Service Name** to **Video Application** → Click **OK** twice.

7. **Save** your project.

Configure the routers:

1. Click on the link connecting the **East** and **West** routers to select it → From the **Protocols** menu choose **IP → QoS → Configure QoS**.
2. Make sure the selected items are as shown in the following *QoS Configuration* dialog box → Click **OK**.

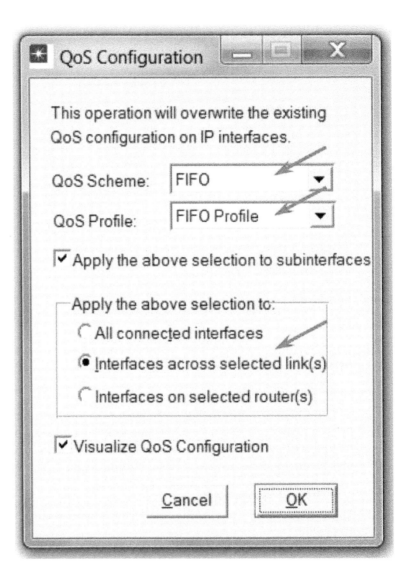

Note: Because the **Visualize QoS Configuration** radio button is checked, the link is colored based on the QoS scheme used (blue for FIFO).

3. **Save** your project.

Choose the Statistics

To test the performance of the applications defined in the network, we will collect some of the available statistics as follows:

1. Right-click anywhere in the project workspace, and select **Choose Individual Statistics** from the pop-up menu.

2. In the *Choose Results* dialog box, select the following global statistics:

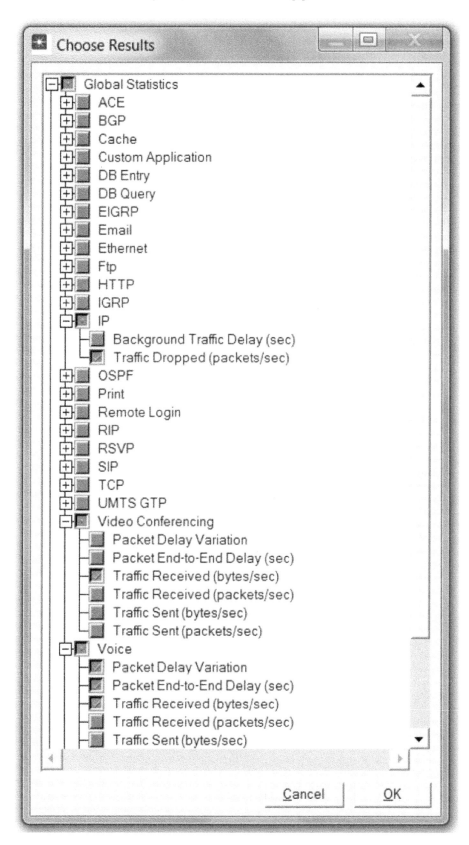

115

3. Click **OK**, and **Save** your project.

Configure the Simulation

Here we need to configure the duration of the simulation:

1. Click on ⬛ and the *Configure Simulation* window should appear.
2. Set the duration to **150 seconds**.
3. Click **OK**.

Duplicate the Scenario

In the network we just created, we used the FIFO queuing discipline in the routers. To analyze the effect of different queuing disciplines, we will create two more scenarios to test the PQ and WFQ disciplines.

1. Select **Duplicate Scenario** from the **Scenarios** menu and give it the name **PQ** → Click **OK**.
2. Click on the link connecting the **East** and **West** routers to select it → From the **Protocols** menu choose **IP** → **QoS** → **Configure QoS**.
3. Make sure the selected items are as shown in the following *QoS Configuration* dialog box → Click **OK**.

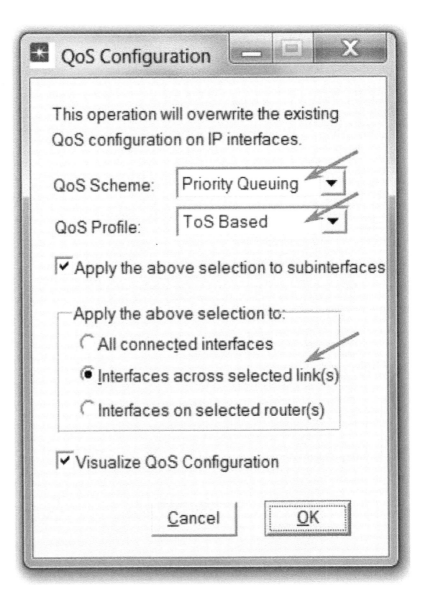

Note: Because the **Visualize QoS Configuration** radio button is checked, the link is colored based on the QoS scheme used (orange for priority queuing).

4. **Save** your project.
5. Select **Duplicate Scenario** from the **Scenarios** menu and give it the name **WFQ** →
   Click **OK**.

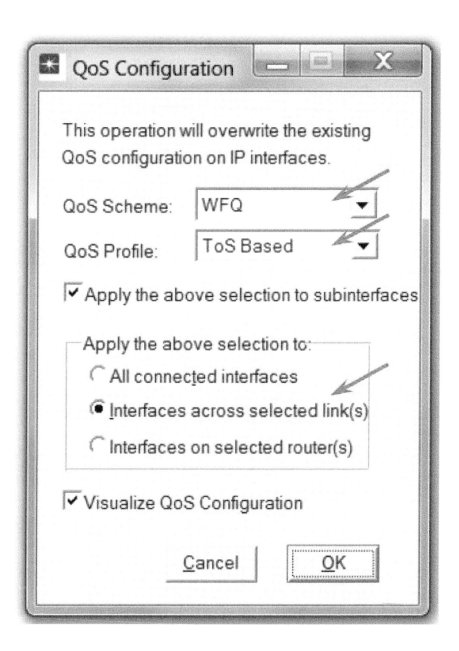

6. Click on the link connecting the **East** and **West** routers to select it → From the **Protocols** menu choose **IP** → **QoS** → **Configure QoS**.
7. Make sure the selected items are as shown in the following *QoS Configuration* dialog box → Click **OK**.

   Note: Because the **Visualize QoS Configuration** radio button is checked, the link is colored based on the QoS scheme used (green for WFQ).

8. **Save** your project.

Run the Simulation

To run the simulation for the three scenarios simultaneously:

1. Go to the **Scenarios** menu → Select **Manage Scenarios**.
2. Change the values under the **Results** column to **<collect>** (or **<recollect>**) for the three scenarios. Compare with the following figure.

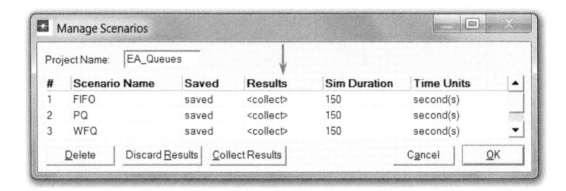

3. Click **OK** to run the three simulations. Depending on the speed of your processor, this task may take several minutes to complete.
4. After the simulation completes the three runs, one for each scenario, click **Close**.
5. **Save** your project.

View the Results

Do the following to view and analyze the results. (*Note:* Actual results will vary slightly based on the actual node positioning in the project.)

1. Select **Compare Results** from the **Results** menu.
2. Select the **IP.Traffic Dropped** statistic and click **Show**. The resulting graph should resemble the one that follows.

Note: The following graph is zoomed into the region of interest on the original graph.

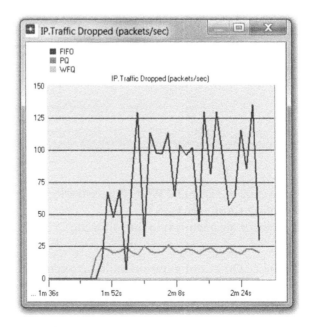

3. Create the graph for **Video Conferencing.Traffic Received**:

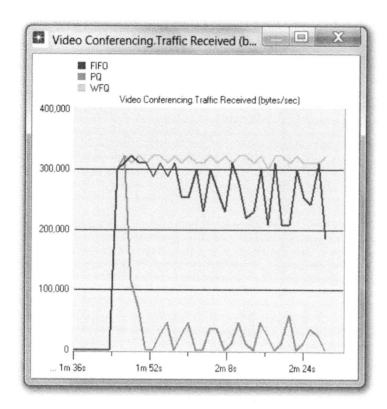

119

4. Create the graph for **Voice.Traffic Received**:

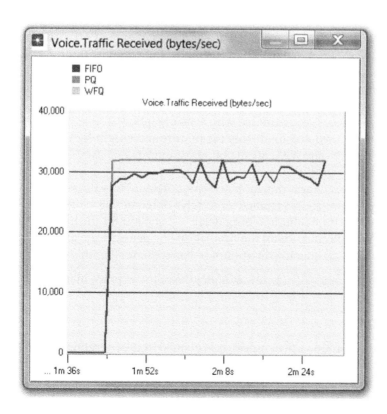

5. Create graphs for **Voice.Packet End-to-End Delay** and **Voice.Packet Delay Variation** as follows. (*Note:* The trace for **WFQ** is not shown on the following graphs because it is overlapped by the trace of **PQ**.)

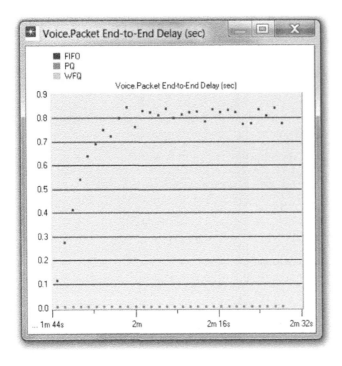

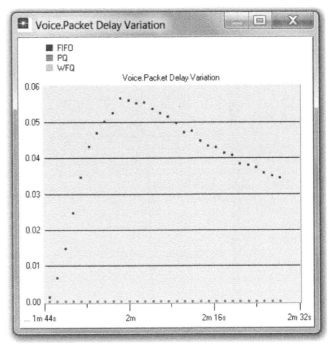

FURTHER READING

The Differentiated Services Field: IETF RFC number 2474 (www.ietf.org/rfc.html).

EXERCISES

1. Analyze the graphs we obtained and verify the overlap of the **Voice.Packet End-to-End Delay** and **Voice.Packet Delay Variation** graphs. Compare the three queuing disciplines and explain their effect on the performance of the three applications.

2. In the implemented project, edit the **Queues** object and check the profiles assigned to the **FIFO**, **PQ**, and **WFQ** disciplines. For each profile, answer the following questions:
   a. How many queues are associated with each discipline?
   b. In this lab, we used **ToS** to identify the priority and weight for the **PQ** and **WFQ** disciplines, respectively. What are the other parameters that can be used to identify the priority and weight?
   c. In **PQ**, how are queues configured to serve different ToS values?
   d. In **WFQ**, how are queues configured to serve different ToS values?

3. For all scenarios, choose the "**queuing delay <--**" statistic for the link that connects **East Router** and **West Router**. Rerun the simulation and generate the graph that compares that queuing delay for all queuing disciplines (scenarios). Analyze this graph.

Hint: The "**queuing delay <--**" statistic is under the point-to-point hierarchy.

LAB REPORT

Prepare a report that follows the guidelines explained in the Introduction Lab. The report should include the answers to the preceding exercises as well as the graphs you generated from the simulation scenarios. Discuss the results you obtained, and compare these results with your expectations. Mention any anomalies or unexplained behaviors.

RSVP: Resource Reservation Protocol
Providing QoS by Reserving Resources in the Network

OBJECTIVES

The objective of this lab is to study the Resource Reservation Protocol (RSVP) as part of the integrated services approach that provides quality of service (QoS) to individual applications or flows.

OVERVIEW

For many years, packet-switched networks have offered the promise of supporting multimedia applications. Multimedia applications combine audio, video, and data. Audio and video applications are examples of real-time applications. In the best-effort model, the network tries to deliver your data but makes no promises and leaves the "cleanup operation" to the edges. This model is not sufficient for real-time applications. What we need is a new service model—one in which applications that need better assurances can request such service from the network. The network may then respond by providing an assurance that it will do better or perhaps by saying that it cannot promise anything better at the moment. A network that can provide different levels of service is often said to support QoS.

Two approaches have been developed to provide a range of QoS: integrated services and differentiated services. The Resource Reservation Protocol (RSVP) follows the integrated services approach, whereby QoS is provided to individual applications or flows. The differentiated services approach provides QoS to large classes of data or aggregated traffic.

Although connection-oriented networks have always needed some sort of setup protocol to establish the necessary virtual circuit state in the routers, connectionless networks, like the Internet, have had no such protocols. One of the key assumptions underlying RSVP is that it should not detract from the robustness that we find in the Internet. Therefore, RSVP uses the idea of soft state in the routers. Soft state—in contrast to the hard state found in connection-oriented networks—does not need to be explicitly deleted when it is no longer needed. Instead, it times out after some fairly short period if it is not periodically refreshed. RSVP adopts the receiver-oriented approach, where the receivers keep track of their own resource requirements, and they periodically send refresh messages to keep the soft state in place.

In this lab, you will set up a network that carries real-time applications and that utilizes RSVP to provide QoS to one of these applications. You will study how RSVP contributes to the performance of the application that makes use of it.

PRE-LAB ACTIVITIES

📖 Read Section 6.5.2 from *Computer Networks: A Systems Approach, 5th Edition.*

💻 Go to www.net-seal.net and play the following animation:
  ○ TCP Flow Control

PROCEDURE
Create the Project

1. Start **OPNET IT Guru Academic Edition** → Choose **Open** from the menu.
2. Select the project you created in the "Queuing Disciplines" lab: **<your initials>_Queues** → Click **OK**.
3. From the **File** menu, choose **Save As** → Rename the project to **<your initials>_RSVP** → Click **OK**.
4. From the **Scenarios** menu, choose **Manage Scenarios** → Click on **FIFO** → Click **Delete** → Click on **PQ** → Click **Delete**.

The idea of the **FQ** (fair queuing) discipline is to maintain a separate queue for each flow currently being handled by the router. The router then services these queues in a round-robin manner. **WFQ** allows a weight to be assigned to each flow (queue). This weight effectively controls the percentage of the link's bandwidth each flow receives. We could use the **ToS** (Type of Service) field in the IP header to identify that weight.

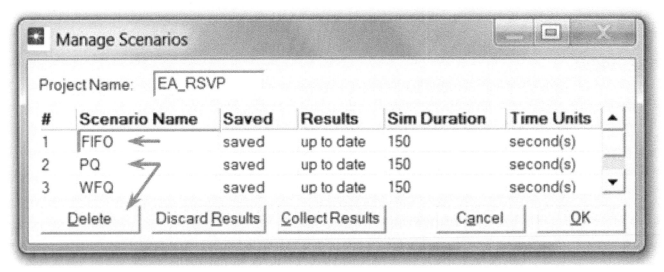

5. Click on **WFQ**, and rename it to **QoS_RSVP** → Click **OK**.
6. Make sure that you have only the **QoS_RSVP** scenario in your project. The following figure shows one way to check the available scenarios in the project.
7. **Save** your project.

Configure the Network

Add more VoIP nodes:

In this project, we will set up the two VoIP nodes so that one will always be the *Caller* party and the other will be the *Called* party. In addition, we will add two new VoIP *Caller* and *Called* nodes. These new nodes will utilize RSVP to reserve their required resources through the network.

1. Right-click on the **VoIP East** node → **Edit Attributes** → Rename the node to **Voice Called** → Assign **None** to the **Application: Supported Profiles** attribute → Assign **Voice Called** to the **Client Address** attribute → Click **OK**.
2. Right-click on the **VoIP West** node → **Edit Attributes**.
   a. Rename the node to **Voice Caller**.
   b. Assign **None** to the **Application: Supported Services** attribute.
   c. Edit the value of the **Application: Destination Preferences** attribute → Set **Rows** to 1 → Assign **Voice Destination** to the **Symbolic Name** of the new row → Edit the **Actual Name** attribute → Set **Rows** to 1 → Assign **Voice Called** to the **Name** attribute of the new row as shown.
3. Click **OK** three times, and **Save** your project.

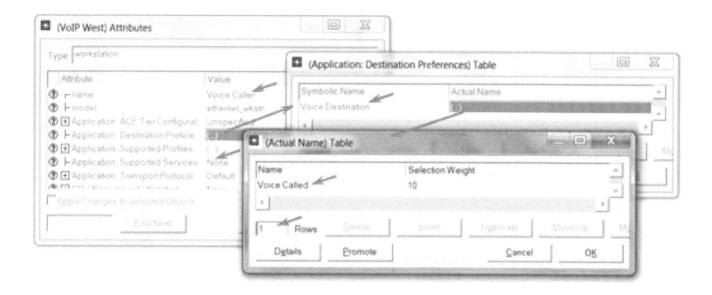

4. Click on the **Voice Called** node to select it → From the **Edit** menu, select **Copy** → From the **Edit** menu, select **Paste** (alternatively, use the standard keyboard shortcuts, **Ctrl + C** and **Ctrl + V**).
   a. Locate the new node somewhere below the **Voice Called** node on the screen → Connect the new node to the **East Router** using a **10BaseT** link.
   b. Right-click on the new node → **Edit Attributes**.
   c. Click on the **ethernet_wkstn** value of the **model** attribute → Select **Edit** → Select the **ethernet_wkstn_adv** model.
   d. Rename it to **Voice_RSVP Called** → Assign **Voice_RSVP Called** to its **Client Address** attribute.
   e. Click **OK**.
5. Copy and paste the **Voice Caller** node:
   a. Locate the new node somewhere below the **Voice Caller** node → Connect the new node to the **West Router** using a **10BaseT** link.
   b. Right-click on the new node → **Edit Attributes** → Click on the **ethernet_wkstn** value of the **model** attribute → Select **Edit** → Select the **ethernet_wkstn_adv** model.
   c. Rename it to **Voice_RSVP Caller**.
   d. Edit the **Application: Destination Preferences** attribute → Open the **Actual Name** table by clicking in the value field of **Actual Name** → Assign **Voice_RSVP Called** to the **Name** attribute (this is to replace the current value, which is **Voice Called**).
   e. Click **OK** three times.

123

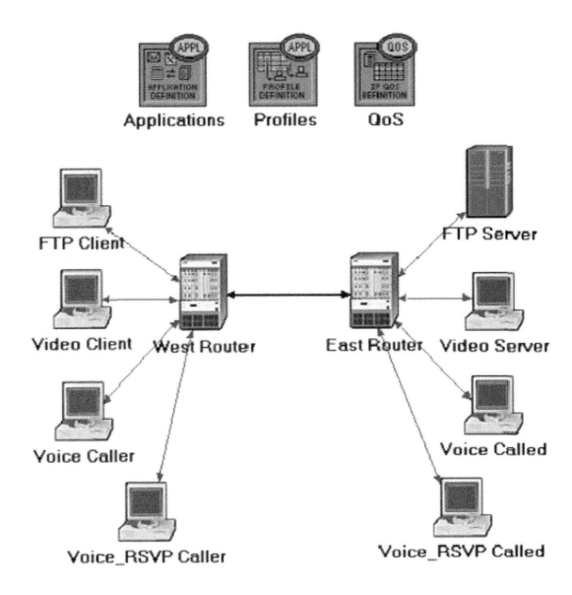

6. Rename the **Queues** node in the project to **QoS**. Your project should look like the diagram shown.
7. **Save** your project.

Define the data flow:

Here we will define the data flow characteristics of the voice traffic in the network. The sender's RSVP module periodically sends RSVP Path messages that use the data flow characteristics to describe the traffic generated by the sender. When the receiver's RSVP module receives the Path message, the receiver host application checks the characteristics of the requested data flow and decides whether resources should be reserved. Once a decision is made, the receiver host application sends a request to the host RSVP module to assist in the reservation setup. The receiver's RSVP module then carries the request as Resv messages to all nodes along the reverse data path to the sender.

The flow is defined by its required bandwidth and buffer size. Bandwidth is set to be the *token bucket rate* in the flow specification of the Path and Resv messages. The buffer size represents the amount of the application "bursty" data to be buffered. It specifies the *token bucket size* that will be set in the Path or Resv messages for the session.

1. Right-click on the **QoS** node → **Edit Attributes**.
   a. Expand the **RSVP Flow Specification** hierarchy and its **row 0** hierarchy → Set **Name** to **RSVP_Flow** → Assign **50,000** to the **Bandwidth (bytes/sec)** attribute → Assign **10,000** to the **Buffer Size (bytes)** attribute.
   b. Expand the **RSVP Profiles** hierarchy and its **row 0** hierarchy → Set **Profile Name** to **RSVP_Profile** → Click **OK**, and **Save** your project.

> **RSVP Flow** defines traffic requirements (bandwidth and requested buffer size) for which RSVP reservation will be attempted.

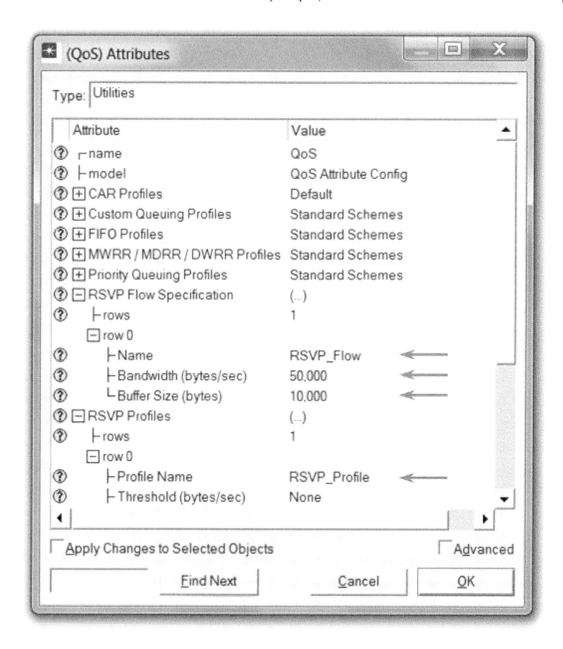

Configure the application:

Here we will create a VoIP application that utilizes the RSVP flow specifications we configured.

1. Right-click on the **Applications** node → **Edit Attributes** → Expand the **Applications Definitions** hierarchy → Set **rows** to 4 (to add a fourth row to the **Application Definitions** attribute).

a. Name and set the attributes of row 3 as shown.

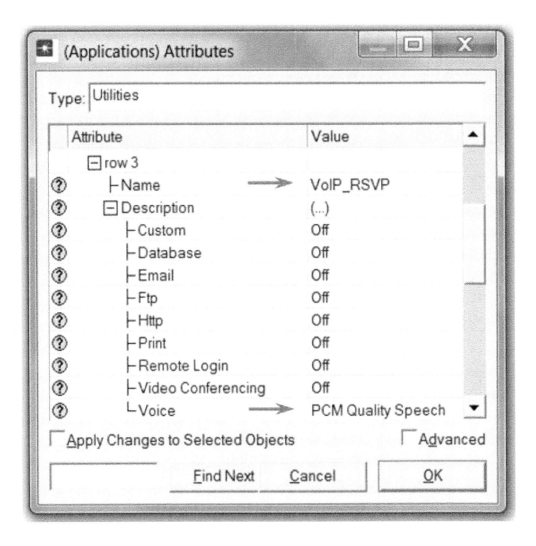

b. Click on the **PCM Quality Speech** value (shown in the previous figure) → Select **Edit** → Edit the value of the **RSVP Parameters** attribute → Assign the following values (recall that we defined the **RSVP_Flow** in the QoS node) → Click **OK** three times.

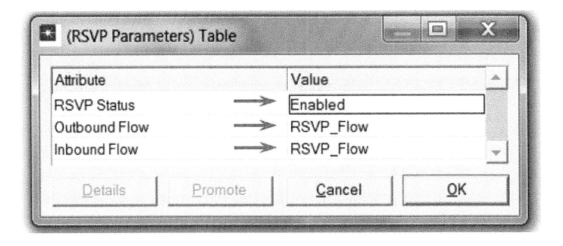

Note that the characteristics of the **Outbound Flow** are carried in the Path messages to be sent from sender to receiver, and the characteristics of the **Inbound Flow** parameters are carried in the Resv messages to be sent from the receiver to the sender.

Configure the profile:

1. Right-click on the **Profiles** node → **Edit Attributes** → Expand the **Profile Configuration** hierarchy → Set **rows** to 4 → Name and set the attributes of **row 0** as shown:

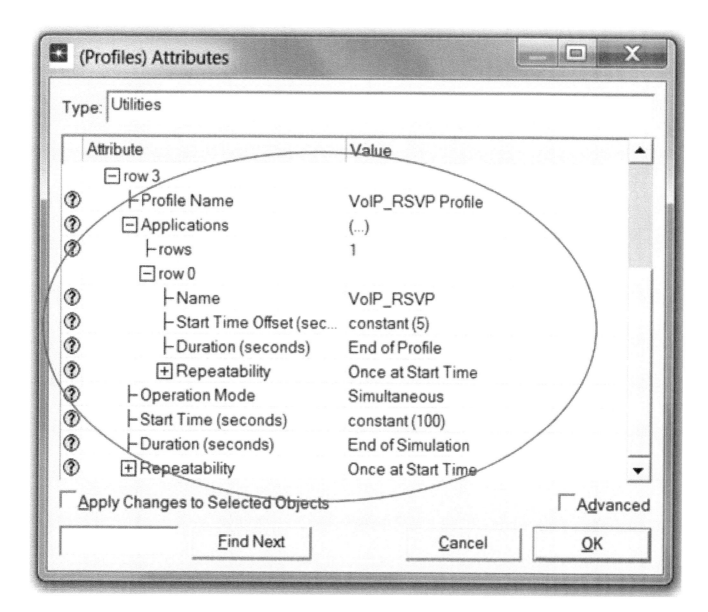

127

2. Click **OK**, and **Save** your project.

Configure the interfaces:

OPNET IT Guru supports RSVP on a per-interface basis; RSVP can be enabled or disabled for each node's interface.

1. Simultaneously select (Shift + left-click) the three links shown:

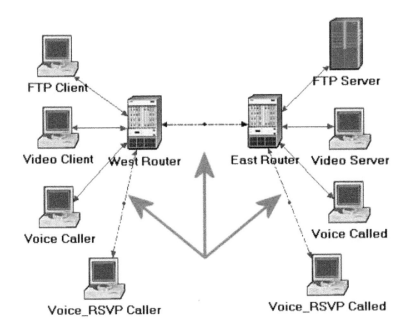

2. From the **Protocols** menu, select **RSVP** → Select **Configure Interface Status** → Make the selections shown in the *Configure* dialog box → Click **OK**, and then **Save** your project.

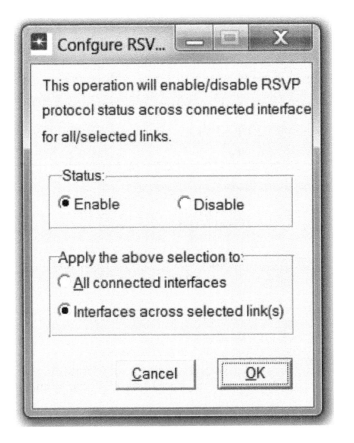

This process enables RSVP on all interfaces along the path between the two voice parties that need to utilize RSVP.

Configure the hosts and routers:

In OPNET IT Guru, the RSVP process runs only in IP-enabled nodes. The advanced versions (***_adv**) of those node models must be used, as we did already, to configure RSVP-related parameters. In addition, the RSVP model in OPNET IT Guru requires either WFQ or custom queuing schemes.

1. Right-click on the **Voice_RSVP Caller** node → **Edit Attributes**.
   a. Expand the **Application: Supported Profiles** hierarchy and its **row 0** hierarchy → Assign **VoIP_RSVP Profile** to the **Profile Name** attribute.
   b. Expand the **Application: RSVP Parameters** hierarchy → Expand its **Voice** hierarchy → **Enable** the **RSVP Status** → Expand the **Profile List** hierarchy → Assign to the **Profile** attribute of row 0 the value **RSVP_Profile** as shown.

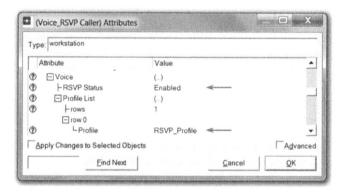

c. Expand the **IP Host Parameters** hierarchy → Expand its **Interface Information** hierarchy → Expand the **QoS Information** hierarchy → Assign **WFQ** to the **Queuing Scheme** attribute → Assign **ToS Based** to the **Queuing Profile** attribute → Assign **RSVP Enabled** to the **RSVP Info** attribute as shown.

Type of Service (ToS) is assigned to the IP packets. It represents a session attribute that allows packets to be provided the appropriate service in the IP queues.

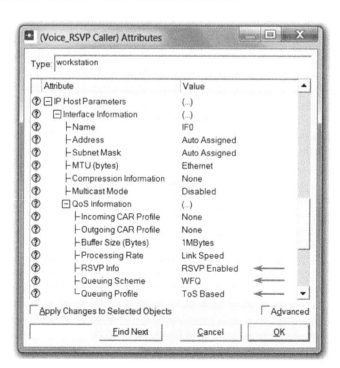

Maximum Reservable BW specifies the percentage of the bandwidth of the connected link that RSVP can reserve on the interface.

Maximum Bandwidth Per Flow specifies the amount of reservable bandwidth that can be allocated to a single flow.

d. Expand the **RSVP Protocol Parameters** hierarchy → Expand the **Interface Information** hierarchy. (You should notice that the word *Enabled* is listed in the summary line. When you expand it, you will see that it is the value of **RSVP Status**. If *Enabled* is not listed, go back to the *Configure the Interfaces* steps.) → Expand the hierarchy of the row of that interface → Assign **75%** to both the **Maximum Reservable BW** and **Maximum Bandwidth Per Flow** attributes as shown:

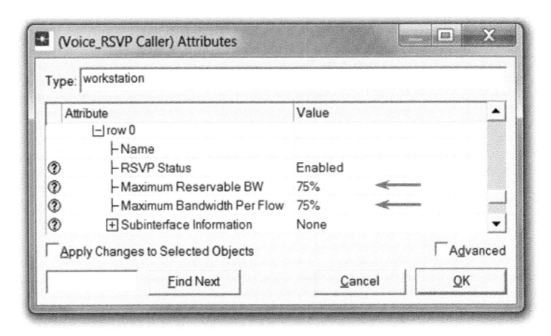

e. Click **OK**.
2. Right-click on the **Voice_RSVP Called** node → **Edit Attributes**.
   a. Edit the **Application: Supported Services** attribute. The *Application: Supported Services Table* will pop up → In that table, replace the **VoIP Application** with **VoIP_RSVP** and click **OK**.
   b. Expand the **Application: RSVP Parameters** hierarchy → Expand its **Voice** hierarchy → **Enable** the RSVP Status → Expand the **Profile List** hierarchy → Edit the value of the **Profile** attribute of row 0 and enter **RSVP_Profile**.
   c. Expand the **IP Host Parameters** hierarchy → Expand its **Interface Information** hierarchy → Expand the **QoS Information** hierarchy → Assign **WFQ** to the **Queuing Scheme** attribute → Assign **ToS Based** to the **Queuing Profile** attribute → Assign **RSVP Enabled** to the **RSVP Info** attribute.
   d. Expand the **RSVP Protocol Parameters** hierarchy → Expand the **Interface Information** hierarchy. (You should notice that the RSVP Status of the interface that is connected to the router is *Enabled*. If not, go back to the *Configure the Interfaces* steps.) → Expand the hierarchy of the row of that interface → Assign **75%** to both **Maximum Reservable BW** and **Maximum Bandwidth Per Flow** attributes.
   e. Click **OK**, and **Save** your project.
3. Right-click on the **East Router** node → **Edit Attributes**.
   a. Click on the **Ethernet4_slip8_gtwy** value of the model attribute → Select **Edit** → Select the **Ethernet4_slip8_gtwy_adv** model.
   b. Expand the **RSVP Protocol Parameters** hierarchy → Expand the **Interface Information** hierarchy. (You should notice that the RSVP Status of two interfaces, which are connected to the **West Router** and the **Voice_RSVP Called** nodes, are *Enabled*. If not, go back to the *Configure the Interfaces* steps.) → Expand the hierarchies

of the rows of these two enabled interfaces → Assign **75%** to both **Maximum Reservable BW** and **Maximum Bandwidth Per Flow** attributes.

    c. Expand the **IP Routing Parameters** hierarchy → Expand the **Interface Information** hierarchy → Expand the hierarchies of the rows of the same two interfaces you configured in the previous step (step b) → Expand the **QoS Information** hierarchy for both → Set **Queuing Scheme** to **WFQ** and **Queuing Profile** to **ToS Based** for both.

    d. Click **OK**, and **Save** your project.

4. Right-click on the **West Router** node → **Edit Attributes**.

    a. Click on the **Ethernet4_slip8_gtwy** value of the model attribute → Select **Edit** → Select the **Ethernet4_slip8_gtwy_adv** model.

    b. Expand the **RSVP Protocol Parameters** hierarchy → Expand the **Interface Information** hierarchy. (You should notice that the RSVP Status of two interfaces, which are connected to the **East Router** and the **Voice_RSVP Caller** nodes, are *Enabled*. If not, go back to the *Configure the Interfaces* steps.) → Expand the hierarchies of the rows of these two enabled interfaces → Assign **75%** to both **Maximum Reservable BW** and **Maximum Bandwidth Per Flow** attributes.

    c. Expand the **IP Routing Parameters** hierarchy → Expand the **Interface Information** hierarchy → Expand the hierarchies of the rows of the same two interfaces you configured in the previous step (step b) → Expand the **QoS Information** hierarchy for both → Set **Queuing Scheme** to **WFQ** and **Queuing Profile** to **ToS Based** for both.

    d. Click **OK**, and **Save** your project.

Choose the Statistics

We will select statistics from three different nodes:

Voice_RSVP caller statistics:

1. Right-click on the **Voice_ RSVP Caller** node and select **Choose Individual Statistics** from the pop up menu.

2. Expand the **RSVP** hierarchy and select **Number of Path States**.

3. Right-click on the **Number of Path States** statistic → Select **Change Draw Style** from the pop up menu → Choose **bar chart**.

4. Right-click on the **Number of Path States** statistic → Select **Change Collection Mode** from the pop up menu → Check the **Advanced** checkbox → From the **Capture mode** drop-down menu, select **all values**, as shown → Click **OK**.

5. Expand the **Voice Calling Party** hierarchy and select the following statistics: **Packet Delay Variation** and **Packet End-to-End Delay (sec)**.

6. Click **OK**.

Voice_RSVP called statistics:

1. Right-click on the **Voice_ RSVP Called** node and select **Choose Individual Statistics** from the pop up menu.

2. Expand the **RSVP** hierarchy and select **Number of Resv States**.

3. Right-click on the **Number of Resv States** statistic → Select **Change Draw Style** from the pop up menu → Choose **bar chart**.

4. Right-click on the **Number of Resv States** statistic → Select **Change Collection Mode** from the pop up menu → Check the **Advanced** checkbox → From the **Capture mode** drop-down menu, select **all values** → Click **OK** twice.

Voice caller statistics:

1. Right-click on the **Voice Caller** node and select **Choose Individual Statistics** from the pop up menu.

2. Expand the **Voice Calling Party** hierarchy and select the following statistics: **Packet Delay Variation** and **Packet End-to-End Delay (sec)** →Click **OK**.

131

Packet Delay Variation is the variance among end-to-end delays for voice packets received by this node.

Packet End-to-End Delay for a voice packet is measured from the time it is created to the time it is received.

Configure the Simulation

Here we need to configure the duration of the simulation:

1. Click on ![icon] and the *Configure Simulation* window should appear.
2. Make sure that the duration is set to **150 seconds**.
3. Click on the **Global Attributes** tab and make sure that the following attribute is enabled:
   a. **RSVP Sim Efficiency = Enabled**. This decreases the simulation time and memory requirements by not sending refresh messages (i.e., Path and Resv refreshes).
4. Click **OK**, and **Save** your project.

Run the Simulation

To run the simulation:

1. Click on ![icon], and then click the **Run** button. Depending on the speed of your processor, this may take several seconds to complete.
2. After the simulation completes, click **Close**, and **Save** your project.

View the Results

To view and analyze the results:

1. Select **View Results** from the **Results** menu.
2. As shown in the following figure, choose the **Packet End-to-End Delay** for both the **Voice Caller** and **Voice_RSVP Caller** nodes. Choose **Overlaid Statistics** and **time_average**.

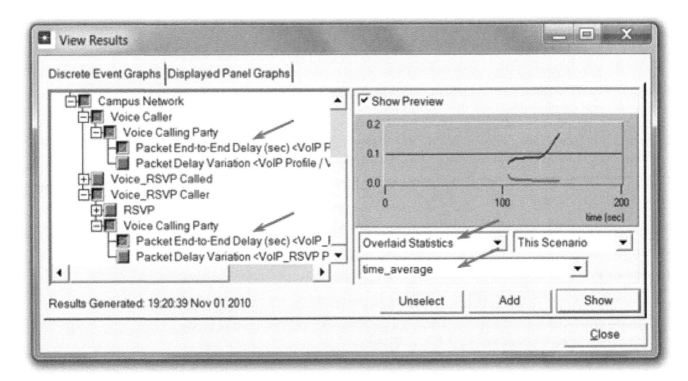

3. Click **Show** to get the following graph. (*Note:* To zoom in on the graph, click and drag your mouse to draw a rectangle around the area of interest and release the mouse button.)

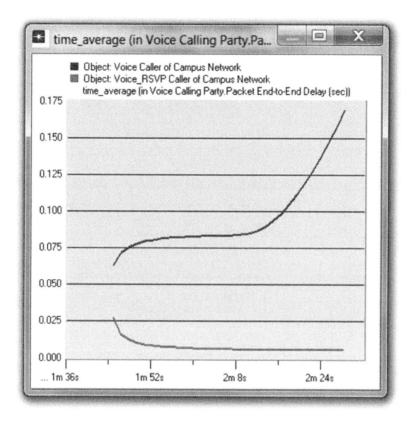

4. Similarly, you can get the following graph that compares the **Packet Delay Variation** for both the **Voice Caller** and **Voice_RSVP Caller** nodes. (*Note*: Make sure to "unselect" the statistics you chose for the previous graph.)

133

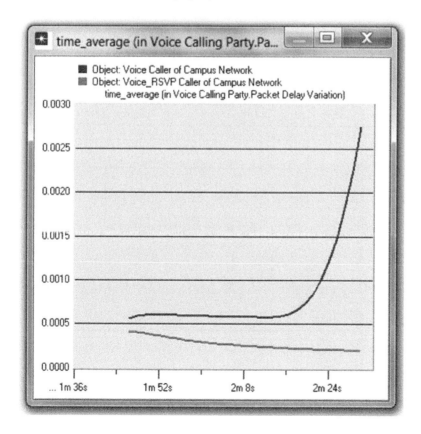

5. Finally, prepare the graph that displays the number of Path and Resv states by selecting the following statistics. Make sure to select **Stacked Statistics** and **As Is** as shown.

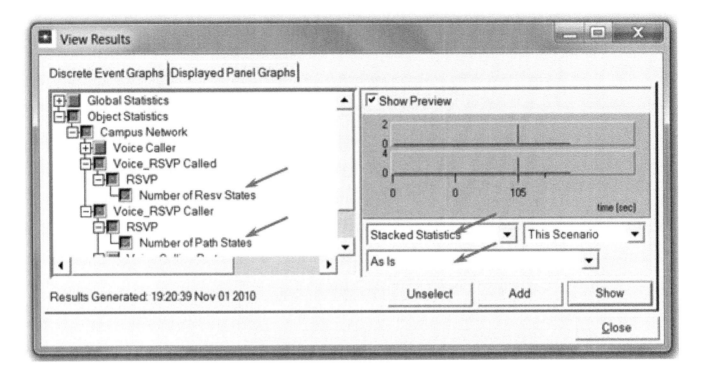

6. Click **Show** and **Right-click** on the resulting graph and choose **Edit Panel Properties** → Change the assigned values to the **Horizontal Min** and **Horizontal Max** fields as shown here:

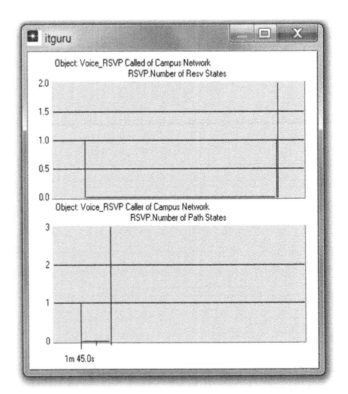

7. Click **OK**. The resulting graph should resemble the one shown.

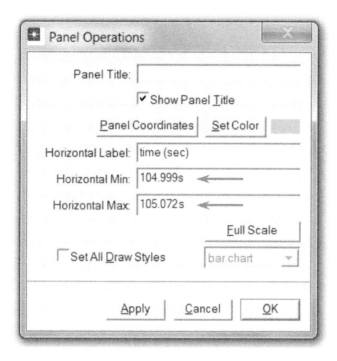

FURTHER READING

OPNET RSVP Model Description: From the **Protocols** menu, select **RSVP → Model Usage Guide**.

EXERCISES

1. Analyze the graphs we obtained in this lab. Show the effect of RSVP on the voice application and explain the obtained numbers of Path and Resv states.

2. How does the data rate of the link connecting the **East** and **West** routers affect the performance (e.g., **Packet End-to-End Delay**) of the voice and video conference applications? To answer this question, create a new scenario as a duplicate of the **QoS_RSVP** scenario. Name the new scenario **Q2_HighRate**. In the **Q2_HighRate** scenario, replace the current **PPP_DS1** link (data rate 1.544 Mbps) with a **PPP_DS3** link (data rate 44.736 Mbps).

LAB REPORT

Prepare a report that follows the guidelines explained in the Introduction Lab. The report should include the answers to the preceding exercises as well as the graphs you generated from the simulation scenarios. Discuss the results you obtained, and compare these results with your expectations. Mention any anomalies or unexplained behaviors.

Firewalls and VPN
Network Security and
Virtual Private Networks

OBJECTIVES

The objective of this lab is to study the role of firewalls and virtual private networks (VPNs) in providing security to shared public networks such as the Internet.

OVERVIEW

Computer networks are typically a shared resource used by many applications for many different purposes. Sometimes the data transmitted between application processes is confidential, and the application users would prefer that others not be able to read it.

A firewall router is a specially programmed router that sits between a site and the rest of the network. It is a router in the sense that it is connected to two or more physical networks, and it forwards packets from one network to another, but it also filters the packets that flow through it. A firewall allows the system administrator to implement a security policy in one centralized place. Filter-based firewalls are the simplest and most widely deployed type of firewall. They are configured with a table of addresses that characterizes the packets they will and will not forward.

A VPN is an example of providing a controlled connectivity over a public network such as the Internet. VPNs utilize a concept called an IP tunnel—a virtual point-to-point link between a pair of nodes that are actually separated by an arbitrary number of networks. The virtual link is created within the router at the entrance of the tunnel by providing it with the IP address of the router at the far end of the tunnel. Whenever the router at the entrance of the tunnel wants to send a packet over this virtual link, it encapsulates the packet inside an IP datagram. The destination address in the IP header is the address of the router at the far end of the tunnel, whereas the source address is that of the encapsulating router.

In this lab, you will set up a network where servers are accessed over the Internet by customers who have different privileges. You will study how firewalls and VPNs can provide security to the information in the servers while maintaining access for customers with the appropriate privilege.

PRE-LAB ACTIVITIES

Read Sections 4.3.3 and 8.4.2 from *Computer Networks: A Systems Approach, 5th Edition.*

PROCEDURE

Create a New Project

1. Start **OPNET IT Guru Academic Edition** → Choose **New** from the **File** menu.
2. Select **Project** and click **OK** → Name the project **<your initials>_VPN**, and the scenario **NoFirewall** → Click **OK**.
3. Click **Quit** on the *Startup Wizard*.
4. To remove the world background map, select the **View** menu → **Background** → **Set Border Map** → Select **NONE** from the drop-down menu → Click **OK**.

Create and Configure the Network

Initialize the network:

1. Open the *Object Palette* dialog box by clicking . Make sure that the **internet_toolbox** item is selected from the pull-down menu on the object palette.

The **ppp_server** and **ppp_wkstn** support one underlying Serial Line Internet Protocol (SLIP) connection at a selectable data rate.

PPP_DS1 connects two nodes running PPP. Its data rate is 1.544 Mbps.

2. Add the following objects from the palette to the project workspace (see the following figure for placement): **Application Config**, **Profile Config**, an **ip32_cloud**, one **ppp_server**, three **ethernet4_slip8_gtwy** routers, and two **ppp_wkstn** hosts.
3. Rename the objects you added and connect them using **PPP_DS1** links, as shown here:

138

Applications   Profiles

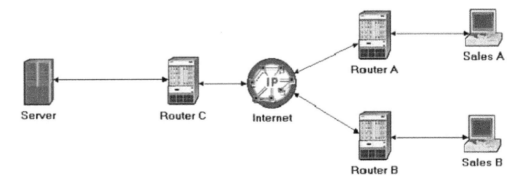

Configure the nodes:

Several example application configurations are available under the **Default** setting. For example, "Web Browsing (Heavy HTTP1.1)" indicates a Web browsing application performing heavy browsing using HTTP1.1 protocol.

1. Right-click on the **Applications** node → **Edit Attributes** → Assign **Default** to the **Application Definitions** attribute → Click **OK**.
2. Right-click on the **Profiles** node → **Edit Attributes** → Assign **Sample Profiles** to the **Profile Configuration** attribute → Click **OK**.
3. Right-click on the **Server** node → **Edit Attributes** → Assign **All** to the **Application: Supported Services** attribute → Click **OK**.
4. Right-click on the **Sales A** node → **Select Similar Nodes** (make sure that both **Sales A** and **Sales B** are selected).
   a. Right-click on the **Sales A** node → **Edit Attributes** → Check the **Apply Changes to Selected Objects** check-box.
   b. Expand the **Application: Supported Profiles** attribute → Set **rows** to 1 → Expand the row 0 hierarchy → **Profile Name** = **Sales Person** (this is one of the "sample profiles" we configured in the **Profiles** node).
5. Click **OK**, and **Save** your project.

Choose the Statistics

1. Right-click anywhere in the project workspace and select **Choose Individual Statistics** from the pop up menu.
2. In the *Choose Results* dialog box, check the following statistics:
   a. **Global Statistics → DB Query → Response Time (sec)**.
   b. **Global Statistics → HTTP → Page Response Time (seconds)**.
3. Click **OK**.
4. Right-click on **Sales A** node, and select **Choose Individual Statistics** from the menu. In the *Choose Results* dialog box, check the following statistics:
   a. **Client DB → Traffic Received (bytes/sec)**.
   b. **Client Http → Traffic Received (bytes/sec)**.
5. Click **OK**.
6. Right-click on the **Sales B** node, and select **Choose Individual Statistics** from the pop up menu. In the *Choose Results* dialog box, check the following statistics:
   a. **Client DB → Traffic Received (bytes/sec)**.
   b. **Client Http → Traffic Received (bytes/sec)**.
7. Click **OK**, and **Save** your project.

> **DQ Query Response Time** is measured from the time when the database query application sends a request to the server to the time it receives a response packet.
>
> **HTTP Page Response Time** specifies the time required to retrieve the entire page with all the contained inline objects.

The Firewall Scenario

In the network we just created, the **Sales Person** profile allows both sales sites to access applications such as database access, email, and Web browsing from the server (check the **Profile Configuration** of the **Profiles** node). Assume that we need to protect the database in the server from external access, including the salespeople. One way to do that is to replace Router C with a firewall as follows:

1. Select **Duplicate Scenario** from the **Scenarios** menu and name it **Firewall** → Click **OK**.
2. In the new scenario, right-click on **Router C → Edit Attributes**.
3. Assign **ethernet2_slip8_firewall** to the **model** attribute.
4. Expand the hierarchy of the **Proxy Server Information** attribute → Expand the **row 1**, which is for the database application hierarchy → Assign **No** to the **Proxy Server Deployed** attribute as shown:

> **Proxy Server Information** is a table defining the configuration of the proxy servers on the firewall. Each row indicates whether a proxy server exists for a certain application and the amount of additional delay that will be introduced to each forwarded packet of that application by the proxy server.

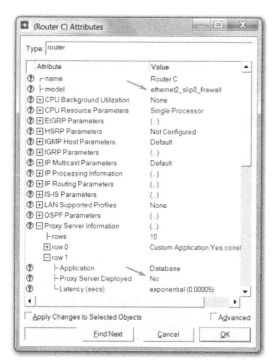

5. Click **OK**, and **Save** your project.

Our **Firewall** configuration does not allow database-related traffic to pass through the firewall (it filters such packets out). This way, the databases in the server are protected from external access. Your **Firewall** scenario should look like the following figure.

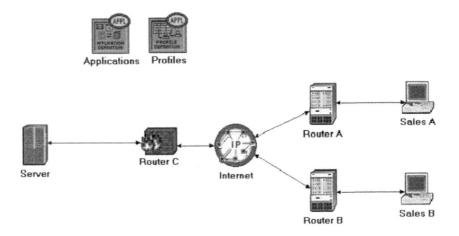

The Firewall_VPN Scenario

In the **Firewall** scenario, we protected the databases in the server from "any" external access using a firewall router. Assume that we want to allow the people in the **Sales A** site to have access to the databases in the server. Because the firewall filters all database-related traffic regardless of the source of the traffic, we need to consider the VPN solution. A virtual tunnel can be used by **Sales A** to send database requests to the server. The firewall will not filter the traffic created by **Sales A** because the IP packets in the tunnel will be encapsulated inside an IP datagram.

1. While you are in the **Firewall** scenario, select **Duplicate Scenario** from the **Scenarios** menu and give it the name **Firewall_VPN** → Click **OK**.
2. Remove the link between **Router C** and the **Server**.
3. Open the *Object Palette* dialog box by clicking ▦. Make sure that the **internet_toolbox** is selected from the pull-down menu on the object palette.

   a. Add to the project workspace one **ethernet4_slip8_gtwy** and one **IP VPN Config** (see the following figure for placement).

   b. From the *Object palette,* use two **PPP_DS1** links to connect the new router to the **Router C** (the firewall) and to the **Server**, as shown in the following figure.

   c. Close the *Object Palette* dialog box.
4. Rename the **IP VPN Config** object to **VPN**.
5. Rename the new router to **Router D** as shown in the following figure:

The **ethernet4_slip8_gtwy** node model represents an IP-based gateway supporting four Ethernet hub interfaces and eight serial line interfaces. IP packets arriving on any interface are routed to the appropriate output interface based on their destination IP address. The Routing Information Protocol (RIP) or the Open Shortest Path First (OSPF) protocol may be used to dynamically and automatically create the gateway's routing tables and select routes in an adaptive manner.

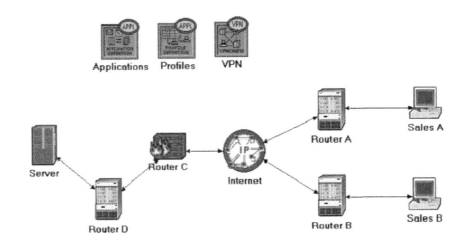

Configure the VPN:

1. Right-click on the **VPN** node → **Edit Attributes**.
   a. Expand the **VPN Configuration** hierarchy → Set **rows** to **1** → Expand **row 0** hierarchy → Edit the value of **Tunnel Source Name** and enter **Router A** → Edit the value of **Tunnel Destination Name** and enter **Router D**.
   b. Expand the **Remote Client List** hierarchy → Set **rows** to **1** → Expand **row 0** hierarchy → Edit the value of **Client Node Name** and enter **Sales A**.
   c. Click **OK**, and **Save** your project.

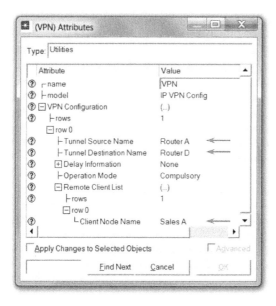

Simulating encryption:

A virtual tunnel between the **Sales A** and the **Server** does not guarantee security for the contents of the transferred database packets. If the contents of these packets are confidential, encryption of these packets will be needed. In OPNET AE, the effect of packet encryption can be simulated by the available compression function. Two of the available compression schemes are the Per-Interface Compression and the Per-Virtual Circuit Compression, as shown in the following figure. Once you edit the Compression Information attribute of an interface, OPNET adds the IP Config node to the project.

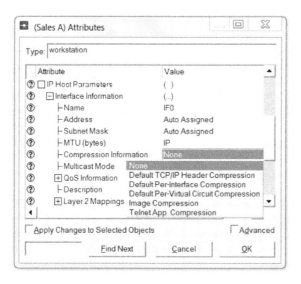

Per-Interface Compression compresses the entire packet (including the headers). This means the packet is decompressed and compressed at each hop on the route. Per-Virtual Circuit Compression compresses the packet payload only. Therefore, compression and decompression take place only at the end nodes. One of the exercises at the end of this lab requires you to create a new scenario to utilize the compression function.

Run the Simulation

To run the simulation for the three scenarios simultaneously:

1. Go to the **Scenarios** menu → Select **Manage Scenarios**.
2. Change the values under the **Results** column to **<collect>** (or **<recollect>**) for the three scenarios. Keep the default value of the **Sim Duration** (1 hour). Compare with the following figure.

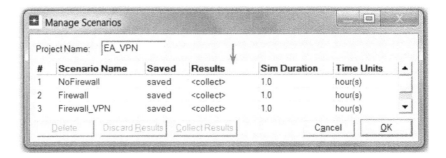

3. Click **OK** to run the three simulations. Depending on the speed of your processor, this task may take several seconds to complete.
4. After the three simulation runs complete, one for each scenario, click **Close**.

View the Results

To view and analyze the results:

1. Select **Compare Results** from the **Results** menu.
2. Expand the **Sales A** hierarchy → Expand the **Client DB** hierarchy → Select the **Traffic Received** statistic.
3. Change the drop-down menu in the middle-lower part of the *Compare Results* dialog box from **As Is** to **time_average** as shown.

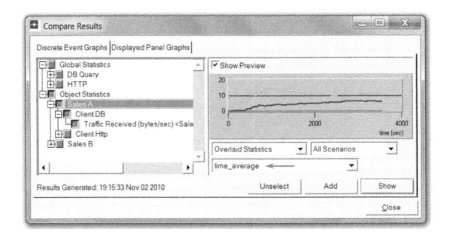

4. Press **Show** and the resulting graph should resemble the following figure. Your graph may not match exactly because of node placement.

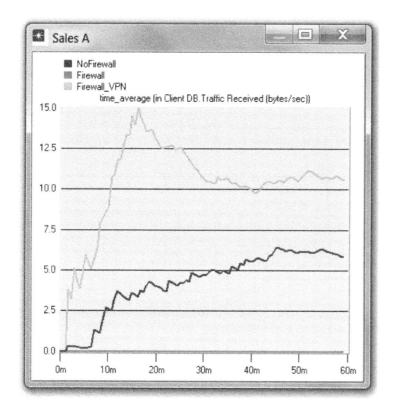

5. Create a graph similar to the previous one, but for **Sales B**:

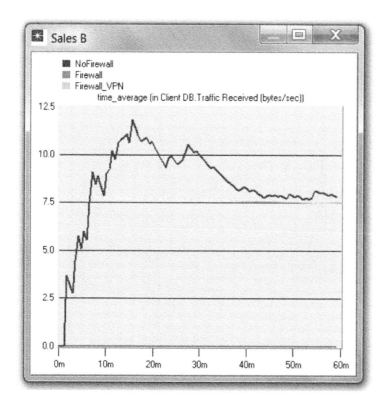

6. Create two graphs similar to the previous ones to depict the Traffic Received by the **Client Http** for **Sales A** and **Sales B**.

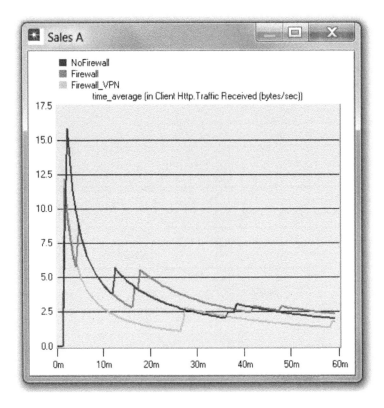

Note: Results may vary slightly because of different node placement.

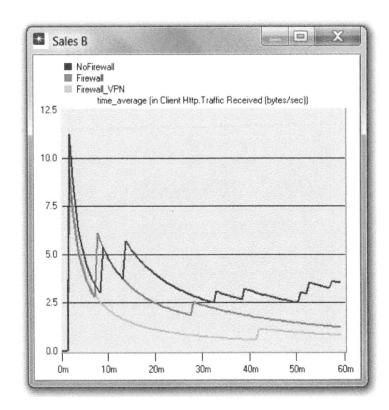

FURTHER READINGS

The Impact of Internet Link Capacity on Application Performance: From the **Protocols** menu, select **Methodologies → Capacity Planning**.

Virtual Private Networks: IETF RFC number 2685 (www.ietf.org/rfc.html).

EXERCISES

1. From the obtained graphs, explain the effect of the firewall, as well as the configured VPN, on the database traffic requested by **Sales A** and **Sales B**.
2. Compare the graphs that show the received HTTP traffic with those that show the received database traffic.
3. Generate and analyze the graph(s) that show the effect of the firewall, as well as the configured VPN, on the response time (delay) of the HTTP pages and database queries.
4. In the **Firewall_VPN** scenario, we configured the **VPN** node so that no traffic from **Sales A** is blocked by the firewall. Create a duplicate of the **Firewall_VPN** scenario, and name the new scenario **Q4_DB_Web**. In the **Q4_DB_Web** scenario, we want to configure the network so that:

    a. The databases in the server can be accessed *only* by the people in the **Sales A** site.

    b. The Web sites in the server can be accessed *only* by the people in the **Sales B** site. Include in your report the diagram of the new network configuration, including any changes you made to the attributes of the existing or added nodes. Generate the graphs of the DB traffic received and the HTTP traffic received for both **Sales A** and **Sales B**, to show that the new network meets the previously mentioned requirements.

5. Create a duplicate of the **Firewall_VPN** scenario, and name the new scenario **Q5_Compression**. In the new scenario, simulate packet encryption between **Sales A** and the **Server** by allowing **Per-Virtual Circuit Compression** in both nodes. Because encryption takes more time than compression, edit the attributes of the Per-Virtual Circuit Compression row (row 3) in the **IP Config** node. Assign 3E-006 and 1E-006 to **Compression Delay** and **Decompression Delay**, respectively. Study the effect of compression on the DB Query response time between **Sales A** and the **Server**.

LAB REPORT

Prepare a report that follows the guidelines explained in the Introduction Lab. The report should include the answers to the preceding exercises as well as the graphs you generated from the simulation scenarios. Discuss the results you obtained, and compare these results with your expectations. Mention any anomalies or unexplained behaviors.

Applications
Network Application Performance Analysis

OBJECTIVES

The objective of this lab is to analyze the performance of an Internet application protocol and its relation to the underlying network protocols. In addition, this lab reviews some of the topics discussed in previous labs.

OVERVIEW

Network applications are part network protocols (in the sense that they exchange messages with their peers on other machines) and part traditional application programs (in the sense that they interact with users).

OPNET's Application Characterization Environment (ACE) provides powerful visualization and diagnosis capabilities that aid in network application analysis. ACE provides specific information about the root cause of application problems. ACE can also be used to predict application behavior under different scenarios. ACE takes as input a real trace file captured using any protocol analyzer or using OPNET's capture agents (not included in the Academic Edition).

In this lab, you will analyze the performance of an FTP application. You will analyze the probable bottlenecks for the application scenario under investigation. You will also study the sensitivity of the application to different network conditions, such as bandwidth and packet loss. The trace was captured on a real network, which is shown in the following figure, and already imported into ACE. The FTP application runs on that network; the client connects to the server over a 768 Kbps Frame Relay circuit with 36 ms of latency. The FTP application downloads a 1 MB file in 37 s. Normally, the download time for a file this size should be about 11 s.

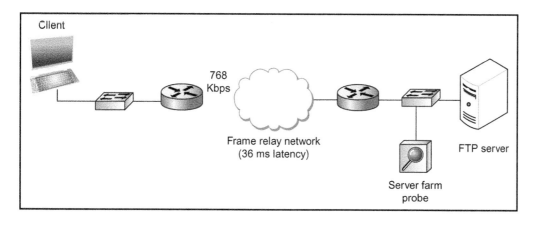

PRE-LAB ACTIVITIES

📖 Read Chapter 9 from *Computer Networks: A Systems Approach, 5th Edition.*

💻 Go to www.net-seal.net and play the following animations:
- o Internet Access
- o Email Protocols

PROCEDURE

Open the Application Characterization Environment:

1. Start **OPNET IT Guru Academic Edition** → Choose **Open** from the **File** menu → Select **Application Characterization** from the pull-down menu.
2. Select **FTP_with_loss** from the list → Click **OK**.

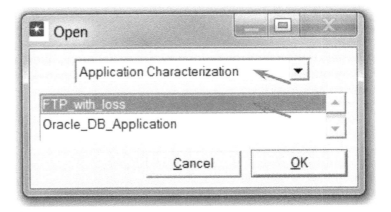

Visualize the Application

ACE shows the Data Exchange Chart (DEC), depicting the flow of application traffic between tiers. Your DEC may or may not show the **FTP Server** tier as the top tier. If it does not, drag the tier label from the bottom to the top, so your screen matches the one shown in the diagram.

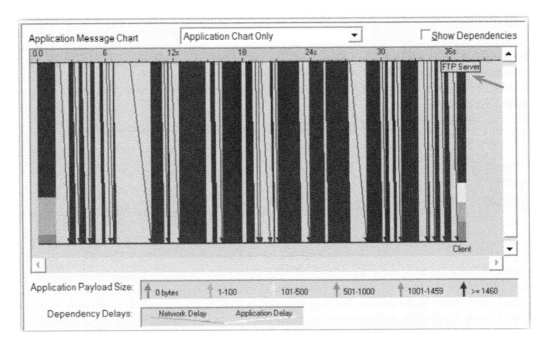

1. Select **Network Chart Only** from the drop-down menu as shown next.
2. To differentiate the messages flow, select **View → Split Groups** as shown.

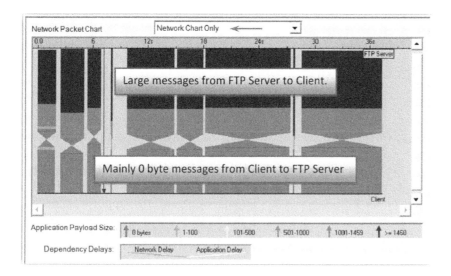

The **Data Exchange Chart** can display the following:

The **Application Chart**, which shows the flow of application traffic between tiers.

The **Network Chart**, which shows the flow of network traffic between tiers, including the effects of network protocols on application traffic. Network protocols split packets into segments, add headers, and often include mechanisms to ensure reliable data transfer. These network protocol effects can influence application behavior.

To get a better understanding of this traffic, you will zoom in the transaction. To understand how the Application Chart and Network Chart views differ, you will view both simultaneously.

1. Select **Application and Network Charts** from the drop-down menu in the middle of the dialog box.
2. To disable the split groups view, select **View → Split Groups**.
3. Select **View → Set Visible Time Range → Set Start Time** to 25.2 and **End Time** to 25.5 → Click **OK**.
4. The Application Message Chart shows a single message flowing from the FTP Server to the Client. To show the size, rest the cursor on the message to show the tooltip. **Client Payload** is shown as 8192.

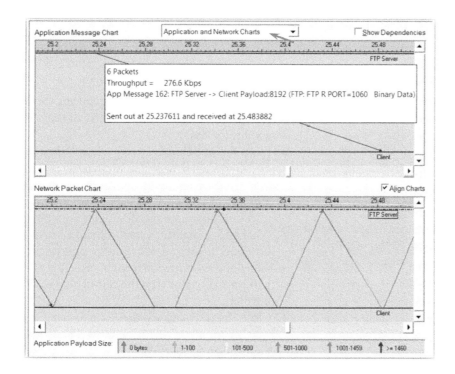

149

The Network Chart shows that this application message causes many packets to flow over the network. These packets are a mix of large (blue and green) packets from the FTP Server to the Client and small (red) packets from the Client to the FTP Server. As the red color indicates, these packets contain 0 bytes of application data. They are the acknowledgments sent by TCP.

Analyze with AppDoctor

AppDoctor's *Summary of Delays* provides insight into the root cause of the overall application delay.

1. From the **AppDoctor** menu, select **Summary of Delays** → Check the **Show Values** checkbox.
   Notice that the largest contributing factor to the application response time is protocol/congestion. Only about 30% of the file download time is caused by the limited bandwidth of the Frame Relay circuit (768 Kbps). Notice also that application delay (processing inside the node) by both the Client and FTP Server is a very minor contributing factor to the application response time.

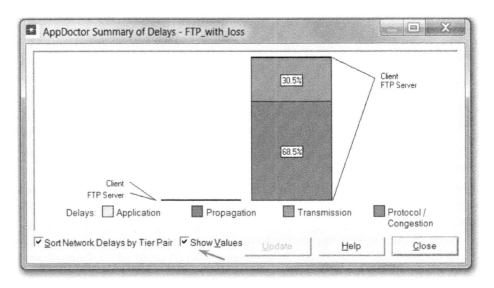

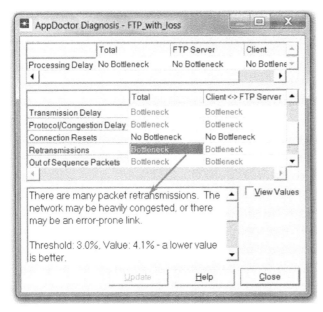

2. Close the *Summary of Delays* dialog box.
   The **Diagnosis** function of AppDoctor should give further insight into the cause of the protocol/congestion delay.

3. From the **AppDoctor** menu, select **Diagnosis**.
   The diagnosis shows four bottlenecks: transmission delay, protocol/congestion delay, retransmissions, and out-of-sequence packets. One factor that contributes to protocol/congestion delay is retransmissions. You can see that the retransmissions are listed as a bottleneck. The out-of-sequence packets are a side effect of the retransmissions. Correcting that issue will probably also cure the out-of-sequence packets problem.

4. Close the *Diagnosis* window.
   AppDoctor also provides summary statistics for the application transaction.

5. From the **AppDoctor** menu, select **Statistics**.

   Notice that 52 retransmissions occurred during a file transfer composed of 1281 packets, yielding a retransmission rate of 4%.

6. **Close** the *Statistics* window.

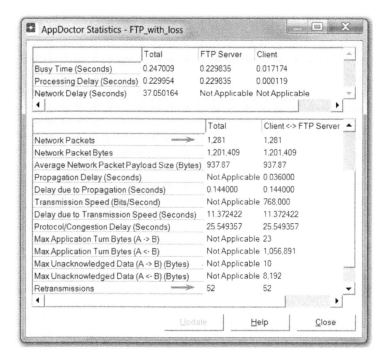

Examine the Statistics

To view the actual network throughput, use the **Graph Statistics** feature.

1. From the Data Exchange Chart, select **Graph Statistics** from the **Graph** menu (or click the button:).

2. Select the both Network Throughput (Kbits/sec): Client to FTP Server and Network Throughput (Kbits/sec): FTP Server to Client → Click **Show**.

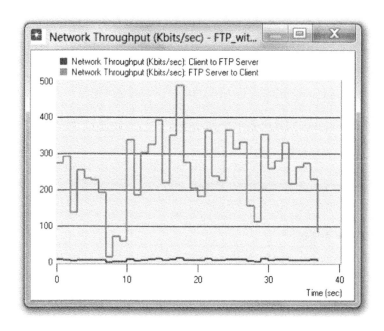

ACE divides the entire task duration into individual **buckets** of time and calculates a mean or total value for each interval. The default bucket width is 1000 ms; you can change this value in the **Bucket Width (msec)** field of the ACE statistic browser.

3. Return to the *Graph Statistics* window → Uncheck the throughput statistics, and select the two **Retransmissions** statistics → Change the **Bucket Width** to **100 ms** → Click **Show**.

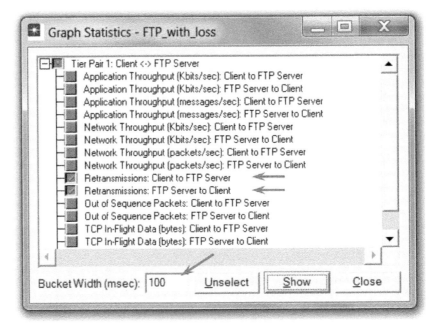

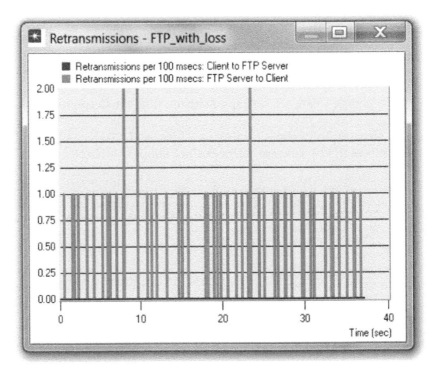

Ideal TCP Window Size

In TCP, rather than having a fixed-size sliding window, the receiver advertises a window size to the sender. This is done using the **AdvertisedWindow** field in the TCP header. The sender is then limited to having no more than a value of **AdvertisedWindow** bytes of unacknowledged data at any given time. The receiver selects a suitable value for **AdvertisedWindow** based on the amount of memory allocated to the connection for the purpose of buffering data. This procedure is called *flow control*, and its idea is to keep the sender from overrunning the receiver's buffer.

In addition, TCP maintains a new state variable for each connection, called **CongestionWindow**, which is used by the source to limit how much data it is allowed to have in transit at a given time. The congestion window is congestion control's counterpart to flow control's advertised window. It is dynamically sized by TCP in response to the congestion status of the connection.

TCP will send data only if the amount of sent-but-not-yet-acknowledged data is less than the minimum of the congestion window and the advertised window. ACE automatically calculates the optimum window size based on the bandwidth-delay product as follows:

The **bandwidth-delay product** of a connection gives the "volume" of the connection—the number of bits it holds. It corresponds to the number of bits the sender must transmit before the first bit arrives at the receiver.

1. Return to the *Graph Statistics* window → Select the **TCP In-Flight Data (bytes) FTP_Server to Client** statistic → Assign **1000** to the **Bucket Width (msec)**.

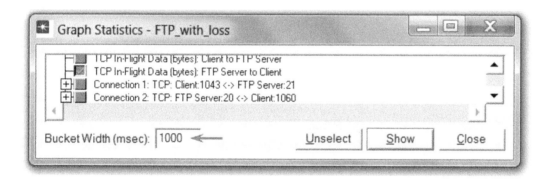

2. Click **Show**. From the graph, the ideal window size calculated by ACE is about 7 KB.
3. You can now close all opened graphs (delete the panel when you are asked to do that) and close the *Graph Statistics* window.

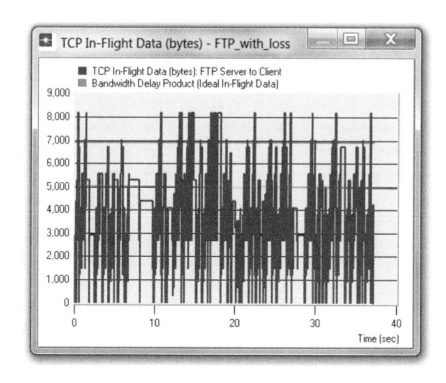

Impact of Network Bandwidth

ACE QuickPredict enables you to study the sensitivity of an application to network conditions such as bandwidth and latency.

1. Click on the **QuickPredict** button: 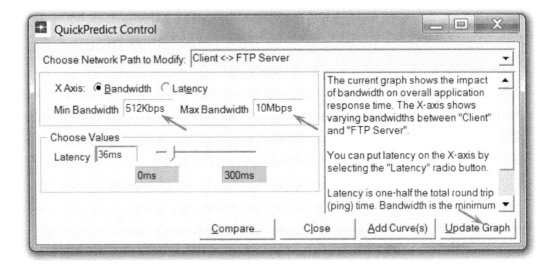.
2. In the *QuickPredict Control* dialog box, assign **512Kbps** to the **Min Bandwidth** field and **10BaseT (10Mbps)** to the **Max Bandwidth** field → Click the **Update Graph** button.

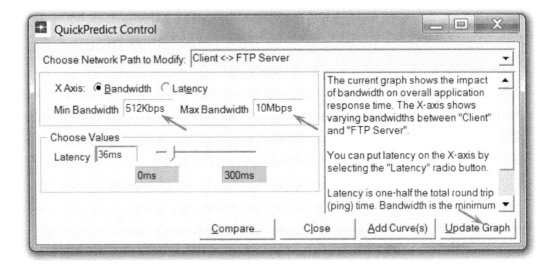

3. The resulting graph should resemble the one shown.
4. Close the graph and the *QuickPredict Control* dialog box.

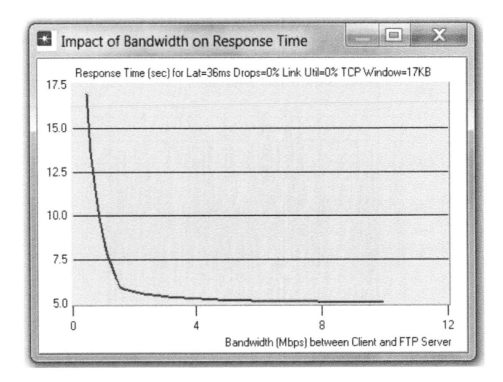

Deploy an Application

OPNET IT Guru can be used to perform predictive studies of applications that are characterized in ACE. ACE uses the trace files to create application fingerprints that characterize the data exchange between tiers. From these fingerprints, a simulation can show how the application will behave under different conditions. For example, the ACE topology wizard can be used to build a network model from the ACE file of this lab, **FTP_with_loss**, to answer the following question: What will the performance of the FTP application be when deployed to 100 simultaneous users over an IP network?

Follow these steps to answer this question:

1. From the IT Guru main window, select **File → New →** Select **Project** from the pull-down menu **→** Click **OK**.
2. Name the project **<your initials>_FTP**, and the scenario **ManyUsers →** Click **OK**.
3. In the *Startup Wizard*, select **Import from ACE** as shown **→** Click **Next**.
4. The *Configure ACE Application* dialog box appears.
   a. Set the **Name** field to **FTP Application**.
   b. Set the **Repeat** application field to **2**. This field controls how many times a user executes the application per hour.
   c. Leave the limit at the default value, **Infinite**.
   d. Click on **Add Task →** In the **Contained Tasks** table, click on the word **Specify... →** Select **FTP_with_loss** from the pull-down menu.
   e. Click **Next**.

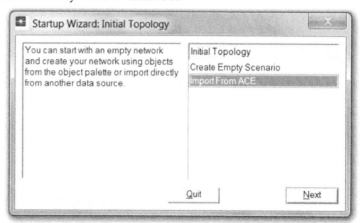

155

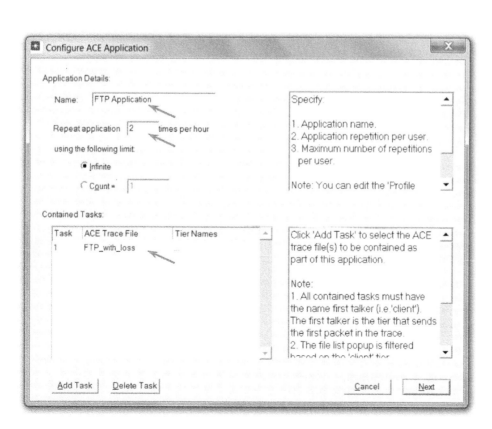

5. The *Create ACE Topology* dialog box appears. Set **Number of Clients** to 100, and set **Packet Latency** to 40. Leave all other settings at the default values →Click **Create**.

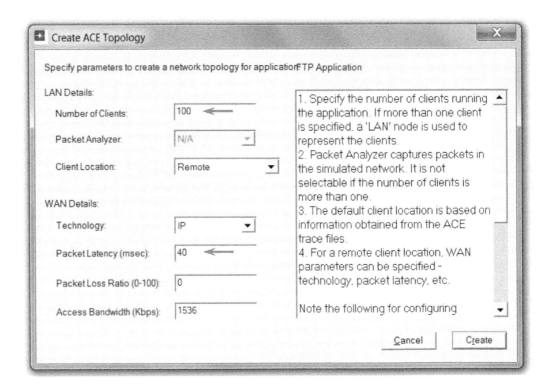

6. Select **File** → **Save** → Click **OK** to save the project.

The ACE Wizard creates a topology similar to the one shown. The **Tasks**, **Applications**, and **Profiles** objects have all been configured according to the trace files and the entries you made in the ACE Wizard. You can customize them further.

Tasks   Applications Profiles

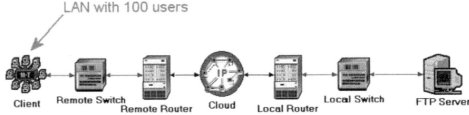

Run the simulation and view the results:

Now that the topology is created, you can run the simulation.

1. Click on the **Configure/Run Simulation** action button:

2. Use the default values. Click **Run**. Depending on the speed of your processor, this task may take several minutes to complete.

3. Close the dialog box when the simulation completes → **Save** your project.

4. Select **View Results** from the **Results** menu → Expand the **Custom Application** hierarchy → Select the **Application Response Time (sec)** statistic.

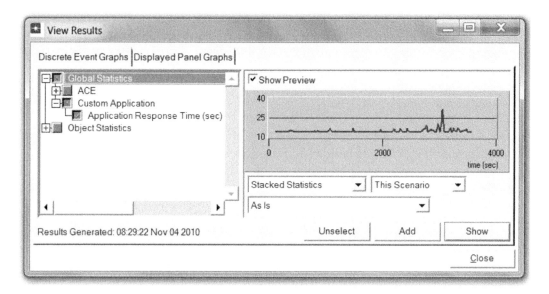

5. Click **Show**. The resulting graph should resemble the following:

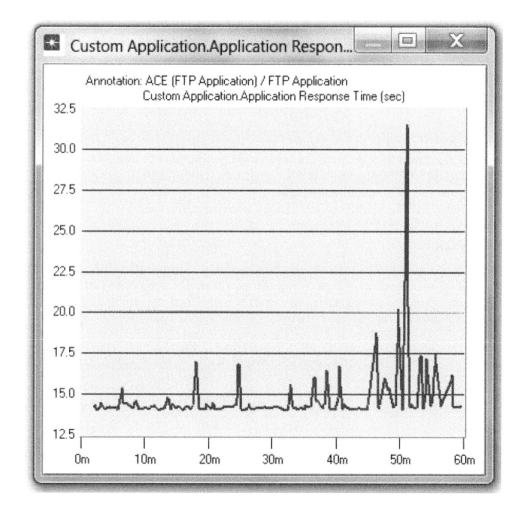

FURTHER READING

File Transfer Protocol (FTP): IETF RFC number 959 (www.ietf.org/rfc.html).

EXERCISES

1. Explain why the Client-to-FTP Server messages are mainly 0-byte messages?
2. Utilizing the AppDoctor's Summary of Delays, what is the effect of each of the following upgrades on the FTP download time?
   a. Server upgrade
   b. Bandwidth upgrade
   c. Protocol(s) upgrade
3. How do retransmissions contribute to protocol/congestion delay? Explain why "out-of-sequence" packets are a side effect of retransmissions.
4. Which protocol is responsible for the retransmission: IP, TCP, or FTP? Explain.
5. In the **Network Throughput** graph, the throughput from the FTP Server to the Client has an average value of about 300 Kbps and has a spike to about 500 Kbps. But the Frame Relay circuit has an available bandwidth of 768 Kbps. Explain why the throughput is not close to the available bandwidth.
6. Explain how the TCP in-flight data is used as an indicator of the TCP window size and how the bandwidth-delay product of the connection is used as an indicator of the ideal window size.
7. Comment on the graph we received that shows the relation between the network bandwidth and the FTP application response time. Why does the response time look unaffected by increasing the bandwidth beyond a specific point?
8. In the "Deploy an Application" section, a network model with multiple users was created based on the ACE file, **FTP_with_loss**. Duplicate the created scenario to create a new one with the name **Q8_ManyUsers_ExistingTraffic**. In this new scenario, add an "existing" traffic of 80% load in the network. Examine how the existing traffic affects the FTP application's response time. *Note:* A simple way to simulate the existing traffic is to apply *background utilization* traffic of 80% to the link between the **Remote Router** and the **IP Cloud**.
9. From OPNET IT Guru Academic Edition, open the Application Characterization for the **Oracle_DB_Application**. Analyze the application performance to find:
   a. The largest contributing factor to the application response time.
   b. The cause of any potential bottlenecks.
   c. The impact of bandwidth on overall application response time.

LAB REPORT

Prepare a report that follows the guidelines explained in the Introduction Lab. The report should include the answers to the preceding exercises as well as the graphs you generated from the simulation scenarios. Discuss the results you obtained, and compare these results with your expectations. Mention any anomalies or unexplained behaviors.

Web Caching and Data Compression
Improving Web Access and Server Performance

OBJECTIVES

The objective of this lab is to study the effect of Web caching and data compression on the response time involved in accessing Web pages and on the load on the Web server.

OVERVIEW

Generally, compressing your data before sending it over the network is a good idea because the network would be able to deliver compressed data in less time than uncompressed data. However, compression/decompression algorithms often involve time-consuming computations. The question you have to ask is whether or not the time it takes to compress/decompress the data is worthwhile given such factors as the host's processor speed and the network bandwidth.

OPNET IT Guru Academic Edition provides two methods of compression: Per-Virtual Circuit (payload) Compression and Per-Interface (entire packet) Compression. In Per-Virtual Circuit Compression, the compression and decompression of the packet payload take place only at the end nodes. With Per-Interface Compression, the whole packet is decompressed and compressed at each hop on the route. Therefore, Per-Virtual Circuit Compression entails fewer additional delays, and Per-Interface Compression results in smaller packets.

Web caching has many benefits. From the client's perspective, a page that can be retrieved from a nearby cache can be displayed much more quickly than if it has to be fetched from across the Internet. From the server's perspective, having a cache intercept and satisfy a request reduces the load on the server. Caching can be implemented in many different places. For example, a user's browser can cache recently accessed pages and simply displays the cached copy if the user visits the same page again. As another example, ISPs can con-figure a node in the network to cache Web pages for their users. This is sometimes called a *proxy*.

In this lab, we will build three scenarios of a network with main clients accessing a Web server across the Atlantic Ocean. We will study the effect of compressing and Web caching on decreasing the response time of accessing Web pages as well as on decreasing the load on the Web server.

PRE-LAB ACTIVITIES

📖 Read Sections 7.2.1 and 9.1.2 from *Computer Networks: A Systems Approach, 5th Edition.*

PROCEDURE

Create a New Project

1. Start **OPNET IT Guru Academic Edition** → Choose **New** from the **File** menu.
2. Select **Project** and click **OK** → Name the project **<your initials>_CachingComp**, and the scenario **NoCache_NoComp** → Click **OK**.
3. In the *Startup Wizard: Initial Topology* dialog box, make sure that **Create Empty Scenario** is selected → Click **Next** → Choose **World** from the *Network Scale* list → Click **Next** three times → Click **OK**.

Create and Configure the Network

Configuring the main network:

1. Open the *Object Palette* dialog box by clicking 📲. Make sure that the **internet_toolbox** palette is selected from the pull-down menu on the Object palette. Add Two **subnets** from the palette, one **Application Config** and one **Profile Config**.
2. Place and rename the added objects as shown in the following figure.

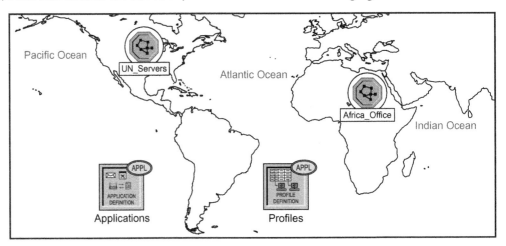

3. Select both subnets simultaneously → Right-click on one of them and select **Advanced Edit Attributes** → Check **Apply Changes to Selected Objects** → Assign to both x span and y span the value **0.001** as shown → Click **OK**.

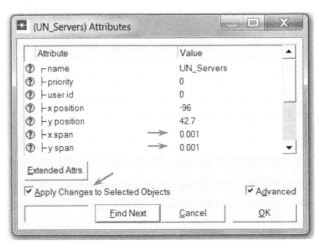

4. Right-click on the **Applications** object → Select **Edit Attributes** → Modify the Attributes as shown → Click **OK** → **Save** your project.

5. Right-click on the **Profiles** object → Select **Edit Attributes** → Modify the Attributes as shown → Click **OK**.

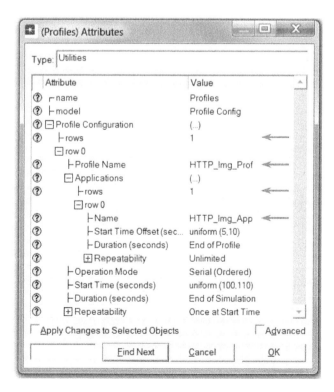

Configuring the UN subnetwork:

1. Double-click on the **UN_Servers** subnet → Open the *Object Palette* dialog box, make sure that the **internet_toolbox** palette is selected from the pull-down menu → Add to the

workspace one **ehternet_server**, one **ethernet4_slip8_gtwy**, and connect them using a **100BaseT** link → Place and rename the added objects as shown.

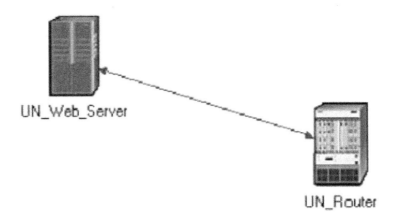

UN_Web_Server

UN_Router

2. Right-click on the **UN_Web_Server** → Select **Edit Attributes** → Assign the value: **UN_Web_Server** to the Server Address → Click on the value of the **Application: Supported Services** attribute → Select **Edit** → Modify the attributes as shown.

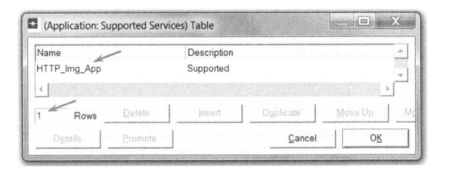

3. Click **OK** twice → Click the **Go to the higher level** 💡 button.

Configuring the Africa subnetwork:

1. Double-click on the **Africa_Office** subnet → Open *Object Palette* dialog box and make sure that the **internet_toolbox** palette is selected from the pull-down menu → Add to the workspace one **10BaseT_LAN**, one **ethernet4_slip8_gtwy**, and connect them using a **100BaseT** link → Place and rename the added objects as shown.

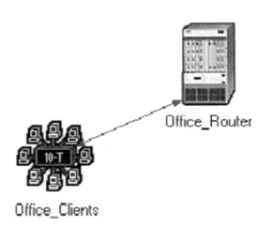

Office_Router

Office_Clients

2. Right-click on the **Office_Clients** → Select **Edit Attributes** → Assign **50** to the **Number of Workstations** attribute.

3. Click on the value of the **Application: Supported Profiles** attribute → Select **Edit** → Modify the attributes as shown → Click **OK**.

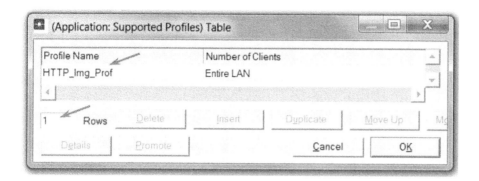

4. Click on the value of the **Application: Destination Preferences** attribute → Select **Edit** → Modify the Attributes as shown.

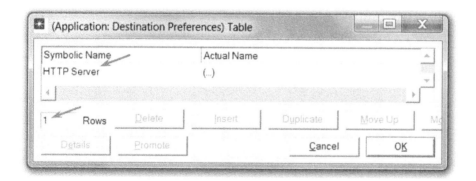

5. Click on the **Actual Name** value → Modify the Attributes as shown.

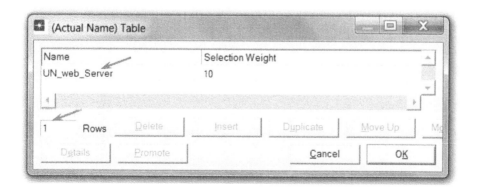

6. Click **OK** three times → Click the **Go to the higher level** 💡 button.

Connecting the subnets:

1. Open the *Object Palette* dialog box, make sure that the **internet_toolbox** palette is selected from the pull-down menu → Use a PPP_DS1 link to connect the two subnets.

Make sure to select the routers in both subnets to represent **node a** and **node b** of the link → Click **OK**.

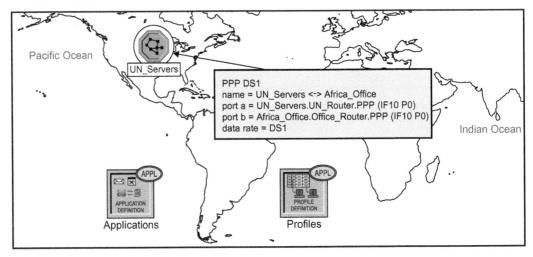

Choose the Statistics

1. Right-click on the **UN_Web_Server** (inside the UN_Servers subnet) → Select **Choose Individual Statistics** from the pop-up menu → Check the **Load (requests/sec)** statistics under the **Server Http** hierarchy as shown → Click **OK**.

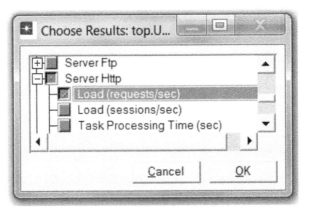

2. Right-click on the **Office_Clients** LAN (inside the Africa_Office subnet) → Select **Choose Individual Statistics** from the pop-up menu → Check the **Page Response Time (seconds)** statistics under the **Client Http** hierarchy as shown → Click **OK**.

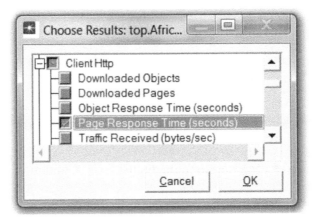

3. **Save** your project.

The NoCache_Comp Scenario

In the network we just created, the clients in the Africa_Office access the Web server in the UN. Because the link between the two subnets is slow and to improve the response time of accessing the Web pages, we will create another scenario for the same network whereby we will utilize the feature of compressing the payload of the IP datagrams. In OPNET, compressing the payload is referred to as Per-Virtual Circuit Compression.

1. Select **Duplicate Scenario** from the **Scenarios** menu and name it **NoCache_Comp** → Click **OK**.
2. In the new scenario, right-click on the **UN_Web_Server** (inside the UN_Servers subnet) → Select **Edit Attributes** → Expand the **IP Host Parameters** hierarchy → Expand the **Interface Information** hierarchy → Assign **Default Per-Virtual Circuit Compression** to the **Compression Information** attribute as shown in the next figure → Click **OK**.
3. Right-click on the **Office_Clients** LAN (inside the Africa_Office subnet) → Select **Edit Attributes** → Expand the **IP Host Parameters** hierarchy → Expand the **Interface Information** hierarchy → Assign **Default Per-Virtual Circuit Compression** to the **Compression Information** attribute as shown in the next figure → Click **OK**.

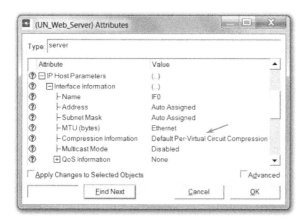

The Cache_NoComp Scenario

Another option to improve the Web page access response time is to utilize a cache server.

1. Press **Ctrl + 1** to go the first scenario (the NoCache_NoComp) → Select **Duplicate Scenario** from the **Scenarios** menu and name it **Cache_NoComp** → Click **OK**.
2. Go inside the **Africa_Office** subnet → Delete the link between the **Office_Clients** LAN and the **Office_Router** → Open *Object Palette* dialog box, make sure that the **Layer_4_switch** palette is selected from the pull-down menu → Add to the workspace one **ehternet64_layer4_switch**, one **ethernet_cache_server**, and connect them using a **100BaseT** link (available in the **Links** palette) → Place, connect, and rename the added objects as shown.

Layer 4 Switch is a switch capable of redirecting application traffic based on the application protocol. Normally we use this switch in conjunction with HTTP traffic to simulate transparent Web caching scenarios.

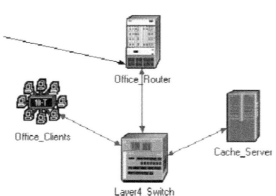

165

Cache Hit Rate determines how often objects are returned from the cache server directly to the client. However, if there is a miss, the cache server will open an HTTP session to the destination server, fetch the object from there, and then forward it to the client.

3. Right-click on the **Cache_Server** → Select **Edit Attributes** → Assign the value: **Cache_Server** to the Server Address → Assign **75%** to the **Cache Hit Rate** attribute.
4. Click on the value of the **Application: Supported Services** attribute → Select **Edit** → Modify the attributes as shown in the following figure → Click **OK** twice.

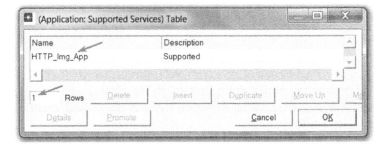

5. Right-click on the **Layer4_Switch** → Select **Edit Attributes** → Assign the values of the **Layer 4 Redirection Information** hierarchy as shown next → Click **OK**.

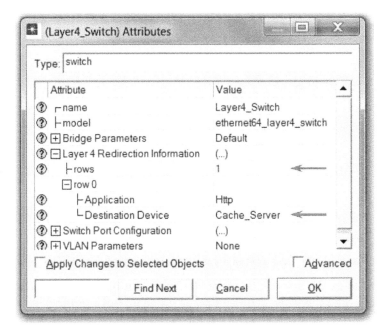

Run the Simulation

To run the simulation for the three scenarios simultaneously:

1. Go to the **Scenarios** menu → Select **Manage Scenarios**.
2. Change the values under the **Results** column to **<collect>** (or **<recollect>**) for the three scenarios. Set the **Sim Duration** to 0.5 hour as shown in the following figure.

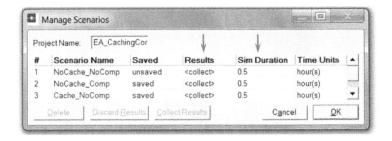

3. Click **OK** to run the three simulations. Depending on the speed of your processor, this task may take several minutes to complete.

4. After the three simulation runs complete, one for each scenario, click **Close**.

View the Results

1. Select **Compare Results** from the **Results** menu.
2. Choose **time_average** from the drop-down menu as shown in the following figure.

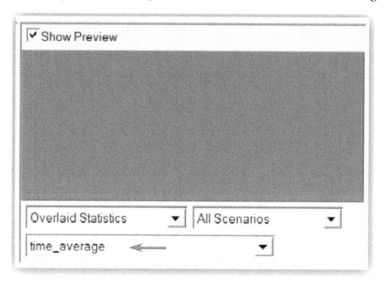

3. Show the results of the following two statistics:
   a. Object Statistics → Africa_Office → Office_Clients → Client Http → Page Response Time (seconds)
   b. Object Statistics → UN_Servers → UN_Web_Server → Server Http → Load (requests/sec)

4. Your results should resemble the following figures:

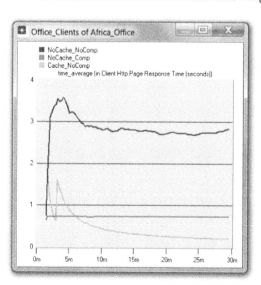

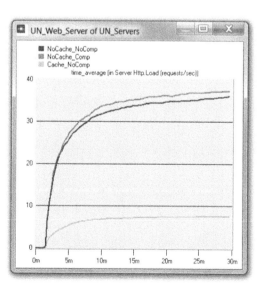

FURTHER READINGS

RFC 3173: IP Payload Compression Protocol (IPComp). http://tools.ietf.org/html/rfc3173.

G. Barich and K. Obraczka: "World Wide Web caching: trends and techniques," *IEEE Communications Magazine*, Vol. 38, No. 5, pp. 178–184, May 2000.

EXERCISES

1. In the graphs showing the Page Response Time (seconds) and Load (requests/sec), explain the difference between these statistics for the implemented simulation scenarios.
2. Create a third scenario called **Cache_Comp**, where both cache server and compression are used. Collect the same statistics, and compare the results to the current ones.

LAB REPORT

Prepare a report that follows the guidelines explained in the Introduction Lab. The report should include the answers to the preceding exercises as well as the graphs you generated from the simulation scenarios. Discuss the results you obtained, and compare these results with your expectations. Mention any anomalies or unexplained behaviors.

Token Ring
A Shared-Media Network with Media Access Control

OBJECTIVES

This lab is designed to demonstrate the implementation of a token ring network. The simulation in this lab will help you examine the performance of the token ring network under different scenarios.

OVERVIEW

A token ring network consists of a set of nodes connected in a ring. The ring is a single shared medium. The token ring technology involves a distributed algorithm that controls when each node is allowed to transmit. All nodes can view all the frames. The destination node, which is identified in the frame header, saves a copy of the frame as the frame flows past the node. With a ring topology, any link or node failure would render the whole network useless. This problem can be solved by using a star topology, where nodes are connected to a token ring hub. The hub acts as a relay, known as a multistation access unit (MSAU). MSAUs are almost always used because of the need for robustness and ease of node addition and removal.

The "token," which is just a special sequence of bits, circulates around the ring; each node receives and then forwards the token. When a node that has a frame to transmit sees the token, it takes the token off the ring and instead inserts its frame into the ring. When the frame makes its way back around to the sender, this node strips its frame off the ring and reinserts the token. The token holding time (THT) is the time a given node is allowed to hold the token. From its definition, the THT has an effect on the utilization and fairness of the network, where utilization is the measure of the bandwidth used versus that available on the given ring.

In this lab, you will set up a token ring network with 14 nodes connected in a star topology. The links you will use operate at a data rate of 4 Mbps. You will study how the utilization and delay of the network are affected by the network load as well as the THT.

PRE-LAB ACTIVITIES

Read Section 2.6 from *Computer Networks: A Systems Approach*, 5th Edition.

PROCEDURE

Create a New Project

To create a new project for the token ring network:

The **tr32_hub** node model is a token ring hub supporting up to 32 connections at 4 or 16 Mbps. The hub forwards an arriving packet to the next output port. There is no queuing of packets in the hub itself because the processing time is considered to be zero.

1. Start **OPNET IT Guru Academic Edition** → Choose **New** from the **File** menu.
2. Select **Project**, and click **OK** → Name the project **<your initials>_TokenRing**, and the scenario **Balanced** → Click **OK**.
3. In the *Startup Wizard: Initial Topology* dialog box, make sure that **Create Empty Scenario** is selected → Click **Next** → Choose **Office** for the Network scale → Click **Next** three times → Click **OK**.
4. Close the *Object Palette*, and **Save** your project.

Create the Network

To create our token ring network:

The **TR4 link** connects two token ring devices to form a ring at 4 Mbps.

1. Select **Topology** → **Rapid Configuration**. From the drop-down menu, choose **Star** and click **OK**.
2. Click the **Select Models** button in the *Rapid Configuration* dialog box. From the *Model List* drop-down menu, choose **token_ring**, and click **OK**.
3. In the *Rapid Configuration* dialog box, set the six values as shown, and click **OK**.

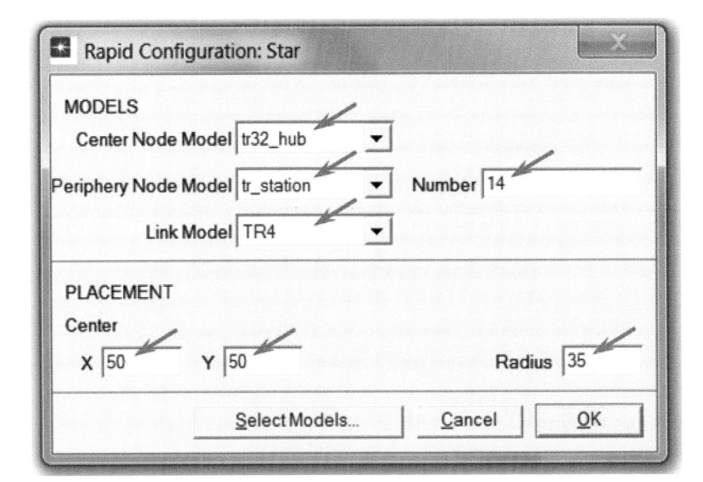

4. You have now created the network, and it should look like the following:

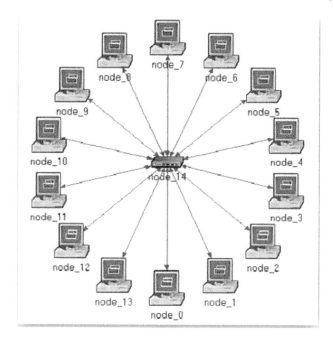

Configure the Network Nodes

Here, you will configure the THT of the nodes as well as the traffic generated by them. To configure the THT of the nodes, you need to use the **tr_station_adv** model for the nodes instead of the current one, tr_station.

1. Right-click on any of the 14 nodes → **Select Similar Nodes**. Now all nodes in the network are selected.

2. Right-click on any of the 14 nodes → **Edit Attributes**.

   a. Check the **Apply Changes to Selected Objects** check box. This step is important to avoid reconfiguring each node individually.

The following figure shows the attributes we will change in Steps 3 to 6:

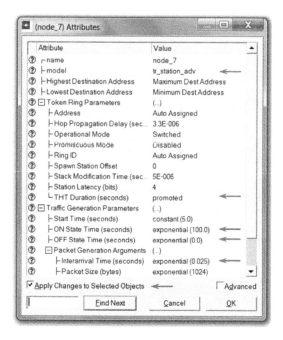

171

The **THT** (token holding time) specifies the maximum amount of time a token ring MAC (media access control) may use the token before releasing it.

The **interarrival time** is the time between successive packet generations in the "ON" state.

3. Click on the model value: **tr_station**, and select **Edit** from the drop-down menu. Now select **tr_station_adv** from the extended drop-down menu.
4. To test the network under different THT values, you need to "promote" the THT parameter. This will allow us to assign multiple values to the THT attribute.
   a. Expand the **Token Ring Parameters** hierarchy.
   b. Right-click on the **THT Duration** attribute → Choose **Promote Attribute** to **Higher Level**.
5. Expand the **Traffic Generation Parameters** hierarchy → Assign **exponential(100)** to the **ON State Time** attribute → Assign **exponential(0)** to the **OFF State Time** attribute. (*Note:* Packets are generated only in the "ON" state.)
6. Expand the **Packet Generation Arguments** hierarchy → Assign **exponential(0.025)** to the **Interarrival Time** attribute.
7. Click **OK** to return to the *Project Editor*.
8. **Save** your project.

Configure the Simulation

To examine the network performance under different THTs, you need to run the simulation several times by changing THT with every run of the simulation. There is an easy way to do that. Recall that we promoted the **THT Duration** attribute. Here we will assign different values to that attribute:

1. Click on the **Configure/Run Simulation** button:
2. Make sure that the **Common** tab is chosen → Assign **5 minutes** to the **Duration**.

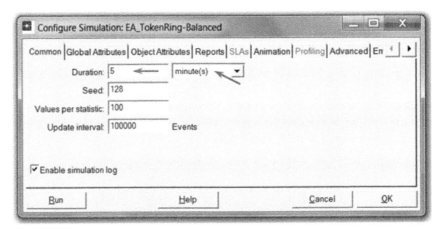

3. Click on the **Object Attributes** tab → Click the **Add** button.
4. As shown in the following *Add Attribute* dialog box, you need to add the **THT Duration** attribute for all nodes. To do that:
   a. Add the unresolved attribute: **Office Network.*.Token Ring Parameters[0]. THT Duration** by clicking on the corresponding cell under the **Add?** column → Click **OK**.

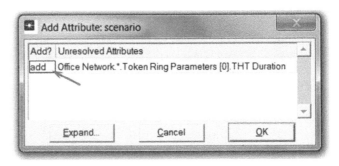

5. Now you should see the **Office Network.*.Token Ring Parameters[0].THT Duration** in the list of simulation object attributes (widen the "Attribute" column to see the full name of the attribute). Click on that attribute → Click the **Values** button, as shown below.

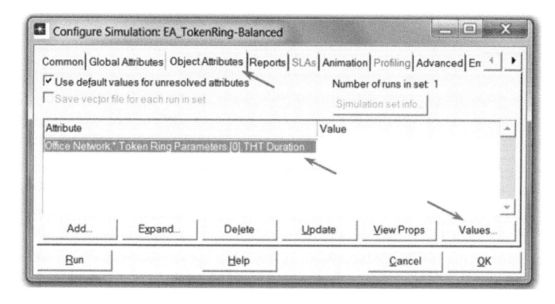

6. Add the following six values. (*Note:* To add the first value, double-click on the first cell in the **Value** column → Type **0.01** into the textbox, and press **Enter**. Repeat this step for all six values.)

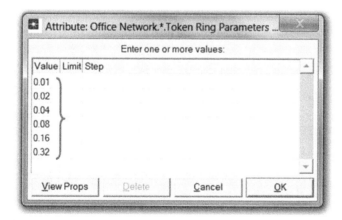

7. Click **OK**. Now look at the upper-right corner of the *Simulation Configuration* dialog box and make sure that the *Number of runs in set* is 6.

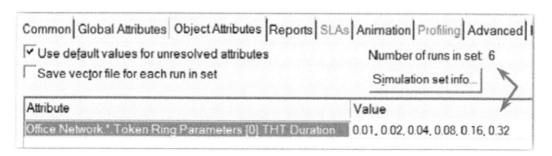

8. For each of the six simulation runs, we need the simulator to save "scalar" values that represent the "average" values of the collected statistics. To save these scalars, we need to configure the simulator to save them in a file. Click on the **Advanced** tab in the *Configure Simulation* dialog box.

9. Assign **<your initials>_Token-Balanced** to the *Scalar file* text field.

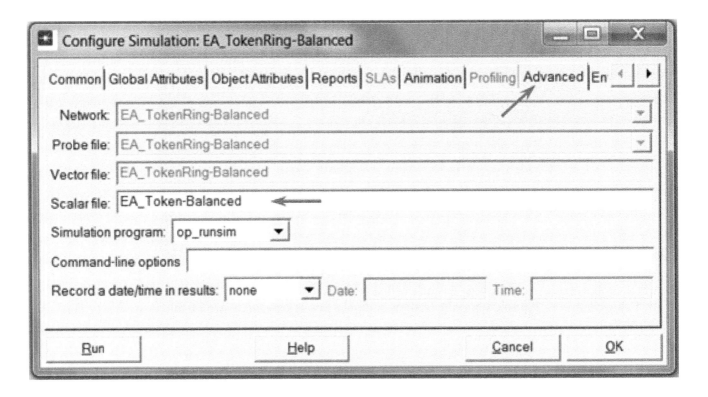

10. Click **OK**, and **Save** your project.

Choose the Statistics

To choose the statistics to be collected during the simulation:

> The **utilization** is a measure of the bandwidth used versus that available on the given ring.

1. Right-click anywhere in the project workspace (but not on a node or link), and select **Choose Individual Statistics** from the pop up menu.
   a. Expand the **Global Statistics** hierarchy:
      - Expand the **Traffic Sink** hierarchy → Select **Traffic Received (packets/sec)**.
      - Expand the **Traffic Source** hierarchy → Select **Traffic Sent (packets/sec)**.
      - Expand the **Node Statistics** hierarchy → Expand the **Token Ring** hierarchy → Select **Utilization**.
   b. Click **OK**.

2. Now we want to collect the average of the preceding statistics as a scalar value by the end of each simulation run.

> A **probe** represents a request by the user to collect a particular piece of data about a simulation.

   a. Select **Choose Statistics (Advanced)** from the *Simulation* menu.
   b. The **Traffic Sent** and **Traffic Received** probes should appear under the Global Statistic Probes. The **Utilization** probe should appear under the Node Statistics Probes.
   c. Right-click on **Traffic Received** probe → **Edit Attributes**. Set the **scalar data** attribute to **enabled** → Set the **scalar type** attribute to **time average** → Compare with the following figure, and click **OK**.

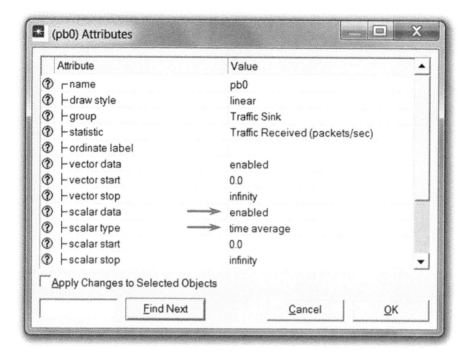

d. Repeat the previous step with the **Traffic Sent** and **Utilization** probes.

3. Because we need to analyze the effect of THT on the network performance, THT must be added as an "input" statistic to be recorded by the simulation. To do that:

a. Select **Create Attribute Probe** from the **Objects** menu. Now a new attribute is created under the **Attribute Probes** hierarchy, as shown in the following figure.

b. Right-click on the new attribute probe, and select **Choose Attributed Object** from the pop up menu → Expand the **Office Network** hierarchy → Click on **node_0** (actually, you can pick any of the network's nodes) → Click **OK**.

175

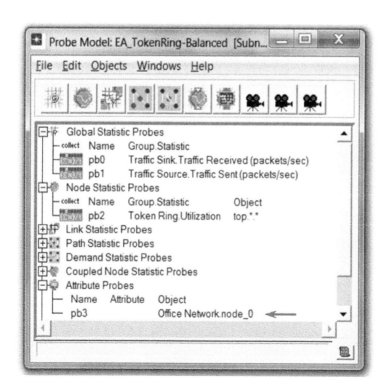

   c. Right-click again on the new attribute probe, and select **Edit Attributes** from the pop up menu → Assign the **Token Ring Parameter[0].THT Duration** value to the "**attribute**" attribute, as shown in the figure → Click **OK**.

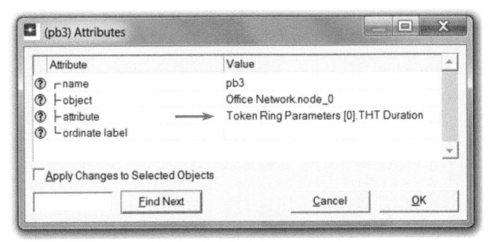

4. Select **Save** from the **File** menu in the *Probe Model* window, and then **Close** the window.
5. Now you are back to the *Project Editor*. Make sure to **save** your project.

Duplicate the Scenario

The token ring network scenario we just implemented is *balanced*: the distribution of the generated traffic in all nodes is the same. To compare performance, you will create an "unbalanced" scenario as follows:

1. Select **Duplicate Scenario** from the **Scenarios** menu and give it the name **Unbalanced** → Click **OK**.
2. Select **node_0** and **node_7** simultaneously → Right-click on one of them and select **Edit Attributes** → Expand the **Traffic Generation Parameters** and the **Packet Generation Arguments** hierarchies → Set **Interarrival Time** attribute to **exponential(0.005)** as shown. Make sure to check the **Apply Changes to Selected Objects** box before you click **OK**.

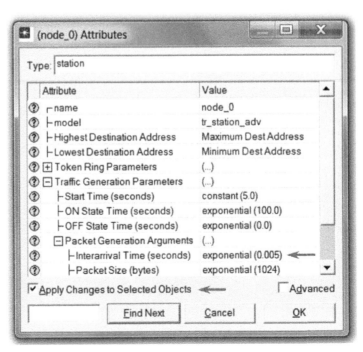

3. Select all nodes except **node_0** and **node_7** → Right-click on one of the selected nodes and select **Edit Attributes** → Change the value of the **Interarrival Time** attribute to **exponential(0.075)** as in the previous step. Make sure to check the **Apply Changes to Selected Objects** box before you click **OK**.
4. Click anywhere in the workspace to unselect objects → Click on the **Configure/Run Simulation** button: 💥 → Click on the **Advanced** tab in the *Configure Simulation* dialog box → Assign **<your initials>_Token-Unbalanced** to the *Scalar file* text field.
5. Click **OK**, and **Save** your project.

Run the Simulation

To run the simulation for both scenarios simultaneously:

1. Go to the **Scenarios** menu → Select **Manage Scenarios**.
2. Change the values under the **Results** column to **<collect>** (or **<recollect>**) for both scenarios. Compare with the following figure.

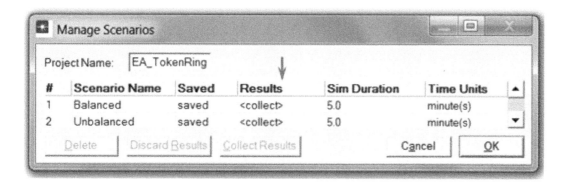

3. Click **OK** to run the simulations. Depending on the speed of your processor, this action may take several minutes to complete.
4. After the simulation completes the 12 runs, six for each scenario, click **Close**.
5. **Save** your project.

When you rerun the simulation, OPNET IT Guru will "append" the new results to the results already in the scalar file. To avoid that, delete the scalar file before you start a new run. (*Note:* If this is your first run, *do not* carry out the following step.)

• Go to the **File** menu → Select **Model Files** → **Delete Model Files** → From the list, choose **other model types** → Select **(.os): Output Scalars** → Select the scalar file to be deleted; in this lab they are **<your initials>_Token-Balanced** and **<your initials>_Token-Unbalanced** → Click **Close**.

View the Results

To view and analyze the results:

1. Select **View Results (Advanced)** from the **Results** menu. Now the Analysis Configuration tool is open.
2. Recall that we saved the average results in two scalar files, one for each scenario. To load the scalar file for the **Balanced** scenario, select **Load Output Scalar File** from the **File** menu → Select **<your initials>_Token-Balanced** from the pop up menu.
3. Select **Create Scalar Panel** from the **Panels** menu → Select the scalar panel data as shown in the following dialog box: **THT** for **Horizontal** and **Utilization** for **Vertical**. (*Note:* If any of the data is missing, make sure that you carried out Steps 2.c and 2.d in the "Choose the Statistics" section.)

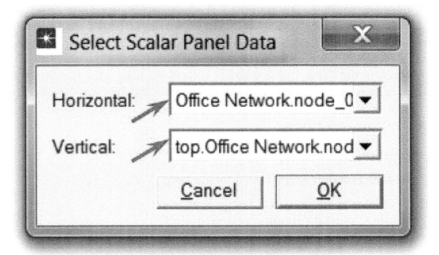

4. Click **OK**.
5. To change the title of the graph, right-click on the graph area, and choose **Edit Graph Properties** → Change the **Custom Title** to **Balanced Utilization** as shown.

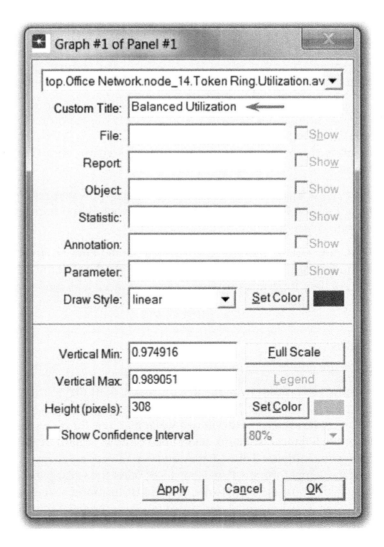

6. Click **OK**. The resulting graph should resemble the one shown. Do not close the graph; continue with the following step.

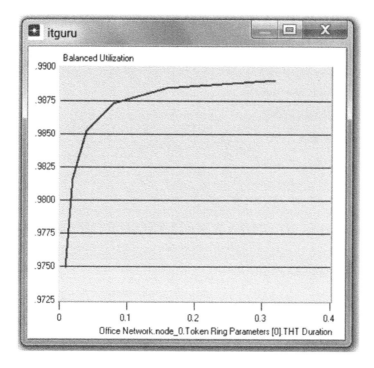

7. To compare with the **Unbalanced** scenario, load its scalar file, select **Load Output Scalar File** from the **File** menu → Select **<your initials>_Token-Unbalanced** from the pop up menu.
8. Select **Create Scalar Panel** from the **Panels** menu → Select the scalar panel data as in Step 3.
9. Click **OK** → Change the graph title to **Unbalanced Utilization** as in Step 5 → Click **OK**. The resulting graph should resemble the one shown. Do not close this graph or the previous one and continue with the following step.

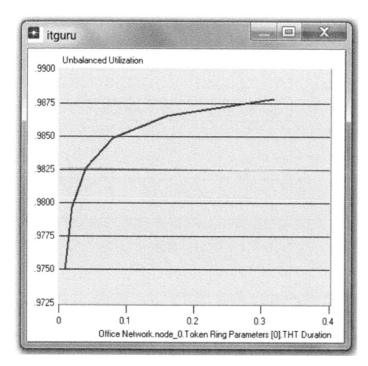

10. To combine the preceding two graphs on a single graph, select **Create Vector Panel** from the **Panels** menu → Click on the **Display Panel Graphs** tab → Select both **Balanced** and **Unbalanced** statistics → Choose **Overlaid Statistics** from the drop-down menu in the right-bottom area of the dialog box as shown.

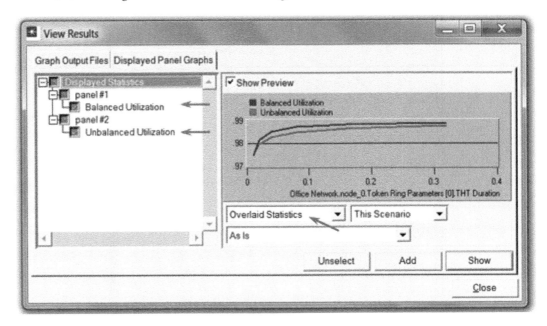

11. Click **Show**, and the resulting graph should resemble the one shown below.

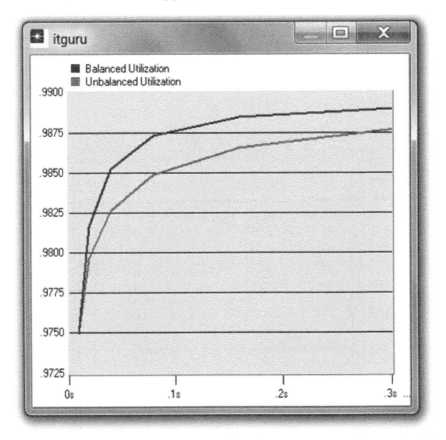

12. Repeat the same process to check the effect of the THT on Traffic Received for both scenarios. Assign the appropriate titles to the graphs.

13. The resulting graph, which combines the Traffic Received statistic for both the Balanced and Unbalanced scenarios, should resemble the following one:

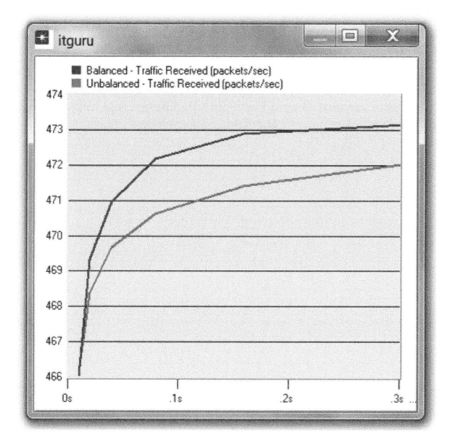

FURTHER READING

OPNET Token Ring Model Description: From the **Protocols** menu, select **Token Ring →
Model Usage Guide**.

EXERCISES

1. Why does the utilization increase with higher THT values?

2. Create a duplicate scenario of the **Balanced** scenario. Name the new scenario
Q2_HalfLoad. In the **Q2_HalfLoad** scenario, decrease the load into the network (i.e.,
load from all nodes in the network) by half and repeat the simulation. Compare the
utilization and traffic received in the **Q2_HalfLoad** scenario with those of the **Balanced**
scenario.

Hints:
- Decreasing the load from a node by half can be done by doubling the "Interarrival Time"
  of the node's **Packet Generation Arguments**.
- Do not forget to assign a separate "scalar file" for the new scenario.

3. Create a duplicate scenario of the **Balanced** scenario. Name the new scenario
Q3_OneNode. In the **Q3_OneNode** scenario, reconfigure the network so that **node_0**
generates a traffic load that is equivalent to the traffic load generated by all nodes in the
Balanced scenario combined. The rest of the nodes, **node_1** to **node_13**, generate no
traffic. Compare the utilization and traffic received in **Q3_OneNode** scenario with those
of the **Balanced** scenario.

Hints:

- One way to configure a node so that it does not generate traffic is to set its **Start Time** (it is one of the **Traffic Generation Parameters**) to the special value **Never**.
- Do not forget to assign a separate "scalar file" for the new scenario.

LAB REPORT

Prepare a report that follows the guidelines explained in the Introduction Lab. The report should include the answers to the preceding exercises as well as the graphs you generated from the simulation scenarios. Discuss the results you obtained, and compare these results with your expectations. Mention any anomalies or unexplained behaviors.

ATM: Asynchronous Transfer Mode
A Connection-Oriented, Cell-Switching Technology

OBJECTIVES

The objective of this lab is to examine the effect of ATM adaptation layers and service classes on the performance of the network.

OVERVIEW

Asynchronous transfer mode (ATM) is a connection-oriented, packet-switched technology. The packets that are switched in an ATM network are of a fixed length, 53 bytes, and are called cells. The cell size has a particular impact on effectively carrying voice traffic. The ATM adaptation layer (AAL) sits between ATM and the variable-length packet protocols that might use ATM, such as IP. The AAL header contains the information needed by the destination to reassemble the individual cells back into the original message. Because ATM was designed to support all sorts of services, including voice, video, and data, it was felt that different services would have different AAL needs. AAL1 and AAL2 were designed to support applications, like voice, that require guaranteed bit rates. AAL3/4 and AAL5 provide support for packet data running over ATM.

ATM provides QoS capabilities through its five service classes: CBR, VBR-rt, VBR-nrt, ABR, and UBR. With constant bit rate (CBR), sources transmit stream traffic at a fixed rate. CBR is well suited for voice traffic that usually requires circuit switching. Therefore, CBR is very important to telephone companies. UBR, unspecified bit rate, is ATM's best-effort service. There is one small difference between UBR and the best-effort model. Because ATM always requires a signaling phase before data is sent, UBR allows the source to specify a maximum rate at which it will send. Switches may make use of this information to decide whether to admit or reject the new virtual circuit (VC).

In this lab, you will set up an ATM network that carries three applications: voice, email, and FTP. You will study how the choice of the adaptation layer as well as the service classes can affect the performance of the applications.

PRE-LAB ACTIVITIES

Read Sections 3.1 and 6.5.3 from *Computer Networks: A Systems Approach, 5th Edition.*

PROCEDURE

Create a New Project

To create a new project for the ATM network:

1. Start **OPNET IT Guru Academic Edition** → Choose **New** from the **File** menu.
2. Select **Project** and click **OK** → Name the project **<your initials>_ATM**, and the scenario **CBR_UBR** → Click **OK**.
3. In the *Startup Wizard: Initial Topology* dialog box, make sure that **Create Empty Scenario** is selected → Click **Next** → Select **Choose From Maps** from the *Network Scale* list → Click **Next** → Choose **USA** from the maps → Click **Next** → From the *Select Technologies* list, include the **atm_advanced** Model Family, as shown in the following figure → Click **Next** → Click **OK**.

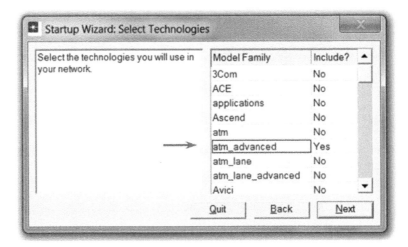

Create and Configure the Network

Initialize the network:

1. Open the *Object Palette* dialog box, if it is not already open. Make sure that **atm_advanced** is selected from the pull-down menu on the Object palette.
2. Add to the project workspace the following objects from the palette: **Application Config**, **Profile Config**, two **atm8_crossconn_adv** switches, and a **subnet**.
3. Close the *Object Palette* dialog box and rename (right-click on the node → **Set Name**) the objects you added, as shown, and then **Save** your project.

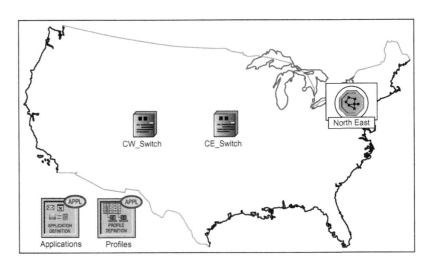

Configure the applications:

1. Right-click on the **Applications** node → **Edit Attributes** → Expand the **Application Definitions** attribute and set **rows** to 3 → Name the rows: **FTP**, **EMAIL**, and **VOICE**.
   a. Go to the **FTP** row → Expand the **Description** hierarchy → Assign **High Load** to FTP.
   b. Go to the **EMAIL** row → Expand the **Description** hierarchy → Assign **High Load** to Email.
   c. Go to the **VOICE** row → Expand the **Description** hierarchy → Assign **PCM Quality Speech** to Voice.
2. Click **OK**.

Configure the profiles:

1. Right-click on the **Profiles** node → **Edit Attributes** → Expand the **Profile Configuration** attribute and assign 3 to **rows**.
   a. Name and set the attributes of row 0 as shown:

> **PCM** stands for pulse code modulation. It is a procedure used to digitize speech before transmitting it over the network.

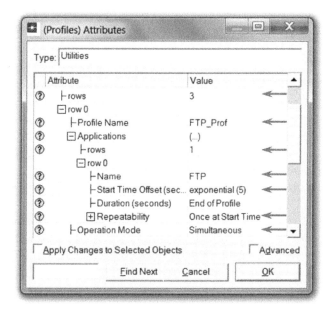

   b. Name and set the attributes of row 1 as shown:

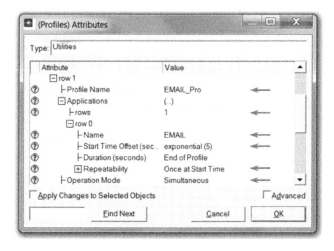

c. Name and set the attributes of row 2 as shown. (*Note:* To set the **Duration** to **exponential(60)**, you will need to assign **Not Used** to the **Special Value**.)

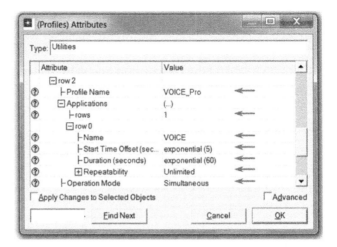

2. Click **OK**.

Configure the NorthEast subnet:

1. Right-click on the **NorthEast** subnet node → Select **Advanced Edit Attributes** → Assign the value **0.001** to both x span and y span (to scale the subnet to an average office size) → Click **OK**.
2. Double-click on the **NorthEast** subnet node. You get an empty workspace, indicating that the subnet contains no objects.
3. Open the Object palette and make sure that **atm_advanced** is selected from the pull-down menu on the Object palette.
4. Add the following items to the subnet workspace: one **atm8_crossconn_adv** switch, one **atm_uni_server_adv**, four **atm_uni_client_adv**, and connect them with bidirectional **atm_adv** links → Close the palette → Rename the objects as shown.

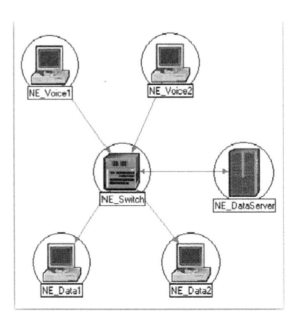

Hint
To edit the attributes of multiple nodes in a single operation, select all nodes simultaneously using Shift and left-click; then **Edit Attributes** of one of the nodes, and select **Apply Changes to Selected Objects**.

5. Change the **data rate** attribute for all links to **DS1**.

6. For both **NE_Voice1** and **NE_Voice2**, set the following attributes:
   a. Set **ATM Application Parameters** to **CBR only**.
   b. Expand the **ATM Parameters** hierarchy → Set **Queue Configuration** to **CBR only**.
   c. Expand the **Application: Supported Profiles** hierarchy → Set **rows** to 1 → Expand the **row 0** hierarchy → Set **Profile Name** to VOICE_Pro.
   d. **Application: Supported Services** → Edit its value → Set **rows** to 1 → Set **Name** of the added row to **VOICE** → Click **OK**.
   e. Expand **Application: Transport Protocol** hierarchy → Set **Voice Transport = AAL2**.
   f. Click **OK**.
7. Right-click on **NE_Voice1** → Select **Edit Attributes** → Set the **Client Address** attribute to **NE_Voice1** → Click **OK**.
8. Right-click on **NE_Voice2** → Select **Edit Attributes** → Set the **Client Address** attribute to **NE_Voice2**→ Click **OK**.
9. Right-click on **NE_DataServer** → Select **Edit Attributes** → Configure it as follows:
   a. **Application: Supported Services** → Edit its value → Set **rows** to 2 → Set **Name** of the added rows to: **EMAIL** and **FTP**→ Click **OK**.
   b. Expand the **Application: Transport Protocol Specification** hierarchy → Set **Voice Transport = AAL2**.
   c. Edit the value of the **Server Address** attribute and write down **NE_DataServer**.
   d. Click **OK**.
10. For both **NE_Data1** and **NE_Data2**, set the following attributes:
    a. Expand the **ATM Parameters** hierarchy → Set **Queue Configuration** to **UBR**.
    b. Expand the **Application: Supported Profiles** hierarchy → Set **rows** to 2 → Set **Profile Name** to FTP_Pro (for **row 0**) and to EMAIL_Pro (for **row 1**).
11. For **NE_Data1**, select **Edit Attributes** → Edit the value of the **Client Address** attribute and write down **NE_Data1**.
12. For **NE_Data2**, select **Edit Attributes** → Edit the value of the **Client Address** attribute and write down **NE_Data2**.
13. **Save** your project.

Add remaining subnets:

1. Now you have completed the configuration of the *NorthEast* subnet. To go back to the project space, click the **Go to the higher level** button.

The subnets of the other regions should be similar to the *NorthEast* one except for the names and client addresses.

2. Make *three copies* of the subnet we just created.
3. Rename (right-click on the node → **Set Name**) the subnets and connect them to the switches with bidirectional **atm_adv** links as shown. (*Note:* You will be asked to pick the

> **Client Address** is the transport adaptation layer (TPAL) address of the node. This value must be unique for each node.
>
> The **TPAL** model suite presents a basic, uniform interface between applications and transport layer models. All interactions with a remote application through TPAL are organized into sessions. A session is a single conversation between two applications through a transport protocol.
>
> The **queue configuration** specifies a one-to-one mapping between output port queues and the QoS that they support. A specific queue may be configured to support a specific QoS.

187

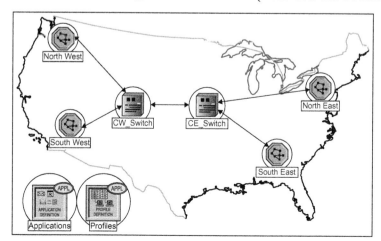

node inside the subnet to be connected to the link. Make sure to choose the "switch" inside each subnet to be connected.)

4. Change the **data rate** for all links to **DS1**.
5. Select and double-click *each* of the new subnets (total four subnets) and change the **names**, **client address**, and **server address** of the nodes inside these subnets as appropriate (e.g., replace NE with SW for the *SouthWest* subnet).
6. For all **voice** stations in all subnets (total of eight stations), edit the value of the **Application: Destination Preferences** attribute as follows:
   a. Set **rows** to **1** → Set **Symbolic Name** to **Voice Destination** → Click on (**...**) under the **Actual Name** column → Set **rows** to **6** → For each row, choose a voice station that is not in the current subnet. The following figure shows the actual names for one of the voice stations in the *NorthEast* subnet:

Hint
To do step 6, you can right-click on any **voice** station and choose **Edit Similar Nodes**. This brings up a table in which each node occupies one row and attributes are shown in the columns.

Follow the same procedure with similar steps in this lab.

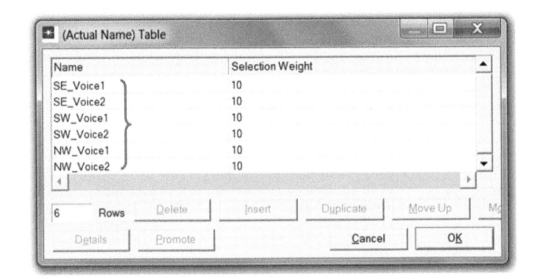

7. For all **data** stations in all subnets (total of eight stations), configure the **Application: Destination Preferences** attribute as follows:
   a. Set **rows** to **2** → Set **Symbolic Name** to **FTP Server** for the one row and **Email Server** for the other row → For each symbolic name (i.e., FTP Server and Email Server), click on (**...**) under the **Actual Name** column → Set **rows** to **3** → For each row choose a data server that is not in the current subnet. The following figure shows the actual names for one of the data stations in the *NorthEast* subnet:

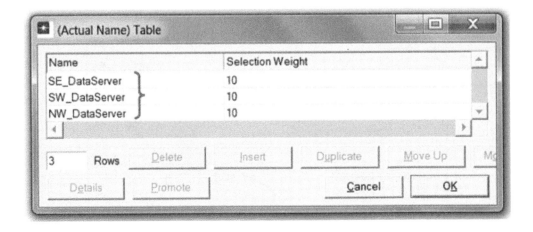

8. For all **switches** in the network (total of six switches), configure the **Max_Avail_BW** of the CBR queue to be 100%, as shown below, and the **Min_Guaran_BW** to be 20%.

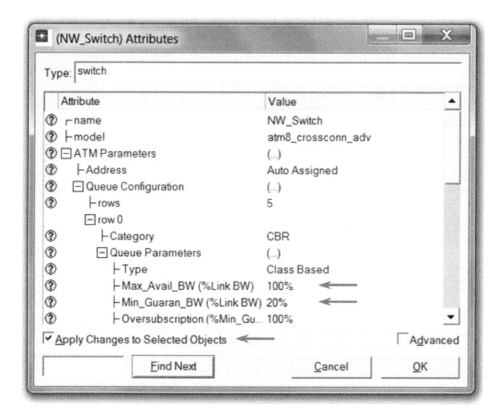

Hint
To do step 8 in a single operation, you can use the right-click menu on any switch to **Select Similar Nodes**; then **Edit Attributes** and check **Apply Changes to Selected Objects**.

This feature does work, even across objects in different subnets.

Max_Avail_BW is the maximum bandwidth allocated to this queue. Calls will be admitted into this queue only if they are within the maximum available bandwidth requirement.

189

9. Click **OK**, and **Save** your project.

Choose the Statistics

To test the performance of the applications defined in the network, we will collect some of the available statistics as follows:

1. Right-click anywhere in the project workspace, and select **Choose Individual Statistics** from the pop up menu.
2. In the *Choose Results* dialog box, choose the statistics shown in this figure:
3. Click **OK**.

Configure the Simulation

Here, we need to configure the duration of the simulation:

1. Click on the **Configure/Run Simulation** button: ⚙.
2. Set the duration to **10.0 minutes**.
3. Click **OK**, and **Save** your project.

Duplicate the Scenario

In the network we just created, we used the CBR service class for the voice application and the UBR service class for the FTP and email applications. To analyze the effect of such different classes of services, we will create

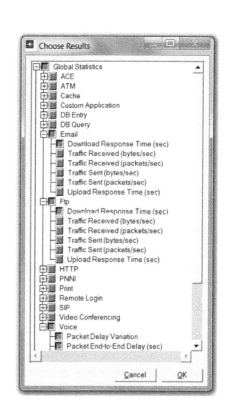

another scenario that is similar to the CBR_UBR scenario we just created, but it uses only one class of service, UBR, for all applications. In addition, to test the effect of the ATM adaptation layer in the new scenario, we will use AAL5 for the voice application rather than AAL2.

1. Select **Duplicate Scenario** from the **Scenarios** menu and give it the name **UBR_UBR** → Click **OK**.
2. For all voice stations in all subnets, reconfigure them as follows. (Check the note below for a faster way to carry out this step.)
   a. Set **ATM Application Parameters** to **UBR** only.
   b. **ATM Parameters** → Set **Queue Configuration** to **UBR**.
   c. **Application: Transport Protocol** → Set **Voice Transport** to AAL5.

Note: One easy way to carry out the preceding step 2 is through the network browser as follows:

- Select **Show Network Browser** from the **View** menu.
- Select **Nodes** from the drop-down menu, and check the **Only Selected** check box as shown in the following figure.
- Type **voice** in the find field, and click **Enter**.
- In the network browser, you should see a list of all voice stations selected.
- Right-click on any of the voice stations in the list → Select **Edit Attributes** → Check **Apply Changes to Selected Objects**.
- Carry out the configuration changes in the preceding step 2.
- To hide the network browser, deselect **Show Network Browser** from the **View** menu.

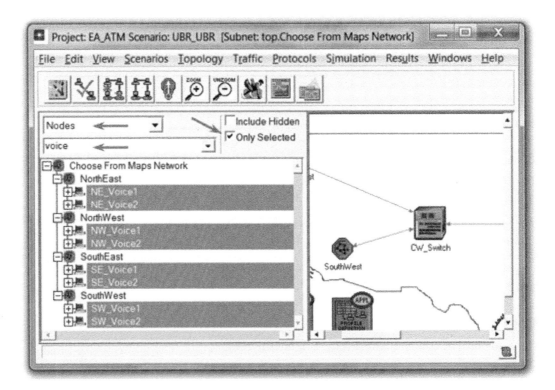

Run the Simulation

To run the simulation for both scenarios simultaneously:

1. Go to the **Scenarios** menu → Select **Manage Scenarios**.
2. Change the values under the **Results** column to <collect> (or <recollect>) for both scenarios. Compare with the following figure.

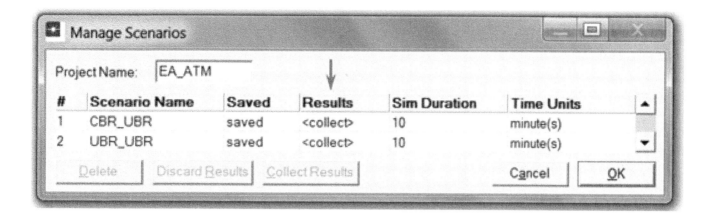

3. Click **OK** to run the two simulations. Depending on the speed of your processor, this task may take several minutes to complete.
4. After the two simulation runs complete, one for each scenario, click **Close**.
5. **Save** your project.

View the Results

To view and analyze the results:

1. Select **Compare Results** from the **Results** menu.
2. Change the drop-down menu in the right-lower part of the *Compare Results* dialog box from **As Is** to **time_average** as shown.

191

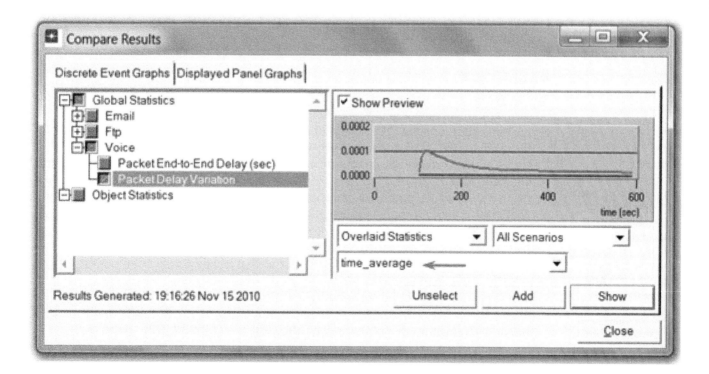

3. Select the voice **Packet Delay Variation** statistic and click **Show**. The resulting graph should resemble the one that follows. (*Note:* Your result may vary slightly because of different node placement.)

FURTHER READING

OPNET ATM Model Description: From the **Protocols** menu, select **ATM → Model Usage Guide**.

EXERCISES

1. Analyze the result we obtained regarding the voice **Packet Delay Variation** time. Obtain the graphs that compare the **Voice packet end-to-end delay**, the **Email download response time**, and the **FTP download response time** for both scenarios. Comment on the results.

Hints:
To set ABR class of service to a node, assign **ABR Only** to its **ATM Application Parameters** attribute and **ABR only (Per VC Queue)** to its **Queue Configuration** (one of the **ATM Parameters**).

For all **switches** in the network (total of six switches), configure the **Max_Avail_BW** of the **ABR** queue to be 100% and the **Min_Guaran_BW** to be 20%.

2. Create another scenario as a duplicate of the **CBR_UBR** scenario. Name the new scenario **Q2_CBR_ABR**. In the new scenario, you should use the **ABR** class of service for data, i.e., the FTP and email applications in the data stations. Compare the performance of the **CBR_ABR** scenario with that of the **CBR_UBR** scenario.

3. Edit the **FTP** application defined in the **Applications** node so that its **File Size** is twice the current size (i.e., make it 100,000 bytes instead of 50,000 bytes). Edit the **EMAIL** application defined in the **Applications** node so that its **File Size** is five times the current size (i.e., make it 10,000 bytes instead of 2000 bytes). Study how this change affects the voice application performance in both the **CBR_UBR** and **UBR_UBR** scenarios. (*Hint:* To answer this exercise, you might need to create duplicates of the **CBR_UBR** and **UBR_UBR** scenarios. Name the new scenarios **Q3_CBR_UBR** and **Q3_UBR_UBR**, respectively.)

LAB REPORT

Prepare a report that follows the guidelines explained in the Introduction Lab. The report should include the answers to the preceding exercises as well as the graphs you generated from the simulation scenarios. Discuss the results you obtained, and compare these results with your expectations. Mention any anomalies or unexplained behaviors.

Printed and bound by CPI Group (UK) Ltd, Croydon, CR0 4YY

03/10/2024

01040315-0016